D1587205

MAGIC REALIST CINEMA IN EAST CENTRAL EUROPE

Traditions in World Cinema

General Editors
Linda Badley (Middle Tennessee State
  University)
R. Barton Palmer (Clemson University)

Founding Editor
Steven Jay Schneider (New York
  University)

Titles in the series include:
Traditions in World Cinema
by Linda Badley, R. Barton Palmer and
  Steven Jay Schneider (eds)
978 0 7486 1862 0 (hardback)
978 0 7486 1863 7 (paperback)

Japanese Horror Cinema
by Jay McRoy (ed.)
978 0 7486 1994 8 (hardback)
978 0 7486 1995 5 (paperback)

New Punk Cinema
by Nicholas Rombes (ed.)
978 0 7486 2034 0 (hardback)
978 0 7486 2035 7 (paperback)

*African Filmmaking: North and South of
  the Sahara*
by Roy Armes
978 0 7486 2123 1 (hardback)
978 0 7486 2124 8 (paperback)

*Palestinian Cinema: Landscape, Trauma
  and Memory*
by Nurith Gertz
978 0 7486 3407 1 (hardback)
978 0 7486 3408 8 (paperback)

Chinese Martial Arts Cinema: The Wuxia
  Tradition
by Stephen Teo
978 0 7486 3285 5 (hardback)
978 0 7486 3286 2 (paperback)

*Czech and Slovak Cinema: Theme and
  Tradition*
by Peter Hames
978 0 7486 2081 4 (hardback)
978 0 7486 2082 1 (paperback)

The New Neapolitan Cinema
by Alex Marlow-Mann
978 0 7486 4066 9 (hardback)

The International Film Musical
by Corey K. Creekmur and Linda Y.
  Mokdad (eds)
978 0 7486 3476 7 (hardback)

American Smart Cinema
by Claire Perkins
978 0 7486 4074 4 (hardback)

Italian Neorealist Cinema
by Torunn Haaland
978 0 7486 3611 2 (hardback)

*Magic Realist Cinema in East Central
  Europe*
by Aga Skrodzka
978 0 7486 3916 8 (hardback)

Forthcoming titles include:
The Spanish Horror Film
by Antonio Lázaro-Reboll
978 0 7486 3638 9 (hardback)

*American Independent-Commercial
  Cinema*
by Linda Badley and R. Barton Palmer
978 0 7486 2459 1 (hardback)

The Italian Sword-and-Sandal Film
by Frank Burke
978 0 7486 1983 2 (hardback)

New Nordic Cinema
by Mette Hjort, Andrew Nestigen and
  Anna Stenport
978 0 7486 3631 0 (hardback)

Italian Post-neorealist Cinema
by Luca Barattoni
978 0 7486 4054 6 (hardback)

*Cinemas of the North Africa Diaspora of
  France*
by Will Higbee
978 0 7486 4004 1 (hardback)

New Romanian Cinema
by Christina Stojanova and Dana Duma
978 0 7486 4264 9 (hardback)

*Contemporary Latin American Cinema:
  New Transnationalisms*
by Dolores Tierney
978 0 7486 4573 2 (hardback)

Visit the Traditions in World Cinema website at www.euppublishing.com/series/TIWC

MAGIC REALIST CINEMA IN EAST CENTRAL EUROPE

Aga Skrodzka

EDINBURGH
University Press

© Aga Skrodzka, 2012

Transferred to digital print 2015

Edinburgh University Press Ltd
22 George Square, Edinburgh EH8 9LF

www.euppublishing.com

Typeset in 10/12.5pt Sabon
by Servis Filmsetting Ltd, Stockport, Cheshire, and
printed and bound in Great Britain by
CPI Group (UK) Ltd, Croydon CR0 4YY

A CIP record for this book is available from the British Library

ISBN 978 0 7486 3916 8 (hardback)
ISBN 978 0 7486 6934 9 (webready PDF)
ISBN 978 0 7486 6936 3 (epub)
ISBN 978 0 7486 6935 6 (Amazon ebook)

The right of Aga Skrodzka
to be identified as author of this work
has been asserted in accordance with
the Copyright, Designs and Patents Act 1988.

CONTENTS

ILLUSTRATIONS

Grateful acknowledgement is made to the following sources for permission to reproduce material previously published elsewhere. Every effort has been made to trace the copyright holders, but if any have been inadvertently overlooked, the publisher will be pleased to make the necessary arrangements at the first opportunity. I would like to thank Piotr Piotrowski from Figaro Film for granting his copyright permission to publish Figures 30, 31, and 32; Rossitsa Valkanova from KLAS Film for allowing me to publish the images photographed by Júlia Kiss as Figures 2, 3, and 10; Zornitsa Sophia for her permission to publish Figures 11, 12, 13, and 14; Film Studio OKO for granting me permission to publish the photographs by Arthur Reinhart as Figures 33 and 34; Rudolf Biermann from IN FILM Praha and Martin Šulík for granting permission to publish Figures 1, 5, 6, 18, 19, and 20; Piotr Bujnowicz for allowing me to publish his photographs, including the portraits of Jan Jakub Kolski, as Figures 16, 17, 21, 35, 36, and 37; and Paul C. Miller for providing Figure 8 and issuing his permission to publish it in this book.

ACKNOWLEDGEMENTS

This book would not have been possible without the many summers of leisure and labour I spent in the company of Aleksander and Nadzieja Zińczuk.

I should like to thank a number of people for their diverse contributions to the production of this book. My deepest gratitude goes to Jeff French, who lived with and supported this project for what seems like too many years. His belief in the book made me envision its completion against all odds. I am indebted to Justine Pekalak for providing me with peace of mind, without which writing would be a taxing process. Sandy Petrey's lessons on making scholarship personal have fostered my stance as an academic writer. I also thank him for teaching me about the importance of expressing oneself clearly and plainly. The series editors, Linda Badley and Barton Palmer, offered continuous, always enthusiastic, words of encouragement and careful editorial advice. Barton's mentorship extends well beyond this project and is a source of continued inspiration. I appreciate the thoughtful suggestions for improving this volume that were delivered to me by the anonymous readers. During the long and laborious process of composing the manuscript, my friends Joanna Borchert, Kette Thomas, Kristin Pape and Lilla Toke sustained my intellectual work with food, conversation and practical advice. The scholarship of Wendy Faris, Katarzyna Marciniak, Anikó Imre, Dina Iordanova, Ewa Mazierska, Peter Hames, Vivian Sobchack and Rosalind Galt has challenged and stimulated my thinking on the issues explored in this volume. Indirectly, the work of Zygmunt Bauman offers a philosophical framework for much of my narrative. Daniel Skrodzki worked hard on providing me with many texts unavailable via the usual library conduits. A debt is also owed to Wlodzimierz Pochmara, who facilitated my efforts at locating film stills that serve here as illustrations, Christina Stojanova, who has kindly assisted me in finding some rare Bulgarian films, and Alexandra Strelková from the Slovak Film Institute, who helped to obtain the necessary copyright permissions. My colleagues at Clemson University – especially Barbara Zaczek, Catherine Paul, Lee Morrissey, Elizabeth Rivlin, Joe Mai, Angela Naimou and Susanna Ashton ('in solidarity') – have contributed meaningful and much-needed professional guidance throughout the course of this project. I am also indebted to Clemson University and its English Department for generous institutional support, which provided me with many course releases, research grants and graduate assistants to ensure the steady progress towards publishing this book. I would like to thank Laura Mogel and David Williams for their patient copy-editing and bibliographic assistance. Finally, I thank Oskar for cooperating!

This book is dedicated to Irena and Eugeniusz Skrodzcy, the two land surveyors who taught me how to mind the ground.

PREFACE

I would like to use this space to inform the reader of what this book is, and what it is not. Rather than describing a well-established tradition in World Cinema, *Magic Realist Cinema in East Central Europe* attempts to recognise a relatively recent tradition that comes from the traumatised territory of post-1989 New Europe. Although the book brings together diverse filmmakers, whose idiosyncratic cinematic worlds could easily constitute unique traditions of their own, I argue that they share an intention to address in their films the monumental transition into the new, post-Wall era of capitalist democracy *without* sacrificing all of the old prejudices, lifestyles, ideas, spirits and things. That intention to preserve the past, whether nostalgically, superstitiously, grotesquely or simply out of habit, is in itself constitutive of tradition. Therefore, this volume not only offers a way to recognise the growing number of East Central European films as partaking in a unique stylistic, political and philosophical formation, but also is a meditation on the value of tradition in the more abstract sense. While tradition usually refers to estimable and celebrated inheritance, the magic realist tradition, which is the subject of this narrative, embraces the shameful, parochial, wrecked, forgotten and naïve. Frequently uncanny, even abject, the characters, events and places featured in the films under analysis speak of the ways in which global political, historical and economic shifts affect local culture. Importantly, despite the local space of enunciation, the films refuse to glorify the indigenous.

Unlike heritage cinema, the cinema discussed in this volume does not sell well, even if it is critically acclaimed on the international film-festival circuit.

It hardly participates in the global marketplace, which is one reason why it is important to popularise it on the pages of this book. Yet, its vernacular perspective sheds new light on the nature of globalisation. Representing the Second World culture of East Central Europe, where (post)modernity is still expected to coexist with premodern thought and practice, magic realist filmmakers (here I include directors who consistently work within the mode of magic realism and those who engage with it occasionally) document and creatively process the encounters of the old with the new. Arguably, these cinematic encounters, captured within the context of the Second World, configure global change as neither the euphoric idea of progress disseminated across the First World, nor the notion of hegemonic domination observed from the Third World's perspective, therefore avoiding what Ella Shohat and Robert Stam recognised as 'the twin pitfalls of euphoria and melancholy'.[1] Similarly, the local periphery that is stuck in time and ensconced in place is neither simply romanticised nor crudely provincialised. It becomes the locus of what can only be described as deliberate stagnation, the form of existence that counters the idea of progress, if progress is attained through technological advancement, scientific discovery, economic growth and the constant improvement of the material conditions of life. The slowing down and staying put that this stagnant periphery speaks of are reactions to the fast and furious manner in which carnivorous capitalism took over the wrecked post-Soviet economies after 1989. The local and the global remain entangled in an imaginary landscape, as fascinating as it is disturbing.

Carefully balancing the magical element with realist representation, the filmmakers manage to avoid the extreme dystopic or utopic idea of change. By first meticulously establishing the solid veneer of the real, and then slowly undermining its firmness through a strategic incorporation of magic – whether it is a supernatural occurrence, enchanting encounter with nature, ethereal apparition, unfathomable sense of mystery, or practice of private ritual – the filmmakers accentuate the process of change itself, a shift from one register of being to another. This investment in visualising metamorphosis is the ultimate value of magic realism in cinema. While all cinema, due to its kinetic nature, highlights the liquid, dynamic and unpredictable aspects of represented reality, magic realist cinema, especially in its East Central European variation, calls attention to the transformative moment itself, when, in a volatile present, the past coexists with the future. As cinema of change, it is a discourse with political potential simply because it contemplates a radical parting with the status quo and a move in the direction of an alternate, less known and less knowable reality.

This book does not pretend to offer an exhaustive survey of all East Central European films that have ever engaged magic realism; nor does it offer a country-by-country catalogue of the filmmakers who have embraced this mode of storytelling. Rather, the analysis offered here introduces a set of carefully selected films that showcase certain important and defining characteristics of magic realism as it operates on screen. In approaching the films under discussion, the national perspective has been abandoned in favour of the transnational framework. In theorising the cinematic version of magic realism, film theory had to be supplemented by critical approaches and methodology borrowed from literary studies. The twofold intention was to write a book that would serve as both a theoretical introduction to magic realism in film and an inquiry into a surprising and consistent appropriation of magic realism by a significant number of East Central European filmmakers in the context of the post-Wall transitions. The following are some of the questions that guided my inquiry: What does the proliferation of magic realism say about the collective identity of post-Wall East Central Europe? What does the East Central European cinematic rendering of magic realism suggest about this representational mode – its role in the creative processing of change and its potential for sustaining hybrid formations that are the fleeting byproducts of change? How do these magic realist films impact the established ways of thinking about the medium of cinema and its purported magic?

A concerted effort has been made to include in this study films and filmmakers from diverse countries within the multicultural and multilingual region of East Central Europe, with some obvious limitations due to the varied output of the national film industries in question and marketing restrictions on distribution. Accordingly, the final list of films under discussion includes works by male and female directors from Bulgaria, Czech Republic, Hungary, Macedonia, Poland, Serbia and Slovakia. In her overview of the history of East Central European cinema, Dina Iordanova asserts that the 'traditions of lyrical cinema, Surrealism, magical realism and experimental avant-garde animation are alive and well'.[2] She is therefore suggesting that these alternative modes of filmmaking have always been a mainstay of the region's cinematic practice. Although *Magic Realist Cinema in East Central Europe* is focused mainly on post-1989 film output as an artistic response to the drastic socio-historical change that followed the collapse of the Soviet Bloc, it is important to mention some of the key precursors of magic realism, with careers well established within the national cinemas of the region. The work of these well-known filmmakers had appealed to the audiences interested in surrealist, lyrical and spiritual depictions of reality on screen for decades prior to the 1990s, when, arguably, these artistic tendencies became more pronounced as well as politically relevant as a result of a transnational collective experience.

To understand better where magic realist filmmakers found their aesthetic and philosophical inspiration, the reader should revisit some of the films that Iordanova isolates as foundational texts for the anti-realist trend in East Central European filmmaking. There are films made by Czechoslovak New Wave directors such as Vojtěch Jasný (*Až přijde kocour / The Cassandra Cat*, 1963), Jiří Menzel (*Rozmarné léto/ Capricious Summer*, 1968), Jan Němec

(*Mučedníci lásky / Martyrs of Love*, 1966), Jaromil Jireš (*Valeria a týden divů / Valerie and her Week of Wonders*, 1970), Juraj Jakubisko (*Tisícročná včela / A Thousand-Year-Old Bee*, 1983, and *Vtáčkovia, siroty a blázni / Birds, Orphans and Fools*, 1969) and František Vláčil (*Marketa Lazarová*, 1967). There is also a number of films by directors associated with Surrealism and Expressionism, such as Wojciech Jerzy Has (*Rękopis znaleziony w Saragossie / The Saragossa Manuscript*, 1965, and *Sanatorium pod klepsydrą / The Hour-Glass Sanatorium*, 1973), Jerzy Kawalerowicz (*Matka Joanna od aniołów / Mother Joan of the Angels*, 1961) and the animators Jan Švankmajer (*Něco z Alenky / Alice*, 1988) and Jiří Barta (*Krysař / The Pied Piper*, 1986), as well as the Hungarian experimental filmmakers Zoltán Huszárik (*Szindbád / Sinbad*, 1971) and András Jeles (*Angyali üdvözlet / Annunciation*, 1984). The metaphysical cinema of Krzysztof Kieślowski should also be mentioned as one of the formative influences. Kieślowski's affinity with magic realism is most traceable in films like *Bez końca / No End*, 1985, and *La Double Vie de Véronique / Podwójne życie Weroniki / The Double Life of Veronique*, 1991. Finally, Fredric Jameson analyses Agnieszka Holland's *Gorączka / Fever*, 1981, as a prime example of magic realism in film in his seminal 1986 essay 'On Magic Realism in Film'.[3]

In her introduction to *A Companion to Magical Realism*, Wen-chin Ouyang writes,

> the spread of magical realism across continents and cultures, and more significantly across media of expression and genres, may be a welcome sign that marks the opening up of the global literary, artistic and visual landscapes to diversification held together by a common core.[4]

Having invested in diversification more than the common core, I hope that this study of the local landscape with global resonance will invite film scholars, film students and film viewers to learn about the new generation of East Central European filmmakers and explore the growing, yet underappreciated, tradition in World Cinema. Since similar traditions are in existence in other cultural contexts, this book will happily engage in future dialogue.

NOTES

1. Ella Shohat and Robert Stam, 'From the Imperial Family to the Transnational Imaginary: Media Spectatorship in the Age of Globalization', in Rob Wilson and Wimal Dissanayake (eds), *Global / Local: Cultural Production and the Transnational Imaginary* (Durham, NC: Duke University Press, 1996), p. 146 (pp. 145–70 inclusive).
2. Dina Iordanova, *Cinema of the Other Europe* (London and New York: Wallflower, 2003), p. 150.
3. Fredric Jameson, 'On Magic Realism in Film', *Critical Inquiry*, 12:2, Winter 1986, p. 311.

4. Wen-chin Ouyang, 'Magical Realism and Beyond: Ideology of Fantasy', in Stephen M. Hart and Wen-chin Ouyang (eds), *A Companion to Magical Realism* (Woodbridge: Tamesis, 2005), p. 14 (pp. 13–20 inclusive).

TRADITIONS IN WORLD CINEMA

General editors: **Linda Badley and R. Barton Palmer**
Founding editor: **Steven Jay Schneider**

Traditions in World Cinema is a series of textbooks and monographs devoted to the analysis of currently popular and previously underexamined or undervalued film movements from around the globe. Also intended for general interest readers, the textbooks in this series offer undergraduate- and graduate-level film students accessible and comprehensive introductions to diverse traditions in world cinema. The monographs open up for advanced academic study more specialised groups of films, including those that require theoretically-oriented approaches. Both textbooks and monographs provide thorough examinations of the industrial, cultural, and socio-historical conditions of production and reception.

The flagship textbook for the series includes chapters by noted scholars on traditions of acknowledged importance (the French New Wave, German Expressionism), recent and emergent traditions (New Iranian, post-Cinema Novo), and those whose rightful claim to recognition has yet to be established (the Israeli persecution film, global found footage cinema). Other volumes concentrate on individual national, regional or global cinema traditions. As the introductory chapter to each volume makes clear, the films under discussion form a coherent group on the basis of substantive and relatively transparent, if not always obvious, commonalities. These commonalities may be formal, stylistic or thematic, and the groupings may, although they need not, be popularly identified as genres, cycles or movements (Japanese horror, Chinese martial arts cinema, Italian Neorealism). Indeed, in cases in which a group of films is not already commonly identified as a tradition, one purpose of the volume is to establish its claim to importance and make it visible (East Central European Magical Realist cinema, Palestinian cinema).

Textbooks and monographs include:

- An introduction that clarifies the rationale for the grouping of films under examination
- A concise history of the regional, national, or transnational cinema in question
- A summary of previous published work on the tradition
- Contextual analysis of industrial, cultural and socio-historical conditions of production and reception
- Textual analysis of specific and notable films, with clear and judicious application of relevant film theoretical approaches
- Bibliograph(ies)/filmograph(ies)

Monographs may additionally include:

- Discussion of the dynamics of cross-cultural exchange in light of current research and thinking about cultural imperialism and globalisation, as well as issues of regional/national cinema or political/aesthetic movements (such as new waves, postmodernism, or identity politics)
- Interview(s) with key filmmakers working within the tradition.

1. VERNACULAR MAGIC REALISM IN GLOBALISING EUROPE

On the map, made in the style of baroque panoramas, the area of the Street of Crocodiles shone with the empty whiteness that usually marks polar regions or unexplored countries of which almost nothing is known. The lines on only a few streets were marked in black and their names given in simple, unadorned lettering, different from the noble script of the other captions. The cartographer must have been loath to include that district in the city and his reservations found expression in the typographical treatment.

Bruno Schulz (*The Collected Works of Bruno Schulz*, p. 100)

The cinema discussed in this volume confronts, but also preserves, what is uncanny about the history and culture of East Central Europe: the sense of being somehow alien in the house of Europe. Through the means of magic realism and a distinct vernacular focus, the films herein question and evoke this uncanny feeling, which somehow appears to be accepted by all within the filmic world, a stance of communal acquiescence more than that of consternation. In this cinematic mode, the uncanny is the status quo, recognised and affirmed by the audience, the filmmaker, the characters within the diegesis, and the symbolic collective. Magic realism reforms and invalidates the representational code of what Robert Stam calls the 'illusionistic realism',[1] much in the way that other postcolonial discourses are parasitic of the code of the coloniser so that they can destabilise this very code from within. Magic realism is realism pushed to the extreme – a hyper-realism. One can see magic as hyper-logic, a way of thinking that overemphasises causality and draws connections that present human life and history as determined by grand determinants (which, in themselves, usually escape definition), bigger than politics and economy. Magic realism helps the provincial subject to make sense of the centre-enforced currents of history by introducing a pause in history, by exposing history as always a mixture of magic and logic. This strategy is especially important when people are victimised by a history that they can neither control nor fully comprehend. Simultaneously, it allows them to avoid the trap of idealising and rationalising, which ultimately cuts the subject away from the living experience. This kind of isolation of the subject from the lived reality happens when fundamentalist religious or nationalist thinking takes over the magical understanding of the world. Magic realism insists on finding connections in structures of polyvalent and irreducible human endeavour, while fundamentalism conceives connections as strictures of dualistic oppositions.

During the post-Communist transitions of the 1990s, East Central Europeans found themselves deeply dissatisfied with the realities of the hard-won freedom: unemployment rates went up, social networks of support quickly unravelled, and the bankruptcy of the state economic system, as well as the shortage of resources, which had been squandered by the inefficient Communist industry, became apparent. The ideal that guided the political opposition and fuelled the hopes of those who jeopardised their lives fighting Communism suddenly revealed its nature as just that – an ideal: a composite of desire, imagination and anarchic construction. The filmmakers discussed in the present study responded with yet another ideal. One 'small' film after another, directors such as Emir Kusturica, Jan Jakub Kolski, Dorota Kędzierzawska, Béla Tarr and Martin Šulík, among others, have created cinematic microcosms, where the source of spiritual, economic and cultural replenishment is found in the rural countryside, provincial town, often the *terra incognita* of childhood, or the margins inhabited by an ethnic community. I analyse these micro-worlds as private enunciations of a regional identity, much determined by an acknowledged peripheral status of East Central Europe.

EAST CENTRAL EUROPE AND ITS REGIONAL IDENTITY

The regional identity in this area of Europe has formed through the common experiences of twentieth-century history, along with the much older common cultural denominators, such as the region's deeply pagan inflections of Christianity and its Byzantine and Ottoman heritage; the long tradition of Jewish, Romani and Islamic settlement; and its geographic location as a buffer zone between the West and the East. Dina Iordanova, one of the leading and most prolific scholars on the cinema of East Central Europe, in her highly comprehensive survey, *Cinema of the Other Europe*, advocates the regional approach as a means for the 'general trends in the film industry and aesthetics to be traced'.[2] She emphasises the twentieth-century '"imposed" togetherness' of East Central Europe, caused by a sequence of political developments: 'the end of Austria–Hungary (1918), the Molotov–Ribbentrop agreement (1939), the Yalta conference (1945), the establishment of Communist regimes in East Central Europe (1945 to 1948), Khrushchev's denunciation of Stalin (1956), the Hungarian Uprising (1956), the Prague Spring (1968), the Warsaw pact invasion (also 1968), or the launch of *glasnost* (1986)'.[3]

In the popular imaginary, especially from the Anglo-American perspective, Europe is configured as a territory of relative homogeneity. This is also the case in much of the recent academic discourse. The Europe of Eurocentrism consists of very few countries, the same countries that are perceived as undoubtedly 'European' by travel agents, and seems to encompass a culture that rose out of ancient Greece, Christianity and the European colonisation of other continents. In a sense, the very discourse of Eurocentrism contributes to the negative and exclusionary politics that it originally set out to criticise. In the hands of some postcolonial scholars, Eurocentrism functions as a way to congeal the dimensions of the enemy and crystallise the binary of the colonising centre and the colonised margins.

This clarifying, conceptualising strategy comes at a great price, however. Europe is reduced to a few politically and economically powerful nations. The intricacy of this continent's multilingual, multidenominational and multicultural identity is greatly limited. The history of the European colonisation of its own European margins is overlooked. The complex hierarchies that exist among the forty-plus different European countries are erased. In *Provincializing Europe: Postcolonial Thought and Historical Difference*, the highly celebrated text of postcolonial theory, Dipesh Chakrabarty criticises European historicism for 'the denial of coevalness' – the myopic vision of European philosophy and history, which limits the developments of capitalism, modernity and the Enlightenment to the geographic territory of Europe, ignoring the role of the overseas colonies, the 'elsewhere', in this narrative of progress, and in the material wealth that benefits Europeans.[4] At the same time as he resurrects the role of the 'subaltern classes of the third world' in the discourse of modernity, Chakrabarty buries the history of European margins (East Central Europe is one of them) and contributes to further idealisation of 'Europe'.[5] In his introduction, he patently admits: 'The Europe I seek to provincialise or decenter is an imaginary figure that remains deeply embedded in clichéd and shorthand forms in some everyday habits of thought.'[6] By implication, this statement attests to Chakrabarty's sense of the existence of the other Europe that does not need provincialising, and that the acknowledgement of this other, already de-centred, Europe somehow undermines the righteousness with which much of the postcolonial scholarship carries out its task.

Created soon after East Central Europe had opened up its borders to the free market economy, increasingly complex networks of international politics, global cultural exchanges, world tourism, and influence of the World Wide Web, the films that are the subject of the present study embrace the stereotype of East Central Europe as provincial, insular and out of date, if not completely out of time.[7] This micro-perspective playfully engaged with the region's existing identity as marginal and inferior to Europe 'proper', but also signalled widespread scepticism towards the new macro-perspective of the globalising world. These cinematic visions have been offered in a gesture of contradistinction to the Western paradigm of freedom, as well as the cinema that reflects it, which time and again turns out to be too out of reach for the exhausted and impoverished Second World society. At the same time, these films came out of a long tradition of the region's subversive art, which gave expression to the worlds and realities hidden from the official discourses of those in control. In the shape of esoteric fables, the carnivalesque and experimental images, the region's aesthetic tradition would often set in motion the repressed religious beliefs, local folklore and indigenous spiritual and hermetic traditions, as well as pagan adoration of nature in order to laugh at, question or reconfigure the official ruling ideology, be it Christianity, the Enlightenment, Positivism, Fascism, Marxism or capitalism.

In his 2000 film *Landscape* (*Krajinka*), Slovak filmmaker Martin Šulík comments on this notion of defiant peripherality. Through an episodic structure modelled on the frame story of Boccaccio's *Decameron*, the film presents ten unrelated stories, whose protagonists are the small people inhabiting the small countryside, presumably rural Slovakia. The heroes of these unheroic tales are madmen, vagabonds, village idiots, children and poachers. They form a decidedly eclectic group. What unites them is their marginality, highlighted by their physical, mental, economic or social handicap, as well as their rootedness in the land and nature that surrounds them. The Slovak word *krajinka* that constitutes the title of the film literally means 'a tiny country'. The narrator who speaks in voice-over, and whose role is to impart a semblance of coherence to the sprawling stories, nonchalantly informs the viewer at the very opening of the film that 'This country never was. And never will be. Nobody talks about it; nobody remembers it. It's like it disappeared from the map forever.' On the one hand, therefore, the narrator is announcing the slight and spectral status of his subject matter. On the other hand, the colourful characters interacting with the natural world, whose earthiness is palpable in every scene shot by the masterful cinematographer Martin Štrba, testify to the authenticity of their minuscule existence, stubbornly entrenched in their hovels (Šulík's countryside is both picturesque and darkly grotesque) against the upheavals of big history.

While the events of that kind of history are directly evoked in the film – the viewer gets a glimpse of the two World Wars, the Holocaust, Stalin's

Figure 1   Imriško on a potty in his parents' orchard in *Landscape* (2000).

Sovietisation and the Prague Spring – it is the local chronicle of private, tragi-comic histories that receives the spotlight. For example, in the first segment of the film, the viewer finds out how the little boy named Imriško, while sitting on his potty in his parents' orchard, is tempted by some unripe fruit, which he pulls off a nearby bush, only to choke on it and drop to the ground uncon-scious. His father, whom the narrator describes as 'the fair sportsman, who could run a 100 metres under 14 seconds . . . and more if the stopwatch had been better', hurries to the nearest town to get the doctor, but not without first ordering a small coffin on his way to the doctor's house, just in case. The Jewish doctor breaks his Sabbath and comes to the boy's rescue immediately. Much like the boy's father, the doctor, too, traverses space in lightning speed. The scene of the doctor dashing through the countryside on his motorcycle is appended with the narrator's comment: 'Dr Roth was the fastest member of the Czechoslovak Automobile Club.' He brings Imriško back to life in a feat of absurd doctoring, by simply blowing cigarette smoke into the child's mouth. The parents are obviously overjoyed and quickly give away the coffin, so reso-lutely purchased in an effort to be prepared for the worst, to the neighbour, whose daughter dies for real.

This and other similarly idiosyncratic stories featured in *Landscape* have been mined by the filmmaker and the screenwriter Dušan Dušek from oral lore, still in circulation among their own family and friends. By bringing these tales to screen, Šulík and Dušek renew the life of the stories, which would be otherwise forgotten, along with the lives of the provincial characters who populate them. The particularity, even strangeness, of the events portrayed in these narratives constitutes a distinctive pleasure for the film viewer, who quickly becomes invested in the fascinating, albeit commonplace, existences of individuals who are unheroic, yet worthy of remembrance. It is possible to see the filmmaker's gesture of evoking big history only to trivialise it by the tall stories of the small people as an oppositional strategy with ideological implications. Although severely criticised by Slovak public opinion for its negative portrayal of the country of Slovakia, *Landscape* is a recuperative text, albeit not in the nationalistic sense. Rather, it seeks to express, through its episodic structure, diminutive content and grotesque stylisation, the importance of the unglamorous, hardly pastoral, rural periphery that miraculously – or, as some might argue, abjectly – persists in the heart of Europe.

In his book *The Art and Politics of Film*, John Orr theorises a Cold War cinematic tradition of such oppositional art, exemplified by directors such as Andrei Tarkovsky, Sergei Paradjanov and Miklós Jancsó, in terms of its resistance to both the calcified Communist ideology and Western modernism, calling it the 'cinema of wonder'.[8] Orr traces the origins of this cinematic trend to Alexander Dovzhenko's 1930 silent feature, *Earth* (*Zemlya*). Different from the futurist urban euphorias of the Soviet montage directors, such as Dziga Vertov or Sergei Eisenstein, Dovzhenko's film, although celebratory of Marxist ideals, constitutes a strikingly poetic contemplation of nature, the Ukrainian steppe and the indigenous folklore of the locals. The film is preoccupied with the metaphysics of life and death, specifically the cyclical rhythm of being in the world. It also functions as a hymn to the ennobling and purifying qualities of nature, a distant echo of Jean-Jacques Rousseau's Romantic primitivism, which contributed to the rise of folklore studies and the spread of neo-paganism across Europe. While *Earth* preaches the superiority of the collective farmers' organic relationship to their means of production, in its cinematography, it is a lyrical and serene sequence of luminous images that capture the transcendence of the natural world.

Dovzhenko's film opens with an extended long shot of a rye field, undulating in the wind. The camera contemplates the sky above, then, very slowly, zooms in on the rye itself, framing the natural movement of the full grain stalks. Next, the camera moves on to showcase a few sunflowers in full bloom, with the multiplicity of ripe seeds in close-up. The viewer must patiently take in these lingering sequences that quietly witness the subtle but steady stirring of nature. The next shot features the heavy branches of an apple tree, with abundant fruit weighing it down. It is the time of harvest, the end of the growing cycle. Underneath the apple tree, an old man, Simon, is lying peacefully. Another old peasant asks, 'You're dying, Simon?' To which he stoically responds 'That I am.' The camera then frames two infants sitting nearby and playing with apples, and goes back to show the calm ebb and flow of the field of rye, as if to suggest that Simon's death is timely and followed by the ascendance of new life. Simon's companion in death states prudently, 'Go ahead, Simon, and after you're dead, let me know where you are there . . . in heaven or hell.' This mixture of acquiescence and spirituality that is deeply invested in natural processes that guide human life outside of technologically enhanced and historically mitigated experience becomes the dominant feature in the films that are the subject of the ensuing narrative.

Unlike Eisenstein's cinema, which mainly mobilises the viewer's consciousness and intellect, Dovzhenko's film operates through affect. In the 'cinema of wonder', Orr explains, the engine of progress comes to a halt, and 'history becomes tragic, yet the marvel of life itself goes on'.[9] This cinema, he adds, generates a perfectly detached cinematic totality – 'the site of an artistic beyond, in which contemplation as a form of witnessing the immediate, the existential, the social, becomes something more, a form of meta-narrative to rival the meta-narrative of the state'.[10]

East Central Europe as a Postcolonial Territory

The twentieth-century common experiences of Communism, the two World Wars and countless revolutions created among East Central Europeans a deep sense of scepticism and ambivalence towards modernity, which, from its nineteenth-century beginnings on, has been shaped by the violent appetites of foreign and domestic aggressors. East Central Europe, especially during its modern period, has been under the direct influence of two powerful centres: the imperial forces of the West (Austro-Hungarian and Prussian Empires, and later the Nazi regime) and, on the other side, the vast and aggressive Russian Empire (later the Communist Soviet Union). The term 'East Central Europe' is itself relatively new and still debated among scholars of the region. Despite the controversy surrounding this term, one observes an increasing acceptance, especially in the discourse of contemporary politics, of the term 'East Central Europe' gradually replacing 'Eastern Europe', which, for decades, linguistically grouped the countries of the Soviet bloc and legitimised their incorporation by the Eastern neighbour, Communist Russia. Not an expert in toponomastics, but a fan of Austin's speech act theory, I consistently use 'East Central Europe' to replace 'Eastern Europe' in an effort to counter this linguistic reminder of Communist propaganda's insistence on the 'organic ties' of the region with the Russian culture,[11] as well as to undermine the West's Orientalist habit of distancing that part of Europe as a remote and exotic frontier. On 9 January 2010, *The Economist* ran an article on the obsolescence of the label 'Eastern Europe' in times when many of the countries in the region are financially more stable than the Western members of the European Union. The author of the article suggests that 'calling them "Eastern Europe" suggests not only a common fate under totalitarian rule, but a host of ills that go with it: a troubled history then; bad government and economic misery now'.[12] Meanwhile, the post-2008 global recession has spared the economic health of many of the countries in question, thus confronting the common assumption about this part of Europe being still weighed down by the common legacy of Communist bankruptcy.

In terms of mythical geography (to recall Norman Davis's term for emotional and intellectual assumptions about location), the region in question is very fluid and might encompass Poland, the Czech Republic, Slovakia, Hungary and Romania, but also Ukraine, Byelorussia, the Baltic states and the Balkans, depending on who is visualising the parameters of the area. For the sake of this project, which deals with the cultural consciousness rather than the socio-economic status of East Central Europe, it is not necessary to define the exact borderlines. Cultural movements are seldom chartable, especially cultural movements among countries whose borders have always posited a challenge to cartographers.

In order to sift through the cultural expansion of the East and the West over this ever-fluctuating terrain and their impact on the identity formation of East Central Europe, I employ some of the methodology and theory of postcolonial studies. The idea of East Central Europe as an object of colonisation is a controversial one. There are some obvious similarities between the colonisation of this region and the colonisation of the Third World: mainly economic exploitation and military control. But there are also important differences that make East Central Europe a site of unique colonialism. This is mostly because, while under the occupation of the foreign forces, East Central European countries remained very conscious, if not overly conscious, of their national identities.[13] Historians hypothesise that this is so because the formation of modern statehood was already well under way in those countries when Prussia, Russia and Austria decided to absorb them into their respective empires (from the late eighteenth century on). When robbed of statehood, these countries continued to work out their identities by emphasising their nationalities, through linguistic, artistic and religious practices. The inhabitants of these countries enjoyed a relative independence in the area of creative expression. Consequently, they were able to interpolate foreign acculturation.

Furthermore, the East Central European countries, unlike most of the Third World countries that fell victim to colonisation, were able to imagine their fate as common (a community of colonised nations) and accompanied by relative sovereignty (when often they had none), due to their common conviction about their own European-ness: their peripheral European-ness, but nevertheless one that carried an important weight. Although both Western Europe and Russia had their appetites for the East Central European territory, they also wished this area to remain apart, as an insulating corridor. The importance of this role as a buffering agent has been recognised by the countries in question and used to negotiate their shared identity. Any dividing zone is characterised by fluidity and dynamism, by the pushing and pulling from opposite directions, but also by a certain amount of abjection that stems from its position as a boundary, which is always preconceived as a visible line of transgression. East Central Europe, through its imposed, yet accepted, liminality, continuously questions and destabilises the meaning of singular European identity. This status of East Central Europe as the 'difference within' has persisted even after the region's integration into the European Union in 2004 and 2007.

In 2001, Iglika Triffonova, a Bulgarian director with a strong background in documentary filmmaking, made her first feature film *Letter to America* (*Pismo do Amerika*). In this film, combining documentary technique with a highly experimental and poetic structure, Triffonova explores matters of spirituality in the context of the quickly globalising, post-1989 Bulgaria. In doing so, the filmmaker comments on the liminality of the post-Communist region with respect to its legacy of Communism and its future of capitalism, as well as its precarious cultural location between the West and the East. *Letter to America* tells the story of a young writer Ivan (Phillip Avramov), who lives modestly with his girlfriend Nina (Ana Popadopulu) in one of the many Soviet-style apartment districts in Sofia. One day, Ivan finds out that his best friend Kamen (Peter Antonov), who emigrated to America and made a successful career as a theatre director in New York City, has ended up in a hospital, with severe car-crash injuries and in a state of coma. Ivan is refused a visa for the United States, and instead of visiting his dying friend, he decides to visit the mountain village where Kamen was born. A video camera in hand, he records the landscape that he traverses and the people that he meets on the way. Ivan's specific quest is to recover the ancient song, often mentioned by Kamen, which is believed to ward off Death. Ivan is travelling to the remote countryside to retrieve this esoteric piece of local poetry in the hope of saving Kamen's life. The two friends are making their journeys in opposite directions. While Kamen's trajectory takes him out of the village and outside of Bulgaria, into the cosmopolitan space of New York City, Ivan is undertaking a trip back to that very village hidden in the Bulgarian mountains, the legendary birthplace of Orpheus. After many frustrations, but also unexpected detours that occasion many endearing encounters with the locals, Ivan meets an elderly woman, who is one of the very few surviving members of the community still to know and remember the lyrics of the healing song. The song is sung to Ivan on the slope of a breathtakingly beautiful mountain, and the viewer soon finds out that it does, indeed, accomplish the miracle for which Ivan was hoping.

The filmic space is liminal in how it simultaneously accommodates the impulse of global expansion and local concentration. It speaks of Bulgaria, and by extension South Eastern Europe, as a place where these two energies coexist, where both a search for new beginnings abroad and the old beginnings in the native back yard are meaningful routes of identity construction

Figure 2   Ivan contemplates premodern and postmodern tools in *Letter to America* (2001).

and creative exploration. The local and the global are signalled throughout the film in the two tropes that Ivan engages in his mission to reinstate Kamen's ties with life: the camera and the song. The first one represents mechanical reproduction, the latter an ancient oral tradition. These two ways of storytelling are not so much contrasted by Triffonova, as they are used side by side as eclectic elements within the hybrid text of her film. Both Kamen and Ivan use the camera as amateur videographers and ethnographers. At the start of the film, we see some of Kamen's videos shot in the streets of New York City upon his arrival there. Kamen curiously documents the metropolitan crowd, showcasing its unique urban intensity (the dialect, the fashion and the body) and ethnic diversity. Although his videos speak of the mosaic of the global village, they frame the subjects as natives, whose fusion with their surroundings (parks, pavements, bridges and buildings) testifies to their rootedness and local attachments. Kamen's recordings are then surprisingly similar to Ivan's videos recorded in the Bulgarian countryside, which portray old peasant women dyeing wool or performing funeral rites at the side of the river. Both men use their cameras to capture the vernacular cultures that they visit and import them to an audience abroad (Kamen sends his films to Ivan as visual postcards from America, and Ivan composes his recordings as the titular letter to America). As a result, Triffonova's film, instead of fetishising the distance between Bulgaria and the United States, brings the seemingly incongruent cultures of East and West closer together. In fact, the film portrays Bulgaria itself as an interstitial territory, where the traditions of Eastern Orthodoxy and ancient Greece have always co-informed the local culture. Correspondingly, the archaic death-defying song, presumably a text of Thracian Orphic poetry, once retrieved by Ivan, travels far and wide and reaches Kamen in the New York City hospital. The song brings him back to life and back to his profession as a director of postmodern theatre. It is significant that, in her ecumenical gesture, the filmmaker scrambles the directionality of the local and the global influence, making any kind of judgement about the prevalence of one over the other irrelevant.

The well-acknowledged difference between the colonisation of the Second World and that of the Third World, rather than prohibiting the postcolonial inquiry, provides points for analysis that could only enrich and problematise the area of postcolonial studies. Investigating the centuries-old history of European colonisation of its local, European, peripheries can only deepen our understanding of different forms of colonialism. Analysing the methods of Soviet ideological colonialism of East Central Europe, on the other hand, allows us to shed more light on the most recent form of cultural and economic imperialism – the surreptitious neo-colonialism – that does not necessarily involve military occupation and war for territorial domination. The fact that, under Communist domination, the countries of East Central Europe remained officially independent nation-states, with periodic incidents of Soviet military incursion, does not cancel out the hidden but painfully real pressures and limitations enforced by the foreign centre of power upon these countries.

Embracing the Periphery in Magic Realist Cinema

In *The Price of Freedom*, Piotr Wandycz carefully reviews the theories of socio-economic and political history of East Central Europe and questions the concept of colonial periphery and its usefulness with regard to this part

Figure 3   The local women who keep the secret of the healing song in *Letter to America*.

of Europe. Nevertheless, he concludes that, historically, countries like the Czech Republic, Hungary or Poland may be viewed as peripheral territory to the European core – the core that, for many centuries, has been located on the strip of land that stretches from Northern Italy, through Northern and Southeastern France, the Netherlands and Western Germany, to Southern England. Interestingly, Wandycz inquires whether the socio-economic model that divides Europe into centre, periphery and semi-periphery could be useful for studying the culture of Europe, and especially the cultural achievements of East Central Europe. He asks: 'Did most of the great cultural currents and movements in Europe originate in the core? Has East Central Europe been mainly an adapter and developer rather than an initiator?'[14] My answer to these questions follows the work of those film scholars who have recently provided excellent studies of the European periphery within the postcolonial perspective. Through their innovative approaches, Luisa Rivi, Anikó Imre, Katarzyna Marciniak and Catherine Portuges, among others, have allowed us to view the European centre as implicated in a complex web of reciprocal cultural dependencies with its most proximate, continental Other.

Understandably, the nature of these dependencies is very different from that of the dependencies of the imperial European core with the colonies set on other continents, but the importance of understanding the former relationships matches the importance of understanding the latter. The goal of such studies is to avoid comparing the taker's and the giver's contributions to the culture. Culture is not limited to cultural achievements. Significant cultural knowledge is to be found in the reasons for a lack of so-called achievements, or in the analysis of normative criteria for what counts as cultural achievement. The study of any one culture is pointless without the study of the subculture that functions as the difference for the negative identification of the dominant culture.

When Milan Kundera wrote his seminal essay 'The Tragedy of Central Europe', published in 1984 in *The New York Review of Books*, the purpose of differentiating East Central Europe from the ideological formation of Eastern Europe was paramount. It seemed at the time that the legacy of this multicultural region was being threatened by slow, almost imperceptible, assimilation into the vast dominion of Russified republics. Therefore, Kundera amplified the Western component in the region's identity, especially its cultural identity, almost as if beckoning the West to come and claim what was always legitimately Western. He spoke of the anti-Communist uprisings in Hungary, Czechoslovakia and Poland as 'a drama of the West – a West that, kidnapped, displaced and brainwashed, nevertheless insists on defending its identity'.[15]

In his impassioned plea for Western support, Kundera othered Russian civilisation as fundamentally alien to the spirit of European egalitarianism and the political system of democracy, a civilisation ultimately pursuing its long-standing imperial appetites. Kundera defined East Central Europe as a 'family of small nations' living under continuous threat, aware that 'their existence may be put in question at any moment; a small nation can disappear and it knows it'.[16] Through this observation, he pointed out to Western Europe the role of marginal European-ness that should not be forgotten so easily. That is the only part of Kundera's reasoning that holds true today. If Europe is to become a sphere of intercultural contact and complex ethnic coexistence, it must pay increased attention to preserving the difference that these small nations bring into its European Union's fold. Kundera's other claims about East Central Europe's inherently Western identity or the alleged history of solidarity among the community of small nations were since then rightfully disclosed as the dramatic exaggerations of an exiled novelist stepping into a politician's shoes when the situation became dire.

While taking into account the fact that postcolonial theorists speak from very specific locations (which often reflect their private positions on the border of their native postcolonial territory and the Anglo-American dominant culture that they now inhabit and speak from), and that cultural study of one group can rarely be applied to that of another, I borrow certain concepts from postcolonial theory and forsake others, depending on their applicability to the culture of East Central Europe. Edward Said's analysis of Orientalism informed my understanding of the relationship between power and knowledge that has dictated Western Europe's image of its Eastern periphery as barbaric and irrational since the arrival of Romanticism. Larry Wolff's tracing of the invention of Eastern Europe back to the Enlightenment, as Western Europe's most immediate savage Other, furthers Said's theory of Orientalism and provides my study with an account of the earliest history of ideological colonisation of the region by its Western neighbour. Gayatri Chakravorty Spivak's concept of the 'subaltern' sheds some light on the disturbing silence of the female voice in the conversations that the male East Central European artists have conducted on the subject of the region's identity vis-à-vis equally male-dominated visions of Western Europe and / or post-Soviet Russia. Katarzyna Marciniak's recent explorations of 'Second Worldness' with regard to transnational crossings (taking place in social reality and cultural representation) inspired my own commitment to preserving the particularity of the post-Soviet heritage in the new, globalising world. Marciniak is puzzled by the unanimous and 'incessant stress on the idea that the "Second World is no more"'.[17] The present study contributes to Marciniak's efforts to question the impulse to erase the interstitial space of Second Worldness by showing that this sphere is not just a reductive socio-political construct, but reflects a difference stronger and older than the Cold War terminology, the difference that stubbornly persists in the era of European integration.

Will the centre–periphery paradigm applied to East Central Europe perpetuate its peripheral status? I believe that an intelligent and creative appropriation of this model, already employed by many of the region's artists, including filmmakers, can help to subvert the very real postcolonial legacy between Western Europe and its adjacent peripheries, or at least change the way we think about imperialism. The same applies to the legacy left by the Soviet Empire. The artists in question practise the East Central European variety of magic realism, sometimes self-consciously, more often completely unaware of the growing theoretical significance and popularity of this aesthetic mode in postcolonial studies. Magic realism, with its smart and always mobile juxtaposition of centre and periphery, offers a very attractive way to oppose the discourses of the centre (for example, European modernism or American postmodernism), and thus gain the space and voice for the periphery. Denying the widely used and intelligible dichotomy of powerful Western Europe and its underdeveloped Eastern European periphery, which has shaped the popular notion of Europe for quite some time now, will not help East Central Europe to gain identity outside of this controlling and compulsive, even if imaginary, mould. What can be done is to enter the mould and attempt to alter its shape from within. Magic realist cinema provides a unique arena for the East Central European (post)colonial subject to claim the remembrance of things and ways of life that were, and still are, carefully censored out by the dominant discourses of the numerous 'great powers' that insist on controlling the cluster of little nations nestled on the cusp of the great civilisations of the Orient and the Occident.

The films discussed in this study regiment the memory of the colonising forces of the nineteenth and twentieth centuries, as well as counter the present global developments by assuming a distinctive style of artistic representation. This aesthetic sensibility has been theorised as magic realism, hyper-realism or the fantastic, among other, less popular, categories that literary scholars have devised to refer to a counter-epistemological impulse that characterises this stylistic mode. This counter-epistemological moment is the 'hesitancy' of representational discourse between mimesis and allegory (Todorov in *The Fantastic*, Jameson in 'Magic Realism in Film', Derrida in 'The Law of Genre', and Freud in his notion of 'psychical reality'). Aided by Stephen Slemon's theory of magic realism as postcolonial discourse, I discuss this special sensibility as a non-genre, or anti-genre, that is used by the artists of East Central Europe as a way to escape the positivist 'reality principle' and to circumvent the aesthetic of (post)modernism, thus expressing the specificity and incommensurability of their condition.

This project does not attempt to enter into debate with the Latin American theories of magic realism. It hopes to enrich the landscape of what is now considered magic realism and contribute to its understanding as an international phenomenon. It also hopes to confirm the validity of seeing magic realism as a representational strategy intrinsic to certain socio-cultural conditions, moments in history that arise in different parts of the world, often simultaneously. Some questions that are at the centre of Latin American conceptions of magic realism are asked and investigated in this project as well, with the hope that the discoveries of the critics who researched and theorised the dynamics of Latin American magic realism can illuminate its occurrence in East Central European art. One such question echoes the old concern of the critics of Latin American magic realism: if both Americas are deeply influenced by the colonial power struggle, multiple-race identity formations and mixing languages, why does magic realism have a significantly stronger presence in South America than in North America? Can one draw a constructive parallel between these different Americas and possibly different Europes?

THE SENSE OF PLACE AND THE POLITICS OF MODERNISATION

Among other complex reasons, the answer to these questions rests in the human experience of the physical space. People of Latin America and East Central Europe have a long history of exhibiting resistance towards a complete transition into modernity, which in both cases coincided with Western imperial rule. Modern governmental legislature and property laws required the complete regimentation of space. The coloniser, along with the local elites, insisted on the use of standardised cartography, uniform state administration and an efficient taxation system. In *Globalization: The Human Consequences*, Zygmunt Bauman comments on the highly systematised organisational effort of the colonising agents, always wrestling with the localities' inscrutable attachments to their material and cultural traditions:

> Territories fully domesticated, thoroughly familiar and intelligible for the purposes of the day-to-day activities of the villagers or parishioners remained confusingly and threateningly alien, inaccessible and untamed to the authorities in the capital; the reversal of that relationship was one of the main dimensions and indices of the 'modernization process'.[18]

Magic realism as a mode of symbolic representation reflects this schism in perception of space. Through its unique sensibility, which combines the sense of the utterly familiar with the otherworldly, magic realism comments on the irreducible gap between those who exploit space and those who inhabit it. As with many other colonial territories, the cultures of Latin America and East Central Europe have always been perched on the cusp between premodernity and modernity, always strangely arrested in a transformation that they make sure will never be completed. Today, this long-standing tradition of resistance, and the economic and technological handicaps that come with it, is aided by contemporary global hegemonies, which equip the privileged few with unprecedented mobility, while grounding the impoverished locals in ghettos. Despite the proliferation of electronic communication systems, the growing speed of transportation and the bewildering transfer of capital around the globe, the majority of today's localities remain poor and isolated, cut off from the expensive technological highways. While the rate of Internet access in East Central Europe is growing fast, the statistics show that broadband connections are limited to a small fraction of Internet users, and the majority of the population has no access at all.

In his 1986 essay 'On Magic Realism in Film', Fredric Jameson envisions magic realism as always emerging from moments of socio-economic transitions and the accompanying coexistence of multiple representational codes, and by extension, the coexistence of different perceptions of space, of the immediate physical reality. He states, 'magic realism depends on a content which betrays the overlap or the coexistence of precapitalist with nascent capitalist or technological features'.[19] In his analysis of some Polish and Venezuelan cinema, Jameson points out that, on the surface, magic realist cinema is very similar to the so-called nostalgia films of the postmodern era. Both seem to pay a lot of attention to material reality and both offer a concentration of enthralling visual detail. But while nostalgia films elicit from the viewer a consuming gaze as 'a formal compensation for the enfeeblement of historicity in our own time', magic realism engages the viewing subject with 'the image in its present time' and, by doing so, allows the viewer to encounter history – 'in that case history with holes, perforated history, which includes gaps not immediately visible to us, so close is our gaze to its objects of perception'.[20] Jameson's conception of magic realism as an encounter with history, before history is smoothed over into a neat narrative propelled by an uninterrupted timeline, brings it back to the moment of its initial formulation as a response to the chaos of historical and economic change in war-torn Europe.

The Great Water (Golemata Voda, 2004), a Macedonian film by Ivo Trajkov, is a good example of magic realism that foregrounds historical change. Shot in 2002, during the civil war in Macedonia (part of former Yugoslavia), and telling a story set in 1946, when the Communist Federal People's Republic of Yugoslavia was formed, the film speaks of the memory of historical unrest from the space of yet another historical conflict. Having just suffered a heart attack and teetering between life and death in his hospital bed, the protagonist Lem Nikodinoski (Meto Jovanovski), a present-day politician in Macedonia, reminisces about the difficult childhood he endured in a Soviet re-education camp. At this state institution, run much like a division of the Hitler Youth, the children whose parents had been identified as 'enemies of the revolution' arrived to undergo a proper Communist upbringing. Lem's voice-over narration takes the viewer back in time to the immediate post-World War II years, and, in a series of flashbacks, delivers the story of a group of children who have to negotiate History and the grand designs of the government in power in an attempt to survive their interrupted childhoods. Along with other unfortunate children, young Lem (Saso Kekenovski) endures with stoic acceptance hours of brutal exercise drill, long sessions of anti-religious propaganda, and arbitrary punishment executed by sadistic wardens. The scenes that portray the regime's abuses of power are painfully realistic and disturbingly explicit; yet, they also preserve the absurdity and dark comedy of the grandiose authority at work. Lem, who is by nature shy, unassertive and physically feeble, appears to be lonelier and sadder than other lonely and forsaken kids in the camp. This changes when a 13–year-old boy, Isaak Keyten (Maja Stankovska), arrives at the re-education facility. He seems to exude some sort of charisma, an unspecified supernatural energy that is detected by all, including the camp headmaster, Comrade Ariton (Mitko Apostolovski), and his deputy, Comrade Olivera (Verica Nedeska). The people who bring Isaak in claim that he was found with the monks, who no longer cared to house him, as they suspected the boy of being 'Satan's seed'. Filmmaker Trajkov translates Isaak's magic to the screen in a subtle and touching way. Through a strategic use of music and a collection of reaction shots that express everybody's unmistaken recognition of the boy's difference, Trajkov manages to stay well within the realist register, while bringing in an unknowable element that cannot be ignored. Isaak's

Figure 4   Lem and Isaak witnessing the starry spectacle of night in *The Great Water* (2004).

otherworldly presence threatens the camp's policy of atheism by casting doubt on Marxist theories of dialectical materialism and humanism. This further complicates the ideological dissension that already exists within the camp, where loyalty to Stalin is undermined by the rising popularity of Josip Tito, and Comrade Ariton's lessons on religion as the opium of the masses are devalued by his own wife's nocturnal practice of Christian liturgy, heavily augmented by pagan rites (she makes the sign of the cross with a figurine of a cat). With the introduction of Isaak's character into the film, socialist realism enters into a strange dialogue with magic realism. The distinction between the two modes of representing reality is signalled by the cinematographer's choice of camera filters. Suki Medencevic consistently uses yellow to show the gruelling daily routine and the utter misery of camp life. He chooses blue to signal the hope that Isaak brings with him to the camp. Medencevic's blue filters are especially effective in poetic long shots of the sky and the great expanse of water (the lake) that surround the camp, providing a visual meditation on alternatives to the claustrophobic system of the camp.

Isaak's radical otherness is summoned to screen by the cross-gender performance of the female actor Stankovska, who plays Isaak as part-human, part-saint and part-Satan. Lem quickly recognises Isaak's spiritual strength and is attracted to it, while others fear it. Lem decides to win the friendship of the mysterious stranger. He eventually succeeds by confronting Comrade Olivera in an act of civil courage. This gesture quickly wins Isaak's trust; he proposes to Lem a pact of blood brothership. During their relationship, Lem and Isaak engage in witchcraft rituals in the attic that strengthen their special bond, bizarre acts of killing and reviving cats in order to shake the authorities out of their atheist comfort, and impressive feats of controlling the weather. While these adventures bring some temporary respite and hope, the film never turns nostalgic. Eventually, the boys' friendship ends because of Lem's heartless betrayal, which results in cruel punishment for Isaak. While Lem is allowed to leave the camp, Isaak is said to have dematerialised in the cell where he was serving his penalty.

The ageing Lem, remembering these events some sixty years later, is full of guilt and as far from any sense of closure as a man with a guilty conscience could be. His thoughtful narrative, although entrancing, does not help us to understand who Isaak was and what eventually happened to him. Nor do we fully understand why Lem betrayed him. One easy explanation is that Isaak was simply the fearful Lem's superior alter ego, a figment of his imagination that made the cruel reality of living in the camp bearable. The film, however, does not directly suggest that interpretation. Rather, it carefully safeguards the open-endedness of Lem's account. The vivid memory of Isaak and his omnipotence is a memory of an alternative to the Communist ideology. Isaak represents a spirited resistance to the system, which even in its early stages was already failing. His impossible actions could have led to a different future. As such, Isaak's character prevents the account from being settled, keeping the past well within the present, and thus asking the viewer to witness the push and pull of history. While the history of the Communist takeover in East Central Europe has been told and documented in the textbooks, Lem's experience of it, as embedded in his private story, remains difficult to comprehend. This incongruence of history in its process of becoming, i.e. history in the making, is expressed in the film through the layering of different registers: the poetic, the realist, the magical and the lyrical. Thus structurally and texturally fractured, the tale speaks of the impossibility of ever ordering one's encounter with history. Still, the overarching realist convention invites the attempt to do so, therefore producing a text hyper-conscious of history, a text that meets Fredric Jameson's definition of magic realism as a response to history that hurts.

Magic Realism's Beginnings in War-torn Europe

It is important to note that the latest studies in magic realism show that the term's genealogy leads us beyond 1940s and 1950s Latin America, back to post-World War I Europe and the anti-modernist impulse in the realm of visual arts. In 1925, Franz Roh, the German art historian, coined the term *Magischer Realismus* to characterise the post-Expressionist direction in European painting that took artists away from Expressionism and abstract art back to Realism. Painters such as Otto Dix, Max Ernst, Alexander Kanoldt, George Grosz and Giorgio de Chirico countered the hyperbolic Expressionist image with a cool and meticulous photographic image of reality focused on the commonplace, the most familiar elements of everyday life, which, paradoxically, in the creative process became imbued with mystery and Freudian uncanniness (*Unheimlichkeit*). There is evidence that shows that the term and the aesthetic of magic realism were then popularised among the members of literary circles. Massimo Bontempelli, the editor and organiser of the magazine *900. Novecento*, which was published in both Italian and French, popularised the term *realismo magico* in 1927 among European poets and writers. Their art, in turn, inspired Latin Americans to transplant this alternative way of representing the quotidian to their native soil, where it was adapted to the local cultural context. Artists such as Miguel Angel Asturias, Jorge Luis Borges, Alejo Carpentier and Arturo Uslar Pietri were all exposed to the new artistic trend of magic realism, either during their sojourns in Europe, or by reading *Revista de Occidente,* which, in 1927, printed the Spanish translation of extensive passages from Roh's 1925 book, *Nach-Expressionismus, Magischer Realismus: Probleme der neusten europäischen Malerei (Post-expressionism, Magic Realism: Problems of the Most Recent European Painting).*

After the traumas of World War I, in times of great political and economic instability, many abstract avant-garde artists felt a need to return to representational art – an art of precision and objectivity. Irene Guenther, who writes about magic realism in the Weimar Republic, describes the pro-realist (but anti-Realist) turn in the interwar period as follows:

> It was an art that was firm in compositional structure and was, once again, representational. In reaction to Expressionism's apocalyptic visions, heated color palette, utopian message, and the shattering disillusionment which followed the war, this post-Expressionist art concerned itself with the tangible real, the familiar. After the emotional fervor of Expressionism, as well as the horrors of the war and subsequent German Revolution, artists searched for 'soberness' and 'freedom from all sentimentality'.[21]

Significantly, the realism that those artists adopted was different from nineteenth-century Realism. In the words of Franz Roh, magic realism, at that time also referred to as New Objectivity (*neue Sachlichkeit*), was to capture 'the clash of true reality and the apparent reality'.[22] Roh believed that 'humanity seems destined to oscillate forever between devotion to the world of dreams and adherence to the world of reality'.[23] Consequently, he found in magic realism a way to recuperate the objective world obliterated by Expressionists and other modernists in order to juxtapose it with its compulsive imitation, or impression, delivered by the human mind. The very same issue of a balance between subjectivity and objectivity, between the 'I' and the world, had been analysed a few centuries earlier by a philosopher of German Idealism, Novalis, who critiqued his teacher's, Johann Gottlieb Fichte's, narrow subjectivism, and who used the term 'magischer Realist' to refer to the quality of a true prophet who can fuse idealism with realism.[24] Roh's new kind of realism represented the 'energetic intensity' of things.[25] He emphasised, however, that this elucidating crystallisation of things always proclaimed it was 'produced artificially', wrestled from 'the midst of general becoming, of universal dissolution'.[26] Temporality was an important element of Roh's definition. He argued that magic realist art offered the 'miracle of an apparent persistence and duration in the midst of a demoniacal flux'.[27]

This 'demoniacal flux' is the flux of history. The history of twentieth-century East Central Europe has been demoniacal and, at times, only impish, but, regardless of the exact proportion of involvement of what seemed at the time to be non-human, otherworldly forces, this history has outgrown its own understanding among those who were most affected by it. My favourite anecdote that illustrates this severance of people from their own history tells the story of the Communist Party apparatchiks who order the city services to paint the dormant lawns green in the middle of winter in preparation for the arrival of a top Communist official from Moscow. The city in this anecdote is sometimes identified as Warsaw, sometimes as Prague, the official as Brezhnev or Khrushchev. When East Central Europeans retell this farce, usually to give Westerners a taste of life under Communism, it is irrelevant who the players were or where it was staged. It does not even matter if this event has really taken place. What matters is the fact that it could have happened in any of the countries in East Central Europe, that the unbelievable and absurd act of painting the brown winter landscape green, turning Winter into Spring, was a possible aspect of that reality. Even if one does not believe in this particular story, who will argue about the absurd history of those days of permanent shortage of everything – the days spent waiting in queues, not knowing whether one would be lucky enough to walk out of the store with yet another hairdryer or maybe a whole couch for the flat that one paid for but would not receive until decades later? What makes magic realism what it is – a fusion of the real and the fantastic, of the plainly familiar and the unbelievable – can be found in abundance throughout the region of East Central Europe in the sudden appearances and disappearances of aspects of material space, cartographic contours, languages, churches, peoples.

VERNACULAR MAGIC REALISM ON SCREEN

The films that I discuss in the present study are vernacular in their devotion to the closest and the most immediate circumstances of life. I am using this term here to signal the filmmakers' complex engagement with the quotidian, the local and the private, on both the level of form and that of content. Their vernacularism seems to arise from the deep-seated disappointment with anything grand or totalising, and from the filmmakers' sympathy for the socially

Figure 5   Martin Šulík's literal vision of groundedness in *Orbis Pictus* (1997).

alienated and culturally dispossessed elements of humanity. The etymology of the word 'vernacular' points to the Latin *verna* – a home-born slave, someone belonging to the place of birth, whose existence and identity is determined, but also very much limited, by that very place. I use it here to valorise these film-makers' art as an ex-centric discourse that challenges the official history (as well as the hegemonic forces that write it) and provides a voice for the inter-nalised Other (the silenced domestic subject whose efforts uphold the master's status). At the same time, the origin of the word is reflected in the charged nature of locality portrayed in the films. This is often the locality left out from the fast-paced flow of globalisation, excluded from the networks of free market mobility, where the inhabitants are literally landlocked. In Zygmunt Bauman's words, they are *'glebae adscripti'*.[28] They did not and will not par-ticipate in the late modern and postmodern processes of exterritorialisation – Bauman's term for the unprecedented mobility and invisibility of power, capital and technology.

In its chthonic character, with the gaze cast downward, looking at the ground, the vernacular cinema of East Central Europe speaks to the region's long history of territorial subjugation by the immediate neighbours from the East and the West but also, more presciently, to the current space confinement of the poorer members of the European Union. This confinement is imposed by the increased mobility of the symbolically and financially endowed agents of consumer capitalism and their economic operations. Largely unregulated by the local laws, these agents have no regard for sustaining local economies and the communities that depend on them. Many of the communities have not yet completed their transition into modernity, let alone late capitalism's postmodernity. The global market forces use up the local labour and resources of Second World society with minimal social commitment, thus exploiting the locality without contributing much to its status as a community. For over a decade now, in their low-wage factories, East Central Europeans have been producing cars, electronics and other goods for Western European corporations for a fraction of the cost that it would take to produce them in France, Germany or Italy, and with greater efficiency. In Spring 2009, as a response to the post-2008 global recession, in a gesture that dealt a blow to the notion of one market and one Europe, the French, Italian and German governments respectively issued protectionist policies encouraging many companies to take advantage of stimulus packages and bailout money on the condition that they stop outsourcing their manufacturing to East Central Europe. The same policies encourage repatriation of the existing manufacturing plants back to Western Europe without any consideration for the local communities that will be affected by the sudden termination of the business relationship.[29]

On the other hand, these same market forces have pushed large numbers of East Central Europeans into a state of temporary or permanent immigration, where mobility becomes a necessity rather than a choice. In the film art of East Central Europe, these two opposing trends with regard to place attachment – the enforced locality and enforced mobility, which are curious symptoms of the same economic system – are translated into an intense preoccupation with the earth-centred spirituality of the local, the idea of being rooted. Zygmunt Bauman describes the growing gap in the nature of territorial attachments between the global and the local as follows:

> If the new exterritoriality of the elite feels like intoxicating freedom, the territoriality of the rest feels like home ground, and ever more like prison – all the more humiliating for the obtrusive sight of the others' freedom to move. It is not just that the condition of 'staying put', being unable to move at one's heart's desire and being barred access to greener pastures, exudes the acrid odour of defeat, signals incomplete humanity and implies being cheated in the division of splendours life has to offer. Deprivation reaches deeper.[30]

Vernacular cinema offers a broad spectrum of responses to the said deprivation, from denial to re-appropriation. Some films discussed in this volume offer a compensatory vision of the locality, where the local is imbued with the meaning of self-sufficient community that inhabits it. Other films represent the current sense of deprivation of the enforced locality, a side-effect of globalisation, hyperbolically, drawing attention to the dark and dismal nature of the local ghetto.

MOSAIC MODERNITY AND THE PERSISTENCE OF THE PREMODERN

Whether the cinematic vision is a compensatory ideal or a hyperbolic dystopia, it is crucial to see the connection between the two; both are ways of re-imagining the unsatisfactory reality. Through their elaborate work of signification, both representational strategies communicate an anxiety over the status of locality and, perhaps more significantly, over one's relationship with the locality that is being inadvertently changed and often severed by the workings of what the sociologist Constantin Schifirnet called 'mosaic modernity', a fusion of socio-economic and cultural premodernism, modernism and postmodernism.[31] Consistently placing their narratives in rural and small-town environments, the filmmakers of East Central Europe are drawing attention to large sections of the region's society, who continue to negotiate top-down modernisation and globalisation in unique, often contrarian, ways. While other media, especially the region's mass media conglomerates, have been co-opted to serve as the organs of top-down modernisation and the Europeanisation project, the vernacular magic realist cinema gives witness to the quiet resistance among the local communities. Schifirnet warns the analysts of the European Community not to assume a uniform absorption of the late modern and postmodern models across the European Union. He argues that, in East Central European countries, 'only part of minority groups, of elites, supports the values of modernity and takes advantage of them. In return, the larger population is only superficially touched by modernity and continues to live in the spirit of ancient values'.[32] Life 'in the spirit of ancient values' can be synonymous with reactionary and patriarchal ideals and lifestyles, and it often is. But, in case of the region in question, it is also an expression of the local scepticism towards imported (and imparted) modernisation, with the concomitant technologies of labour, space, time and resource regimentation. 'The spirit of ancient values' that Schifirnet speaks of refers to the prominent spiritual element in the East Central European culture, which has a distinct countercultural formation. Often related to marginalised peasant traditions and the silenced (neo-)pagan folk beliefs and practices, which invest nature with divinity, this well-established trend emerged in opposition to the institutions of Christianity and the Enlightenment. Although diverse and hardly reducible to one worldview, the indigenous traditions that comprise this cultural formation share the impulse to keep *technē* – instrumental rationality as technical knowledge – in check and question its ever-increasing dominance over *physis* – nature as ineffable being.

A film that showcases this conflict between premodern spirituality and the culture of rationality is Petr Zelenka's brilliant *Year of the Devil (Rok*

Figure 6   The Slovak countryside with its premodern rituals in *Landscape*.

Ďábla, 2002). The film, which uses elements of magic realism within the generic framework of a mocumentary, was a box-office success and winner of the main prize of the Crystal Globe at the 37th Karlovy Vary International Film Festival. Although highly sophisticated formally (intertextual and meta-cinematic), *Year of the Devil*, like Zelenka's other films, explores very basic and universal themes, such as life, death, friendship, man's search for God and creative fulfilment. The complex premise of Zelenka's experimental film can be summarised as the story of a Dutch documentary filmmaker, Jan Holman (Jan Prent playing a fictitious character), who is struggling with alcohol addiction and embarks on a creative project to film a documentary about a Czech alcohol rehab facility because he hears that, in the Czech Republic, they actually know how to cure alcoholics successfully. While working on his project, Holman meets the famous singer and lyricist Jarek Nohavica (artist played by himself), who happens to be a patient at the facility. In the course of filming his documentary, Holman finds Nohavica's enigma seductive enough to derail him from his intended project. Holman thus decides to follow the musician on his concert tour after he is released from the facility. This narrative framing allows for Zelenka to address Nohavica's legendary status as a musician and a revered cult figure within the Czech art scene. As Holman is trying to understand Nohavica's mythical status, he becomes privy to a series of mystifying occurrences. For a start, Nohavica's guitarist Karel Plíhal (playing himself) stops talking for one year and gradually becomes shy of the stage. Medical intervention is unsuccessful. The viewer later finds out that Plíhal is Nohavica's guardian angel, gifted to him in childhood by his younger brother, who loses

Figure 7   Postmodern shamanism in *Year of the Devil* (2002).

a game of chess to Nohavica. The angel stops talking simply because he likes occasionally to 'hear the melodies that people give off'.

When Plíhal finally breaks his silence, he asks Nohavica to invite the struggling folk band Čechomor (in reality a very successful band that combines traditional Czech music with rock arrangements) to join them on a tour. Nohavica discovers that the lead musician of Čechomor, Franta Cerný, works at a cabaret club as a doorman. Wishing to carry out Plíhal's request, Nohavica goes to the club to recruit Cerný. To his surprise, that night, Cerný is actually performing on stage, in drag, to fill in for a drag queen who was suddenly rushed to the hospital. While this is going on, another musician from Čechomor, the violinist Karel Holas, who is working at a hotel, making live elevator music, meets the Killing Joke's vocalist Jaz Coleman (playing himself), who is in town to work with the Prague Symphony Orchestra. A punk musician, composer, orchestra conductor and self-proclaimed shaman, Coleman hears Holas play the violin in the lift and invites him, along with Čechomor, to perform on the symphony's world tour. Happenstance brings these characters together. New friendships are forged and music provides the glue for the new alliances that take the men on a journey that offers much more than professional opportunities. The film contemplates the possibility of reactivating the sensuous, primordial impulses of human communication and group interaction that are largely lost to modern man.

As the narrative progresses, Čechomor's musicians embark on tour with the charismatic Nohavica and, winning the applause of thousands of enchanted fans, begin to experience first-hand the aura of the bard. Soon their music and the sense of togetherness contribute to a unique blend of spirituality that they partake in and share with others. Zelenka's talent as a filmmaker rests in the fact that he conjures the collective spirit on screen without making it look corny or false. The spirituality that the musicians cultivate together, on and off stage, seems to have eclectic sources that include music, poetry, folklore, religion, nature, consciousness-altering drugs, astrology and more. In time, Cerný starts seeing an ensemble of ghosts that joins the band on stage, Holas becomes a healer, channelling cosmic energy through his hands, and Plíhal self-combusts in front of the entire band. After they complete their engagement with Nohavica and before they embark on world tour with a symphonic orchestra, Jaz Coleman takes the musicians to a Czech 'desert' (an open pit mine), where they engage in a shamanic ritual that requires them to wear face paint as 'masks of hellish astral entities' that will help them reach higher levels of consciousness, and therefore musicianship. As outlandish as these plot developments sound, the film manages to make them commonplace in a true magic realist style. The ghosts receive a designated corner on stage at every performance to help them feel welcome. Holas gives up his healing as soon as he runs out of cosmic energy. Plíhal receives a proper burial despite having dematerialised. Nothing strikes the viewer as fantastic or incredible because it is not presented as such within the text of the film. The poetic, slightly lyrical, lens translates the supernatural into spiritual, making questions of rationality superfluous. The emphasis for Zelenka and his viewer remains on the human relationships and the energy that a group of friends can create in a specific time and place, when united by a song or a ritual from the collective memory of a given culture. Not without a good dose of dark comedy, the film seems to suggest that coming together and paying close attention to one another and the place of the encounter is the surest way to transcendence. This attention allows one to meet an alcoholic and recognise in that person an artist or an angel. The faith in the collective spirit resonates in the film's credits, which announce *Year of the Devil* as 'A Film by Petr Zelenka and his Friends'.

The Greek word *technē* shares its stem with the verb *tikto*, which means simply to 'bring forth', as in making something appear. In philosophical discourse about technology, *technē* is often associated with appearance, while *physis* gains its status as the essence from dis-appearance.[33] The two elements in the binary are not strict opposites, but they become opposites when one element in the pair takes over, rhetorically or historically. Modernity, through the advancements of the scientific and the industrial revolutions, allowed for the domination of *technē*. Cinema, as the emblematic medium of modernity and a technology that is singularly equipped to summon appearances, has been used to 'bring forth' this domination into the centre of modern imagination. On some level, cinema is a meta-technological discourse that documents the supreme mobility, dexterity, precision and reproducibility of mechanical visuality. The existence of mosaic modernity in East Central Europe problematises that domination. It also questions the role that cinema plays in modernity's challenges to the human. The region's history conveniently attests to the occurrence of every appearance always being followed by a dis-appearance, frustrating progress every so often, and leaving material vestiges of failed, often lethal, technology: concentration camps, collective farms, military bases, heavy industries' water / soil pollution, and so on. It would be hardly surprising to recognise and even sympathise with this cautionary impulse (frequently interpreted as reactionary) among East Central Europeans, whose most recent experiences with technocentric reforms include such extremes as the mandatory Soviet-era industrialisation, which lead to the near-destruction of the natural environment by the heavy industries, or the post-1989 bout of carnivorous capitalism, with its rampant exploitation of labour and increasing commoditisation of social and cultural existence.

In his extensive philosophical study of the impact of technics on human consciousness, Bernard Stiegler acknowledges 'multifarious reactions of resistance to development' on the part of those inhabitants of the globalising world who believe that 'it is no longer obvious that progress is tantamount to benefit for the human race'.[34] Vernacular magic realism is one such reaction of resistance to development. Interestingly, in the same work, Stiegler also argues that human consciousness is inherently cinematic, thus implying that *technē* permeates the modern human *physis*, that human interiority is formatted by the materially external modes of technics, an argument that echoes Jean-Louis Baudry's apparatus theory and Plato's model of human consciousness, as well as Derrida's deconstruction of speech as always relying on the prosthesis of writing. The assumed normative scope of Stiegler's notion of cinematisation of consciousness posits a degree of conflict with his earlier claim about the possibility of, and indeed the existence of, 'multifarious reactions of resistance to development'.[35] Where and how can these reactions of resistance be conceived if modern consciousness has been immersed in the flux of cinema?

Stiegler's blind spot, much like Plato's, Derrida's or Baudry's, stems from ignoring the element of socially constituted embodiment. Stiegler conceptualises cinema as transcendental and abstract, with an unidentified viewing position, as perception externalised. Vernacular cinema, on the other hand, puts emphasis on the body and the act of embodiment as placement in a given set of material conditions. These very conditions, illustrated by the images of marginal bodies inhabiting rural and peripheral landscapes strewn with traces of ramshackle vestiges of failed technology, testify to consciousness that is refusing the totally cinematic constitution, if cinema is to be defined in a limited way as purely optical, disembodied visuality. The viewing position, the place of enunciation, and the direct narrative emphasis on the very idea of the place contribute to the sense of groundedness, understood as a complex emotional and symbolic connection with the physical reality, which characterises vernacular magic realism. The marginal status of the bodies represented on screen is partially derived from the shoddy and crippling *mise-en-scène*, which alternates with vignettes of thriving nature that continues to absorb the mistakes of technology. In turn, this act of absorption validates the marginal bodies as witnessing bodies.

To construct his analogy between consciousness and cinema, Stiegler isolates three common features: much like consciousness, cinema reproduces a temporal stream, operates through montage of images, and preserves an ontological connection to recorded reality. Stiegler's notion of cinematically constituted consciousness might apply to contemporary culture rather well. Its general applicability in contexts other than the postmodern technoculture, however, must be debated.

Firstly, montage as a cinematic feature is far from cinema's quintessence; thus Stiegler's analogy remains highly selective and hardly original. It greatly limits the cinematic to one editing technique and the modern consciousness to one of its symptoms, the one that was diagnosed by the early critics of modernisation: alienation through fracturedness. Already in 1924, in his review of Karl Grune's film, *Die Straße* (*The Street*, 1923), Siegfried Kracauer equated montage with modern consciousness when he argued that there is something in the technique of montage that is uniquely fashioned to capture, 'empty as a tin can, a life which instead of internal connections knows nothing but isolated events forming ever new series of images in the manner of a kaleidoscope'.[36] The fast-cut, fragmented experience of (post)modern consciousness resonates well, one must agree, with the kaleidoscopic aspect of film. The Soviet Montage cinema and Hollywood action films utilise this aspect to duplicate as well as promote that certain model of consciousness, with a difference in ideology but not in the work of propaganda that they ultimately accomplish. But a single editing technique can hardly define all of cinema, and Soviet Montage films or Hollywood blockbusters are hardly predisposed to documenting the oppositional impulse of (post)modern consciousness.

Furthermore, one can easily argue that the montage technique precedes cinema and is always already imbedded in human imagination and the cognitive structures of the mind. Against popular assumptions, montage is not synonymous with visual technology or the modern vision, for that matter. Although seriously conceptualised only in the 1920s by the Soviet Montage theorists, the montage technique had been present in literature (Gustave Flaubert) and still photography (Victorian photomontage), and had been discussed as a mnemonic feature of human consciousness (Freud's free associations) long before the technology of cinema popularised it. As André Bazin convincingly argued, the alternatives to montage, deep focus and the long take, are equally important cinematographic strategies. Among these alternatives, I would also list the long shot, which, as 'a distanced view of a natural landscape', Rosalind Galt theorises as a complex spatio-temporal trope that captures the tension between the filmic and the profilmic.[37] Unlike montage, they promote democratic gaze and preserve the unity of space and the material and temporal relations of the space and the objects inhabiting it. These strategies have been adopted by vernacular cinema, in its magic realist rendition, to slow down, reverse or simply frustrate the compulsive cutting of much of contemporary commercial cinema, also, to offer a certain totality of vision that poses a challenge to the viewer in terms of decoding the hierarchy of the discursive and material spaces.

Secondly, in terms of Stiegler's account of technological projection always interjecting the act of perception, the analogy between cinema and consciousness breaks down when one considers the losses, omissions and unique fluctuations that escape perception before projection mechanisms can make them reproducible. The ability of cinema to offer an endless and exact repetition of a recorded temporal experience is well noted by Stiegler, who uses this feature of cinema to correct Husserl's account of the workings of human memory. Modern recording technology's ability to reproduce the exact same temporal sequence, yet provide a different perception with each act of reproduction, is Stiegler's proof of the always changing and always already externally modified memory of temporal experience, thus non-existence of a pure perception. This paradigm suggests the primacy of projection over perception, but it does not concern itself with the question of whether perception can ever retain the precision and mechanical reproducibility inherent in projection. Stiegler occludes the fact that there are aspects of human consciousness that are unlike cinema in their relational positioning towards material space and inability to unfold temporally with the consistency of cinema. There is an element of situational dependence and therefore radical loss and forgetting in human consciousness that is irreproducible. The following questions need to be asked: can cinema, with its mechanical bias, attempt to represent this performative and elusive aspect of human consciousness? Does film's potential at the infinite repetition in reproducibility become a handicap when the filmic object is spiritual, ritualistic, polyphonic and semantically diffused? Against the common assumption about film as a tool of culture industry, can cinema be employed to show the *physis* in its resistance to *technē*? Can the filmmaker use the modern technology of film to preserve and contemplate premodern aspects of the East Central European mosaic modernity?

UTOPIA, NOSTALGIA AND THE WORK OF IMAGINING A FUTURE

In 1932, in his essay, 'Nonsynchronism and the Obligation to its Dialectics', Ernst Bloch, the controversial Marxist philosopher of hope and utopia, wrote about the German reactions of resistance to capitalism and modernity. The resistance, in his view, bifurcated into the totalitarian ideology of National

Socialism, which, at the time of Bloch's writing, was using German folklore to incite the inert minds and hearts of the bourgeois youth and the more authentic 'nonsynchronism' – the out-of-time-ness – of the rural population, whose continued resistance had nothing to do with Hitler's movement. Bloch saw the peasant's attachment to premodern ways of life as a vision with a potential for social change, not a simple reactionary fantasy. The edge that the peasant's resistance had over that of the National Socialist was to be found in the peasant's ownership of the land, the possession of the means of production, and the grounded nature of the rural non-synchronism. The peasant's 'sobriety', as opposed to the National Socialist's 'foam at the mouth and the dimming eye', stems from the peasant's 'bound existence' that obeys the demands of the soil and the calendar cycle.[38] Bloch argues that the peasant's soil is not the Germanic earth of the Third Reich. Rather, it is the place of the 'unsettled past', a site of non-synchronic existence, where the memory of the past provides room for values and experiences that were made distant and inaccessible by the alienating lifestyles of the capitalist modernity.[39] The sober memory of the better past does not lead to the reactionary nihilism brought on by the Nazis. Living in the past, Bloch suggests, does not have to equal anachronism. Another way of understanding non-synchronism is to view it as a projection of the desired state of affairs on to the future, not a straightforward regression into the premodern era but a creative incorporation of the desired elements of premodernity in the project of forging a different future.

Much of the vernacular cinema of East Central Europe invites resistance to consumer capitalism through its non-synchronic vision of life in the European peripheries. Through this vision, the filmmakers counter the pull of what Stephen Bertman diagnosed as our society's preoccupation with the moment, a side-effect of the proliferation of new information technologies: 'The social consequence of connectivity and speed is a synchronous society, a society unified by instancy and acutely attuned to the moment.'[40] The information society's emphasis on the moment and on continuous change paradoxically ejects the human subject from the experience of the present (if there ever was such an experience), creating a host of social and individual pathologies related to time compression, of which political apathy and chronic stress are two examples. If living in the moment breeds disconnect, living in the past, with much of its energy invested in cultivating a connection to that which no longer is, can be used as a coping strategy, at worst, and an oppositional practice, at best.

Offering both utopic and dystopic reconfigurations of the post-1989 present, this cinema complicates temporality, making the presented vision of reality both present and absent, both now and then, equipped with essence and non-essence, thus making the represented reality open to potential change, encouraging the re-envisioning of that very reality, and stressing the process of negotiation that is still under way in the region. The nature of the medium itself contributes to this subversive non-synchronic impulse. Continuing the theoretical project of André Bazin and Siegfried Kracauer, Stanley Cavell embraces the film's spectral presence as a means to strengthen the viewer's connection with the world. Echoing Bazin and Kracauer, Cavell emphasises the medium's ontological connection to filmed reality. Through the complex chemical and optical processes involved in film photography, cinema as organic technology preserves traces of the filmed object. At the same time, it always shows the object as already diffused and displaced. Cavell says,

> Photography maintains the presentness of the world by accepting our absence from it. The reality in a photograph is present to me while I am not present to it; and a world I know, and see, but to which I am nevertheless not present (through no fault of my subjectivity), is a world past.[41]

The filmic image speaks of the past; it is non-synchronic in its tendency of depicting Bloch's 'unsettled past' – an image of an object that hovers between the past and present, in its ambiguous temporal status demanding a decision made in the future.

The non-synchronism imbedded in the vernacular magic realism needs to be differentiated from the celluloid returns to the glorious past of the fetishised fatherland peddled via the vehicle of heritage cinema. Relatively new to the region, but already widely popular in British, French and Indian national cinemas, heritage genre envisions premodernity as times of truer, purer and more stable collective identity. The surrounding discourse in the mainstream media across East Central Europe links the local variety of heritage cinema with rebuilding national character and reawakening patriotic sentiments, both allegedly depleted by the long Communist tenure and recently, once again, jeopardised by the greed of multinational corporations. The naïve conviction that the gravity centre of the fast and furious globalising world may be found in one's nostalgically embellished back yard, packaged in heritage films as glossy, sepia-steeped images of epic battles, collective sacrifices and births of nations, is, by now, a common symptom of the postmodern condition, equally alarming among the societies of the First, Second and Third Worlds. What makes the East Central European variety of nationalist nostalgia perhaps more forgivable, but at the same time much more politically dubious due to its act of collective repression, than the commercial nostalgias of Western mass culture is the region's need to re-appropriate its post-World War II memory from the imaginary wreckage of the Communist era.

Different versions of the national ideal proliferated in the East Central European arts immediately upon the dissolution of the homogenised world-view (and its equally monotonous aesthetics) imposed by the Communists.

At the time (early 1990s), the very act of re-imagining the nation in contrast to the Communist doctrine of internationalism served an important function of allowing East Central Europeans to regain their unique sense of place in the otherwise uniformly drab reality left by the dying regime. In Poland, for example, Stanisław Vincenz's concept of the 'small fatherland' – a private sense of local belonging – earned a renewed popularity in the Poles' struggle to re-imagine themselves and their country against the pervasive and equalising bleakness of Socialist Realism's legacy. Interestingly, the concept's populist appeal peaked again around 2002 to 2004, when Poland, among other East Central European countries, debated whether to join the European Union. This time, the issue of preserving the national identity in the face of globalisation became paramount, and 'small fatherland' was used to propagate the reactionary impulse.

The discourse of 'small fatherland' has been a source of comfort (real or imagined) for those who managed to survive Communism by firmly holding on to their memories of the prewar geography, customs, language and people, and by ignoring the hiatus introduced in the name of Karl Marx. Characteristically, in the 1990s, those who offered their visions of 'small fatherland' (visual artists, writers, TV personalities and politicians) would often link them with their own (real or imagined) ties to aristocracy. This rhetorical move was common enough to be recognised as a symptom of a general desire on the part of the post-Communist society to diversify socially – by identifying one's roots, establishing once again a class hierarchy, and locating a community tradition that was somehow older and more authentic than the Communist classless 'tradition'.

From the beginning, however, much of the 'small fatherland' imaginary circulating in the 1990s Polish media leaned towards somewhat sentimental reminiscences that idealised religious holidays; glorified the conquests of the grandfathers who partook in various independence movements; mourned the national shrines destroyed by the Nazis and Communists; and lamented over the general bastardisation of the old way of life during most of the twentieth century. Here, it is necessary to note that the original notion of the 'small fatherland', as defined by Vincenz in his ethnographic narrative about the Hutsuls, *On the High Uplands. Sagas, Songs, Tales and Legends of the Carpathians* (1938–79), resonated with a rather well-established trend of localism, understood as an intimate connection to one's place of origin, in European literature championed by writers like Franz Kafka, Thomas Mann, I. B. Singer, Bruno Schulz, Bohumil Hrabal, Tomas Venclova, Tadeusz Konwicki, Czesław Miłosz and Marcel Proust. For these writers, the locus of their childhood, where most of the formative social, cultural and geographic attachments were formed, along with the tastes, colours, smells and sounds of that unique place, became a lasting source of artistic inspiration. In their prose, these authors went about meticulously recreating the memory of that first, most important place of belonging. This fictional place always has a certain mythical quality (if myth is to be understood as a sacred story of world's creation) because it functions as a compass for navigating the larger universe, in all its senses: psychological, emotional, social, geographical, political and, most importantly, metaphysical. It is a place of primary rootedness.

This creative construct so keen on preserving the memory of home can be seen as an escape from all ideologies and history into a transgressive, often stylistically excessive, private microcosm; by far, however, the more common critical interpretation sees this impulse as reactionary and deeply supportive of patriarchy. After all, the trajectory of these private worlds takes one back into the past; there is something prelapsarian about these visions. In trying to see the difference between the two interpretations, it might be useful to recognise the difference between Proust's Combray and Schulz's Drohobych in terms of Deleuze and Guattari's contrast between the master and minor literatures. Master literature authenticates the official culture from which it derives. Deleuze and Guattari define this act of symbolic confirmation as 'territorialization'.[42] Minor literature, on the other hand, is the literature that uses the language of the official culture in order to create a vision of the world that subverts the official culture. It 'deterritorializes' it.[43] Both Proust and Schulz are deeply nostalgic for the lost times and places, but Proust's fictitious fatherland was based on the prosperous town of Illiers in the Third French Republic, at the time the second largest empire in the world, while Schulz's Drohobych was a Jewish *shtetl* in Galicia, one of the poorest and most backward provinces in East Central Europe, which changed hands three times during the first four decades of the twentieth century between the Austro-Hungarian Empire, Poland and the Soviet Union. The image of the world created by Proust is a nostalgic elaboration of a sovereign community. For Proust's narrator, the greatest challenge is to recover the lost time that is the private experience of a place whose continuity in time and space carries on uninterrupted. Schulz's nostalgic vision offers a semblance of sovereignty for a community that was unable to claim its rightful territory in the world. In fact, Schulz's fictitious construct, at least for some readers, would stand in for the real place, whose geographic, economic and political status was too often under erasure. For these two writers and their readers, the relationship between the fiction and the world cannot be equivalent, most significantly because history made Schulz's actual homeland into fiction, while protecting Proust's world from the same fate. The contrast between Schulz's use of nostalgia to create a mythical place in the face of the dissolution of the real place and Proust's use of nostalgia to create a mythical place on the foundation of the real place is what distinguishes the minor discourse from the master discourse. The same contrast synthesises the distinction between the cultural identity of East Central Europe and that of Western Europe.

The complicated difference between these two inflections of nostalgia, which, for the sake of this argument, I would like to define as a desire to return to the wholeness of lost home, can be traced on the continuum that links localism with tribalism. In today's globalising world, these two notions are typically seen in contrast to one another. Localism stands for the community's desire to regain sustainability, native merchant / agricultural traditions and intimate community ties. Tribalism is a highly pejorative term with connotations of religious fanaticism, chauvinism and ethnocentrism. Both, however, require a certain amount of separatism (as in rejection of global networks) and narcissistic gaze upon one's own back yard. The difference in how localism romanticises the community's roots versus how tribalism does it rests, to a large extent, in the rhetoric used. Localism is portrayed as a rational movement of enlightened and environmentally concerned individuals, often liberal, politically correct and carefully secular. Tribalism is shrouded in the discourse of religious zealotry, pack mentality and unsanctioned violence. Another key difference is in the attitudes that the respective communities have towards the land they occupy. Both localism and tribalism are about rootedness. Calmly and reasonably, localists go about rediscovering their roots in the land whose autonomy has not been questioned in generations. Those afflicted with tribalism usually cannot afford to be quite as comfortable about their search for roots. The land that they inhabit might be theirs to put the roots in today but not tomorrow. Their affect is visible, their fear demonised, their reason questioned. Once again, this is the difference between the minor and the master discourse. During the last military conflict in Europe, the interests of the people of the former Yugoslavia, in contrast to those of Europe 'proper', were quickly dismissed as the blood lust of the Balkan tribes. Today's globalising Europe is very much caught up in the conflicting rhetoric of localism versus tribalism. This schizophrenic rhetoric was pointed out in 1997 by historian Norman Davis in 'West Best, East Beast?' – his evaluation of the great divide within Europe. In his essay, Davis argues: 'Western or civic nationalism is allegedly constructive, progressive, and peaceful. Eastern or ethnic nationalism is presented as destructive, regressive, disruptive, divisive, and destabilising, not to say murderous, anti-Semitic, hateful and generally nasty.'[44]

In the vernacular magic realism of East Central European cinema discussed here, this tension of paradigms receives a complex and intriguing artistic treatment. Local culture and ethnic identity had been celebrated for decades before the collapse of Communism in both the literature and the cinema of East Central Europe. Without directly evoking the concept of 'small fatherland', numerous filmmakers have centred on minority communities, village life and local folklore. In her study of East Central European cinema, Dina Iordanova devotes a section to a nuanced discussion of the representation of village life and minority culture on screen by a diverse group of directors working under

Communist rule, including Andrzej Wajda, Dušan Hanák, László Ranódy, Zoltán Fábri, Kazimierz Kutz, Ferenc Kósa, Jiří Menzel, Vojtěch Jasný, Péter Bacsó, László Vitézy, Jan Rybkowski and Krzysztof Zanussi. These filmmakers often used their films to explore the provisional nature of the Communist state and to criticise the ethnic policies and collectivisation reforms instituted by the Communist regime. One might see the cinematic vernacularism of the 1990s as a continuation of this critically inclined 'peripheral vision'.

The visual universe created by 1990s filmmakers of vernacular magic realism is often discussed as a version of 'small fatherland', but there are crucial differences that make this cinematic vision singular and its impact more complex than a romanticised expression of national identity mixed with a fierce anti-Communist stance. The latter sentiments have been monopolised by the East Central European variety of heritage cinema (costume dramas, biographies, new interpretations of famous historical events, and adaptations of classic national epics), which Ewa Mazierska identifies as a product of the 'nostalgia business', keen on perpetuating the right-wing, conservative, religiously fundamentalist and misogynist agenda, which aligns itself with restrictively nationalist politics.[45] The vernacular films, on the other hand, showcase the particular and the local, but at the same time they manage to deconstruct the nostalgic impulse that would otherwise lock this vision into a dogmatic statement. Both vernacular and heritage cinemas share an expansive, elaborate and often-pastoral *mise-en-scène*, which critics, from Fredric Jameson to Antoine de Baecque, identified as a trope used to flatten and romanticise the history and the specificity of a place. But as Rosalind Galt argues, the lush *mise-en-scène* can also be used in art house and counter-cinema to reconsider issues of postcolonial identity and gender, as well as political and economic transformations. Galt suggests that master shots of landscape can express the physical loss suffered by a community. Therefore, these images exceed the pure spectacle, and instead of arresting the narrative for moments of visual fetishism, they can mobilise the affective realms of cinema.[46]

Additionally, on the level of form, while heritage cinema utilises harmonious and glossy stylistics that consists of linear plots and pictorialist camera techniques to create an extravagant *mise-en-scène* that seduces the spectator's senses into a synaesthetic frenzy and a resulting intellectual coma, vernacular cinema *undermines* its own nostalgic impulse by mixing a healthy dose of East Central European miserabilism into the frequently pastoral aesthetics. Tony McKibbin has isolated this negative current in the cinema of Béla Tarr, Sharunas Bartas and Fred Kelemen specifically, dubbing it the 'cinema of damnation',[47] in contrast to the 'cinema of wonder' – John Orr's designation for the work of directors such as Tarkovsky and Jancsó, whose films convey a sense of epiphany and religious transcendence. In the abject microcosm of the cinema of damnation, McKibbin argues, misery, poverty, illness, immorality and oppressive landscape, which the characters are subject to, resonate well with the post-Communist sense of collective 'material collapse and the spiritual bereft'.[48] Also, in contrast to heritage cinema's preoccupation with grand and glorious events (history is problematised only on the surface for the sake of narrative suspense) and edifying characters, vernacular cinema engages with the quotidian, the local and the private, on both the level of form and that of content. The filmmakers in question express their disappointment with anything grand or totalising and instead focus their cameras on the socially alienated and culturally dispossessed elements. The main characters here are often village idiots, orphans, whores, ethnic minority members, the crippled and the old.

Traumatic History and the Politics of Magic Realism

Despite all the beauty and stylisation, cinematic vernacularism self-consciously questions the localised with the historicised and the politicised. These filmmakers avoid the elitism of the typical heritage construct by placing the subjects of their stories either on the margins of society or at the bottom of the class structure. Mazierska points out that heritage cinema's retrograde politics is largely due to its class elitism, the fact that the subjects are always noblemen and / or members of the intelligentsia, while the lower classes are 'only commodities to use in battle'.[49]

Vernacular cinema, much like the old picaresque tradition, laughs off all strict social divisions and often devotes much screen time to scenes of anarchy and social chaos. With regard to Communism, these filmmakers often conflate humour, kitsch aesthetics and carnivalesque playfulness in their evaluation of the failed leftist project. In contrast to heritage cinema's almost phobic denunciation of the Communist past, vernacular cinema attempts to salvage a positive aspect of the lived Communist experience, even if it is to be found in the memory of drunken camaraderie and the outrageous antics of the corrupt party officials. By approaching the painful and rather awkward subject of the moral bankruptcy of the survivors of Communism through the use of humour, vernacular cinema manages to revalorise most people's silent complicity with this totalising system, in turn allowing film audiences to account for their own responsibility. In the dialectics between heritage and vernacular cinemas, post-Communist East Central Europe is once again polarising its artistic expression between the sacred and the profane, or what Julia Kristeva saw as 'the epic and the carnivalesque ... the two currents that formed European narrative, one taking precedence over the other'.[50] I echo Kristeva in her conviction that the carnivalesque trend, much more so than the epic, is 'the life source' of innovative art that challenges the status quo and pushes creative imaginations 'towards new perspectives'.[51] I believe that the carnivalesque element so vibrant in East Central European vernacular magic realism positions it as an exciting and unique screen tradition, a truly innovative aesthetic that is well equipped to reflect on the vicissitudes of a society in transformation.

In 1996, one of the masters of Hungarian cinema, Péter Gothár, made the highly entertaining, formally experimental and politically provocative film *Letgohang Vaska* (*Haggyállógva Vászka*), which provides an excellent example of a historical narrative that resorts to the carnivalesque tradition in an effort to account for the wildly imaginative and playful ways in which people cope with the harsh conditions of life and ideological strictures under authoritarian rule. The film reformulates the legacy of Communism, asking the viewer to think of the regime as a force that fostered human ingenuity and a spirit of solidarity, and offered many an opportunity to think outside the box, even if that meant embracing the absurd, in order to outsmart and laugh off the dogma of the ruling Communist Party. Narrated in Hungarian voice-over, Gothár's film is a delightful, at times gruesome, tale of two thieves who form an unusual alliance between the living and the dead. The somewhat depressed and disillusioned city thief, Vaska (Maksim Sergeyev), meets the village thief, Vanya (Evgeniy Sidikhin), and their new friendship takes them on a spree of outrageous exploits in the streets of 1930s Leningrad (present-day St Petersburg). While the setting and the characters are decidedly Russian, it is not difficult to think of the two thieves, who drive their arch-enemy, Commissar Zinoviev (the historical figure of Bolshevik revolutionary Grigory Zinoviev), into a frenzy, as allegorically representing all of the unhappy and dissenting citizens living under the Soviet regime, including the countries of the Soviet bloc. Engaging in endless drunken orgies, roof chases, political parades and religious processions, Vaska and Vanya do not miss a single opportunity to spread anarchy across town. With every new antic, they wreak havoc in the carefully choreographed official fabric of the state apparatus. Their erratic behaviour is matched by the equally jumbled storyline. The text of the film is further estranged by the director's choice not to dub or subtitle the Russian dialogue among the characters, instead making the off-screen voice-over narration in Hungarian responsible for keeping the viewer informed about the madcap adventures.

The script, by László Bratka, is based on a prison yarn that circulated among the inmates of the White Sea Canal gulag (heard by the Voltaire scholar Lev Semenovich Gordon during his imprisonment and recorded in writing by his daughter Maryana Kozyreva), and it therefore resonates as a narrative of resistance against the repressive Communist state. One might imagine that the political prisoners and the 'enemies of the revolution' who were forced into the Soviet penal colonies to perform back-breaking labour under extremely harsh conditions found solace in this and similar stories about daredevil characters successfully sabotaging the system with the use of folk wisdom and street grit.

Figure 8   Two thieves flying over St Petersburg in *Letgohang Vaska* (1996).

Combining urban legend with fairy-tale motifs, Gothár's film begins with a grotesque scene of a funeral procession that passes by Vaska's communal block of flats. The mourners cause such a racket that Vaska, who just woke up with a massive hangover, runs out into the street to check on the commotion. What he witnesses is a carnivalesque reversal of the typically solemn and tranquil death ritual. Instead of a dignified march of death, Vaska watches a spectacularly wretched bunch of peasants who are following a horse-drawn carriage that is transporting a coffin, clamouring over something in total disregard for the sacred rite of passage. Instead of lamenting the dead, the peasants are angrily beating on the coffin with sticks and cursing the dead man's existence. When Vaska finds out that the reason for their wrath is a large debt that the man owed the people, he decides to give out his last money to send the

Figure 9   Pagan funeral procession in the heart of the city in *Letgohang Vaska*.

dead off in peace, and more importantly to stop the noise responsible for his escalating hangover. Soon after he returns to his drab, communal apartment, where his sweetheart Luvnya (Valentina Kasyanova) is nagging him about the lean times, a visitor appears out of thin air. It is Vanya, the village thief, and, as the viewer eventually finds out, the dead man spared by Vaska.

Quickly, an alliance between the thieves is formed and celebrated with copious amounts of vodka and herring. The partners in crime set to work immediately, but not without a refreshing outing into the countryside. In what follows the viewer watches the audacious rascals steal the Tsar's treasures from the heavily guarded National Bank of the Soviet Union and get away with it. This is accomplished with the use of two magical objects that the thieves fortuitously find in the griffin's nest, which they shoot off the Scrape-the-Sky Tree during their picnic in the countryside. The two objects are the Bloodied Sardine Tin key and the ball of the Guiding Thread. They use the key to open the bank's roof and descend into the vault down the Guiding Thread, suspended from the ceiling. Their robbery and Zinoviev's frenzied pursuit constitute the majority of the plot in the film; however, most of the spectatorial pleasure comes from the extended scenes of collective excess, which include marching, singing, feasting and drunken merrymaking. The director uses some very clever special effects (revolving tables, bottles of vodka used as camera filters, varied film speed and canted frames) to enhance the Dionysiac atmosphere, which seems to follow Vaska and Vanya wherever they go. At some point, the chase takes the protagonists to the famous Aurora cruiser, where the October Revolution of 1917 commenced. The scene re-imagines the origins of the Communist regime as a slapstick charade, with Zinoviev and his Red Brigade running in circles. Gothár's film revisits history through a carnival re-appropriation, which combines magic, parody and comedy in a surprising tribute to the times of Soviet rule.

Vernacular films operate well within the realm of nostalgia, if by nostalgia we mean an ability to travel towards a place of belonging that is separated from us by a period of time, when it is painfully understood that the time barrier cannot be removed, as time can hardly be reversed. The journey can be accomplished with the help of the imagination, a creative leap of faith, but the circumstance of the place always being somehow out of reach cannot be removed. Furthermore, much of the place's desirability as a travel destination lies in its ultimate inaccessibility. One can approach this place but never arrive at it. The nostalgic gaze is inward and toward. It is both less and more than what the rules of optics allow for the interaction of light with matter. The nostalgic gaze never truly beholds. Its energy comes from visual expectation, not a realised vision. The object of the nostalgic gaze is the Derridean trace, a presence that is already somewhat absent. In a sense, all cinematic gaze is nostalgic gaze: it documents a trace of an object while marking the already forming remoteness of the said object, its distance in time, the irreversibility of the passing moment when the camera was actually beholding the object. It resides on the cusp of the past and the present; it implies both coming into being and the transcendence of being. In Derrida's own words:

> As soon as there is a trace, whatever it is, it implies the possibility of its being repeated, of surviving the instant and the subject of its tracing, and it thereby attests to the death, the disappearance, or at the very least the mortality of that tracing.[52]

Vernacular cinema as nostalgic medium is as much about an instant gain of the coveted place of belonging as it is about its simultaneous loss. It invents a memory of a place while expressing an awareness of the ephemeral nature of this very place. The vision of East Central Europe depicted through the vernacular lens evokes the sense of authentication and concurrent recognition of the possibility of dissolution. In terms of cinematic time, its absent presentness confronts the time signatures of the other two popular genres in the region: the technological future of action films and the nationalist past of heritage cinema.

Vernacular magic realism consciously avoids referring to the immediate contemporary reality of the post-Communist era, with its array of harsh socio-economic transitions. Instead, these films offer an encounter with a microcosm that is somewhat frozen in a nondescript mid-twentieth-century past and a locale that is marked as simultaneously remote and proximate, the small village, provincial town or deserted outskirts of a city. As a result of a clever rhetorical move, the singularity of the psychological struggle of an individual facing the post-Communist crisis is eclipsed by the comforting metaphysical totality: a collective that shares the same sense of being somehow alienated, not yet ready to partake in the fast-moving world of international democracy

Figure 10   Bulgarian village as the sleepy and stagnant East Central European
periphery in *Letter to America*.

and the swift transactions of a capitalist economy. This microcosm is a trace
of East Central Europe as a place of belonging. It is an ideal, without being
idealistic. The cinema's focus on the notion of place, along with its ability to
construct the place on screen, makes it an ideal medium for negotiating the
region's new, post-Communist identity. Providing a celluloid home for the
fragmented identity is an enabling mechanism that masks over the epistemological and ontological void encountered by the post-Wall societies. During
the challenging period of sudden, often dizzying shifts in cultural paradigms,
vernacular cinema's ability to construct a spectre of an isolated periphery,
more stagnant than stable, offers an invaluable space for renewed imaginary
investment and the collective cathexis required to move beyond the rubble of
a bankrupt system.

Interestingly, the nostalgia of the 1990s was never restricted to the Second
World. During that decade, the First World began cultivating its own strand
of symbolic representation based on a sense of loss generated by the closing
stages of the millennium, the postmodern crisis of representation, and the
escalation of ethnic, political and economic conflicts. Western popular culture
embraced the nostalgic impulse and commercialised it in the form of all kinds
of retro trends in fashion, car design, architecture and diet. One might also
interpret it as a symptom of a general anxiety caused by the unprecedented
succession of technological advancements, a reactionary fixation on things
past in the face of mass proliferation of time–space compression produced
by communication technologies. This recent nostalgia is rather similar to the
late nineteenth-century scepticism regarding the changes brought about by
the Industrial Revolution. That rejection of industrial technologies and the
growing saturation of the decadent urban lifestyle culminated in the prolific
cultural movement of the *fin-de-siècle* period. Art Nouveau embodied the

nostalgia of this historical moment in its turn to nature, sentimentalised folk culture and organic form in design. Arguably, both the twentieth- and the nineteenth-century nostalgic trends in the West should be analysed as symptoms of affluence, certain exhaustion generated by abundant wealth, and the accompanying decadence. Paradoxically, then, this nostalgia has more to do with the experience of gain than that of loss. If there is any loss registered here, it is the loss of the less.

When analysing the nostalgic impulse of East Central European vernacular cinema, one has to determine to what degree it resonates with the parallel Western condition if it rose from the very different circumstances of economic deprivation, rhetorical desiccation, civil apathy and a general shortage of productive energy. How does it then relate to something like postmodern nostalgia, which is born of material and symbolic excess? Is it an earlier or later version of the same basic psychosocial mechanism? And, perhaps, the notion of desiring less, of wanting to experience something smaller, scarcer and without too many options, is where the two discourses meet. On some level, through its darker, more destitute images that evoke the idea of a wasteland, vernacular cinema becomes a complex interpolation of the region's encounter with the sudden flood of commercial goods and services that keeps pouring in, through the open borders, including the toxic refuse produced by the West. The purer, simpler microcosm is not only created to react against the flood of literal and metaphoric garbage imported from the West, but also to offer an escape from the region's own post-Communist waste inheritance that continues to pollute the environment of East Central Europe in the form of heavy industry's chemical waste, Communist memorabilia, Social Realist art / architecture and the morbidly inefficient bureaucracy.

Linda Hutcheon focused on nostalgia's ability to rarefy and cleanse. 'Nostalgic distancing sanitizes as it selects,' she observes.[53] Nostalgia is not only about time and space. Its mechanism involves quantity adjustments, often subtracting, throwing away and occluding. This aspect of nostalgia is what earns it its bad reputation as the populist discourse of simplifying the complexities of representation. The nostalgic 'less' is never more in the eyes of its critics. This 'less' is the sentimental abbreviation of everything that matters in critical thought. The energy of this unacceptable 'less', lament the critics, is that of a Disney cartoon artist who traces his pencil over the contours of reality, smoothing over the imperfections in order to rescue the cartoon world from the 'complicated, contaminated, anarchic, difficult, ugly, and confrontational' present.[54]

In the context of vernacular magic realism, nostalgia's ability to sanitise can and should be reconsidered as a salutary gesture that holds off the barrage of cultural paradigms, the new ones and the used, making room for an authenticity search, these days an unfashionable quest among the technologically levitating inhabitants of the First World, but an increasingly important pursuit among the displaced subjects of the rest of the world, whether the displacement is physical, the lot of political refugees and migrant workers, or symbolic, as in the case of post-Communist societies. The displaced identity will utilise the sanitised, the slimmed-down version of the memory of home, in order to amplify the connection with the adopted home. For nostalgia vacillates between mental operations of subtraction and addition. It can be a constructive process, or 'active attribution', as Hutcheon argues, and not just succumbing to an illusion, in resignation.[55] Nostalgia may be incorporated into progressive politics, when the desire for home, and the sense of belonging that comes with it, are no longer framed by nationalism, but instead it is translated into a much more abstract, and ironically more basic, notion of groundedness. That which is grounded implies connections, as opposed to that which is ungrounded, which can only refer to itself, and thus barely be identified as human. The humanity of the displaced subject depends on the ability to re-establish a web of connections. The connections that allow the subject to be grounded in reality are symbolic ties that secure a sense of continuity with the place, and by extension the earth. Nostalgic images often serve as means to regain the sense of groundedness, which is best defined as the practice of gathering one's experiences of the local and the nearest in the form of an individual orientation in space.

Accompanied by magic realist sensibility, vernacular cinema, which emerged during the period of turbulent post-Wall transitions, admittedly offers a somewhat compensatory image of the East Central European region, suggesting a far-reaching frame of reference for the dislocated members of the post-Communist societies. Images of peripheral life and landscape conjure a spiritual presence that mildly mutes the void of the Communist past. The images of groundedness enable a smoother path through transitions that are still under way in that part of Europe. At the same time, these images form a context in which the filmmakers address the current tensions that exist at the heart of the globalising locality. In how it activates the notion of space, the vernacular magic realism in East Central European cinema is decidedly European if one agrees with Rosalind Galt's assessment that '[in] the early 1990s, Europe became, as if it had not been so before, a question of space'.[56]

NOTES

1. Robert Stam, *Literature Through Film: Realism, Magic and the Art of Adaptation* (Malden, MA, and Oxford: Blackwell, 2005), p. 307.
2. Dina Iordanova, *Cinema of the Other Europe* (London and New York: Wallflower, 2003), p. 173.
3. Ibid. p. 173.
4. Dipesh Chakrabarty, *Provincializing Europe: Postcolonial Thought and Historical Difference* (Princeton: Princeton University Press, 2007), p. 8.

5. Ibid. p. 8.
6. Ibid. pp. 3–4.
7. Temenuga Trifonova laments this tendency in Bulgarian cinema in 'Stoned on Mars: Home and National Identity in Bulgarian Post-Communist Cinema'. She speaks of the 'Bulgarian filmmakers' almost masochistic willingness to conform to Western stereotypes of the Balkans as the epicentre of uncontrollable urges, irrational violence, deep-seated fatalism, a generally premodern way of life' in *Cineaste*, 32:3, June 2007, p. 33.
8. John Orr, *The Art and Politics of Film* (Edinburgh: Edinburgh University Press, 2001), p. 52.
9. Ibid. p. 52.
10. Ibid. pp. 52–3.
11. Piotr Wandycz, *The Price of Freedom: A History of East Central Europe from the Middle Ages to the Present* (London and New York: Routledge, 2001), p. 2.
12. 'Wrongly Labelled', *The Economist*, 394:8664, 9 January 2010, p. 50.
13. See Steven Tötösy de Zepetnek, 'Comparative Cultural Studies and the Study of Central European Culture', in Steven Tötösy de Zepetnek (ed.), *Comparative Central European Culture* (West Lafayette: Purdue University Press, 2001), pp. 1–32.
14. Piotr Wandycz, *The Price of Freedom*, pp. 4–5.
15. Milan Kundera, 'The Tragedy of Central Europe', *The New York Review of Books*, 31:7, April 1984, pp. 33–8.
16. Ibid. p. 33.
17. Katarzyna Marciniak, 'Second World-ness and Transnational Feminist Practices: Agnieszka Holland's *Kobieta Samotna* (*A Woman Alone*)', in Anikó Imre (ed.), *East European Cinemas* (New York: Routledge, 2005), p. 6.
18. Zygmunt Bauman, *Globalization: The Human Consequences* (New York: Columbia University Press, 1998), p. 33.
19. Fredric Jameson, 'On Magic Realism in Film', *Critical Inquiry*, 12:2, Winter 1986, p. 311.
20. Ibid. pp. 303–4.
21. Irene Guenther, 'Magic Realism in the Weimar Republic', in Lois Zamora and Wendy Faris (eds), *Magical Realism: Theory, History, Community* (Durham, NC: Duke University Press, 1995), p. 37.
22. Franz Roh, 'Magical Realism: Post-Expressionism', in Lois Zamora and Wendy Faris (eds), *Magical Realism: Theory, History, Community* (Durham, NC: Duke University Press, 1995), p. 20.
23. Ibid. p. 17.
24. See Christopher Warnes, 'Magical Realism and the Legacy of German Idealism', *The Modern Language Review*, 101:2, April 2006, pp. 488–98.
25. Franz Roh, 'Magical Realism: Post-Expressionism', p. 20.
26. Ibid. pp. 20, 22.
27. Ibid. p. 22.
28. Zygmunt Bauman, *Globalization: The Human Consequences*, p. 105.
29. See Kurt Tsuo, 'Unity Under Siege: The European Single Market after the Financial Crisis', *Harvard International Review*, 31:1, Spring 2009, pp. 32–5.
30. Zygmunt Bauman, *Globalization: The Human Consequences*, pp. 23–4.
31. Constantin Schifirnet, 'The Mass Media and Tendentious Modernity in the Transition Process from the National Society to the European Community', *Civitas*, 9:1, January 2009, p. 57.
32. Ibid. p. 53.
33. See Martin Heidegger, 'Building, Dwelling, Thinking', in *Poetry, Language,*

Thought, trans. Albert Hofstadter (New York: Harper Colophon, 1971), pp. 143–61.

34. Bernard Stiegler, *Technics and Time: The Fault of Epimetheus* (Stanford: Stanford University Press, 1998), p. 95.
35. Ibid. p. 95.
36. Miriam Hansen, 'Decentric Perspectives: Kracauer's Early Writings on Film and Mass Culture', *New German Critique*, no. 54, Autumn 1991, p. 49.
37. Rosalind Galt, *The New European Cinema: Redrawing the Map* (New York: Columbia University Press, 2006), p. 66.
38. Ernst Bloch, 'Nonsynchronism and the Obligation to its Dialectics', *New German Critique*, no. 11, Spring 1977, pp. 24, 26, 24.
39. Ibid. p. 29.
40. Stephen Bertman, 'Warp Speed: How Fast Times Are Changing Our Personal Values', *Humanities Research Group Working Papers*, vol. 8, 1999, p. 9.
41. Stanley Cavell, *The World Viewed: Reflections on the Ontology of Film* (Cambridge, MA: Harvard University Press, 1979), p. 23.
42. Gilles Deleuze and Félix Guattari, 'What is Minor Literature?', *Mississippi Review*, 11:3, Winter / Spring 1983, pp. 13–33.
43. Ibid.
44. Norman Davis, 'West Best, East Beast', *Oxford Today*, 9:2, 1997, pp. 28–31.
45. Dina Iordanova, *Cinema of the Other Europe*, p. 50.
46. Rosalind Galt, *The New European Cinema: Redrawing the Map*, p. 68.
47. Tony McKibbin, 'Cinema of Damnation', *Senses of Cinema*, December 2004, at http://archive.sensesofcinema.com/contents/05/34/cinema_of_damnation.html (accessed 2 June 2010).
48. Ibid.
49. Ewa Mazierska, 'In the Land of Noble Knights and Mute Princesses: Polish Heritage Cinema', *Historical Journal of Film, Radio, and Television*, 21:2, June 2001, p. 172.
50. Julia Kristeva, *The Kristeva Reader*, ed. Toril Moi (New York: Columbia University Press, 1986), p. 50.
51. Ibid. p. 50.
52. Jacques Derrida, *Paper Machine* (Stanford: Stanford University Press, 2005), p. 158.
53. Linda Hutcheon, 'Irony, Nostalgia, and the Postmodern', in Raymond Vervliet and Annemarie Estos (eds), *Methods for the Study of Literature as Cultural Memory* (Amsterdam: Rodopi, 2000), pp. 189–207. I relied on the online version of this text, made available by the University of Toronto English Library at http://www.library.utoronto.ca/utel/criticism/hutchinp.html (accessed 10 June 2010).
54. Ibid.
55. Ibid.
56. Rosalind Galt, *The New European Cinema: Redrawing the Map*, p. 1.

2. THEY LIVE ON MARS: THE MAGIC OF THE PERIPHERY

It was Western Europe that invented Eastern Europe as its complementary other half in the eighteenth century, the age of Enlightenment. It was also the Enlightenment, with its intellectual centers in Western Europe, that cultivated and appropriated to itself the new notion of 'civilization,' an eighteenth-century neologism, and civilization discovered its complement, within the same continent, in shadowed lands of backwardness, even barbarism. Such was the invention of Eastern Europe.

Larry Wolff[1]

How to define 'provincialism'? As the inability (or the refusal) to see one's own culture in the large context. There are two kinds of provincialism: of large nations and of small ones [. . .] Small nations are reticent toward the large context for the exact opposite reasons: they hold world culture in high esteem but feel it to be something alien, a sky above their heads, distant, inaccessible, an ideal reality with little connection to their national literature.

Milan Kundera[2]

In *Mila from Mars* (*Mila ot Mars*), the 2004 debut feature by Bulgarian director Zornitsa Sophia (artistic alias of Zornitsa Popgantcheva), a remote Bulgarian village is playfully coded as the place that is so physically and culturally removed from the modern-day European metropolis that it might as well be Mars. Filming on location in the stunning Rhodope Mountains, the filmmaker conjures a place where dramatic nature mingles with the splendour of the ancient Thracian culture as well as the feeling of utter dejection. The village and its few aged inhabitants go on against the forces of nature and history but only barely so. Their existence is marked as precarious, hazardously perched between times and changing political systems. The proximity of the border with Greece and Turkey marks the village as an interstitial territory. It is located both centrally, at the crossroads of differently European nations, and peripherally, tucked away so safely that it is possible for the villagers, who have given up traditional farming, which they are now too few and too frail to carry out, for illicit marijuana cultivation, to participate in the global economy and sustain their traditional way of life. Paradoxically, the village is reachable enough for the drug lord to set up his illegal operation there but unreachable for anyone else – or, rather, not worth reaching. This Bulgarian village figures in the film as the face for the countless East Central European villages that were depopulated during Communism due to the forced industrial reforms or were driven to bankruptcy by collective farming. The population is ageing and shrinking. The schools, churches, grocery stores and public transportation no longer operate in these settlements. The narrative of Zornitsa Sophia's film directly confronts the endangered status of this kind of settlement and the welfare of its inhabitants in globalising Europe. The filmic characters, the villagers and the outside observers, the diegetic city-dwellers who watch the villagers on TV, in a programme that looks like an ethnographic documentary, express their awareness of the village being out of time and out of space in the New Europe. They refer to the village as 'wasteland' and 'Mars'.

Arguably, in the era of global cyber-connectivity, the East Central European village remains the habitat of the disconnected. Yet, time and again, filmmakers from the region revive this remnant of premodernity to suggest its continued significance in the region's identity. In their magic realist films, they connect the disconnected in what becomes an oppositional discourse, which paradoxically reaches into the past, arresting some of its markers and memories, in order to contemplate alternative options for the future that are more desirable, even if seemingly out of touch. These post-Communist filmmakers imbue the village, the countryside, the provincial town – the locus of premodernity – with a pronounced sense of wonder, spanning from the pastoral enchantment found in Martin Šulík's cinema to that of the hypnotic hauntedness present in Béla Tarr's films, oscillating their screen manifestations of the vernacular dream from utopic to dystopic.

It is this very location, with its heavy air of degradation and isolation, that Zornitsa Sophia, among other filmmakers, chooses as the dramatic setting for her tale of a young woman's coming of age. Her protagonist, Mila (Vesela Kazakova), is a teenage orphan, involved with a criminal, Alex (Lyubomir Popov), who is acting as her sugar daddy. He is the man who buys Mila out of

Figure 11   Villagers transport marijuana in pillowcases in *Mila from Mars* (2004).

Figure 12   Entrepreneurial elders welcome Mila into their midst.

the orphanage, promising her greener pastures in the big world. Ironically, he does bring Mila to literal pastures, indirectly, through his brutalising treatment of her. He abuses Mila physically and emotionally, and the filmic text intimates Mila's initiation into prostitution, with many scenes resonant of the growing body of cinematic commentary on the region's problem of sex trafficking.[3] The background for this part of the narrative consists of petrol stations and night clubs, signalling the transience, glitz and alienation of the newly capitalist metropolitan area. Eventually, bruised and pregnant with Alex's child, Mila escapes her captor by hitching a ride with the driver of a Groceries-on-Wheels truck, a one-man retail institution that periodically connects the global world of the free market economy with the local community, which becomes more distant and unreachable with every new wave of the time–space compression caused by globalisation.

The Groceries-on-Wheels driver brings Mila into the village of pot growers, where she will hide from her oppressor and give birth to his child. In the process, she will experience the wonders of a simple life and repeated spiritual epiphanies (with a host of accompanying frustrations), which ultimately show her that the world of the disconnected offers communal bonds and security that make life on Mars a viable alternative, if not a choice per se. Can this life become a matter of choice for Mila and other young East Central European women like her? When Mila, along with the film viewer, has her first glimpse of the villagers, they form a dignified and likable collective. Cracking dirty jokes, smoking cigarettes (soon to be identified by the viewer as marijuana joints), these elderly people are a sight to behold; shrouded in their traditional all-black garb, their stern faces creased with time and emotional baggage, their bodies diminished by age but imbued with surprising guile and energy, they are characters like no others in contemporary cinema. Instead of representing the bygone era of blissful national belonging, governed by the order of patriarchy, these villagers stand as active participants in the global economy. Significantly, however, they are on the side of the transgressive operations that have been enabled by the porous borders and the diminishing national control over the ever-expanding free market, the same market that made their traditional farming methods obsolete. In a sense, these are old rebels for the new times.

Dina Iordanova, in her extensive analysis of Balkan intercultural cinema, has identified the village as the 'true site of memory' and observed how the village, through its fragile status as a locality on the brink of extinction, becomes 'the center of the universe' in narratives of exile and displacement. She writes: 'The monotony of village life is more emotionally charged and eventful than the dynamism of any metropolis. The village is deserted, but it is precisely its forsaken status that makes it so important and places it in the core of the protagonists' identity,'[4] Through her reading of the village as a pictorial category that serves as a symbol of exilic memory, Iordanova dismisses the charge expressed by many critics who see the village motif, so strongly present in the recent cinema of the region, as a gesture of reactionary fetishism, a search for purer and simpler values that, in turn, boil down to veiled chauvinism and nationalism. Although mainly preoccupied with matters of history, Iordanova not only sees the importance of the village in terms of renegotiating the past but, more importantly, she assigns this pictorial category a crucial role in confronting the present, with all of its challenging transitions that ensued after the dissolution of Yugoslavia and the devastation left after the Balkan wars of the 1990s. Through this interpretive gesture, Iordanova makes room for a much more subtle approach to the conflicted nature of regional identity defined through self-acceptance of European-ness that is marginal, non-essential and sometimes barely tolerable. While in much of the national cinema the village setting figures, via its symbolic stasis, as the seat of national memory and the right-wing value system, in the recent vernacular cinema from East Central Europe, the village is a site of a dynamic value re-adjustment, a filmic space where the

Figures 13 and 14   Mila makes a new start on 'Mars'.

peripheral complex of East Central Europe gains a spatial articulation much in line with the territorial inflection of the complex itself. Iordanova points out this dynamic affect invested in the images of the village when she qualifies the 'monotony of the village life' as 'emotionally charged' and 'eventful'.

Unlike critics who dismiss *Mila from Mars* as an exercise in recuperative Bulgarian nationalism, I would like to read this film as a contemplation of a broader, more regional issue: the highly controversial presence of the peripheral aspect in the identity of East Central Europe. In her analysis of the film, Temenuga Trifonova charges the filmmaker with 'willing participation' in the project of exoticising Europe. This charge raises the same concerns that some critics of magic realism raise with regard to its alleged 'anthropological admiration for the primitive'.[5] This criticism is often in line with the charge that magic realism is a quintessentially modernist movement, mimicking the latter's fascination with indigenous mythologies and folklore. Other critics interpret magic realism as an anti-modernist stance that re-appropriates the modernist distortions of the indigenous in order to correct them.[6] Is the recurrent peripheral motif embraced by filmmakers from East Central Europe a sign of commercialised primitivism or a site of contestation?

Trifonova sees Zornitsa Sophia as one of the many filmmakers who exaggerate 'the cultural divide between East and West, thereby sabotaging the argument for affinity with Europe'.[7] Trifonova's evaluation frames the film as a chaotic postmodern posturing that ultimately does nothing to challenge a straightforward compensatory nostalgia. Mila's, and by extension the film-maker's, embrace of the 'Martian' status of the Balkan village is, for Trifonova, an expression of a typical affective stance characteristic of the Balkans and East Central Europe in general – the 'mixture of hurt pride, low national self-esteem, and an exaggerated sense of entitlement'.[8] According to Trifonova, this stance goes hand in hand with the highly ironic, therefore necessarily ethi-cally dubious, cinematic deployment of the stereotype of this part of Europe as being 'the perennial theater of the absurd', populated with 'off-the-wall, vulgar, idiotic characters incapable of rational thought but very good at dress-ing exotically, cursing profusely, blowing things up, and having brutal sexual encounters', in films where history functions as a 'cabinet of curiosities'.[9] Regarding the proliferation of the stereotype, Trifonova is correct on three accounts. Firstly, the stereotype has a long-standing tradition in the cinema (and literature, one might add) of the region. Secondly, this very stereotype aligns well with Western Europe's stereotype of its eastern periphery. Thirdly, the filmmakers deploy the stereotype by coating it in irony. In conjunction with irony, Trifonova also mentions categories of camp and the grotesque to qualify the playful application. In her final tally, however, Trifonova blames the film-makers for further inculcating the highly pejorative and narrow view of East Central Europe, especially the Balkans, ignoring what the imaginative stylistic and formal resolutions might contribute to the processing of the stereotype.

In addition to Trifonova's valid assessment of the compulsive and recurrent engagement of the 'wacky backwaters' stereotype, I believe that one must ask the question of why the stereotype is so popular among the artists who repre-sent the culture being stereotyped, and what exactly is gained from the ironic reformulation of the stereotype. In an attempt to delve into this issue, I would like to point out that the popularity of the direct, yet playful, engagement with the stereotype is reflected in box-office figures and the audience demographic. *Mila from Mars*, for instance, turned out to be a huge success at the box office, becoming the best-selling Bulgarian film in over a decade.[10] Films by other filmmakers who employ vernacular magic realism, such as Jan Jakub Kolski, Martin Šulík or Béla Tarr, have also gained both popular and critical acclaim, significantly among younger audiences. The attention that the younger popula-tion of film viewers bestows upon these films further complicates the argument about the films' popularity stemming from the nostalgic impulse. The young viewers are obviously not drawn to these films in search of the older ways of life and traditional values that would bring back the taste of the Proustian 'lost time'. Village life is something that they hardly know from first-hand experi-ence. The appeal of the cinematic village rests in its peripheral symbolism that resonates rather strongly with the younger viewers' recognition of their delayed start in the postmodern race. Coming into the race so late (arguably only after 1989, deferred by decades of Communist limbo), however, has its undeniable benefits. Unlike the Western participants, these East Central European latecomers can enter the race from a privileged position, having a knowledge of both the advantages and the disadvantages of earnestly participating in the race. The vernacular microcosm – the European periphery – offered in the region's cinema becomes a site where these viewers can reflect upon the face of globalisation and the pull of (post)modernity. In that sense, the filmic periphery becomes an anteroom, where the gains and losses that come with the new phase of modernity are carefully weighed, and where the connection with the premodern is anything but severed.

Emir Kusturica's 1995 film, *Underground* (*Bila jednom jedna zemlja*), contemplates this belatedness in conjunction with the European periphery (the Balkan periphery, to be specific). The titular underground space is a huge basement hideout in war-torn Belgrade, circa 1941. Initially, the two protagonists, Marko (Miki Manojlović) and Blacky (Lazar Ristovski), enter the war as Communist resistance fighters and use the basement to escape Nazi persecution and to protect their families and friends during the bombardment of the city. Soon, the shelter becomes a prison, although the inmates are completely unaware of the enforced nature of their confinement. Cunning Marko persuades everybody, including his now-injured comrade Blacky, to stay permanently underground for the next fifty years (for the duration of the Cold War) on the pretext of the continued Nazi occupation. He sets up a munitions factory in the basement and exploits the underground dwellers as his unpaid labour. It is important to note that Kusturica goes to great lengths to visualise the underground space as an everlasting carnival, rather than a dismal sweat shop. Over time, Marko becomes a senior apparatchik in Tito's Government and lives a life of luxury above ground, while his army of slaves become convinced that their safety depends on their subterranean isolation and continued manufacturing of weapons that will eventually help the Communist partisans on the ground to eradicate the Nazi regime from the Kingdom of Yugoslavia. Eventually, after long decades of Marko's charade, his best friend Blacky emerges from the basement, only to witness what he takes to be the uninterrupted battleground of World War II but is, in fact, the Bosnian war of 1992. In the end, Marko meets his punishment at the hands of his own brother, and Blacky survives. In a highly surreal scene that concludes the film, Blacky reunites with his deceased relatives and friends at a sumptuous feast. As the revellers eat, drink and dance, the piece of land where their celebration is taking place becomes detached from the mainland and drifts off into the waters of the Danube. The floating island becomes a prison, but Blacky and his guests are, once again, too busy feasting and merrymaking to care.

Different, often ideologically opposing, interpretations of the film's central conceit – the figure of the frozen-in-time subterranean microcosm – abound, ranging from Luisa Rivi's reading of the underground space as a critical appraisal of the destructive fabrications of Communism, and history in general, to Dina Iordanova's claim that the underground represents a harmful caricature of Balkan moral character, to Slavoj Žižek's condemnation of the underground as the balkanising vision of the former Yugoslavia as the space of a gory and frenzied spectacle – Europe's Balkan Other.[11] I could also mention the documented multiplicity of voices, including those of Alain Finkielkraut, André Glucksmann, Stanko Cerović, Peter Handke and Bernard-Henri Lévy, that have debated the political merits of Kusturica's film, and the director's alleged pro-Serbian sentiments, soon after it was awarded the Palme d'Or at the Cannes Film Festival in 1995 and around the time when Yugoslavia was partitioned into several independent nations and autonomous regions. While most critics understandably focus on the film's pronounced socio-political and historical subtext, few, with the notable exception of Rosalind Galt, analyse Kusturica's signature exuberance of style.[12] In fact, those who have debated the political bias of *Underground* choose to ignore altogether the highly self-referential and grotesque impetus of the film, or comment, like Žižek, on the film's 'aestheticist attitude' as if Kusturica employed it that one time only as a cunning strategy to 'depoliticise' his war film.[13]

Kusturica's films yield more if one treats their formal and aesthetic code as an entryway into the narrative meaning and the socio-political vicissitudes that shed light on to that meaning. One of the ways in which this unique relationship of form to content in Kusturica's work can be brought up to the surface is to be found in the framework of magic realism and the category of the baroque. Both concepts have been discussed by the authors of the two major monographs on Kusturica published in English: Dina Iordanova in *Emir Kusturica* and Goran Gocić in *The Cinema of Emir Kusturica: Notes from the Underground*.[14] Both categories are discussed separately but not in conjunction with each other. Iordanova also points out that the two concepts are consciously employed by the director, who, in his interviews, explicitly mentions his admiration for the Latin American magic realists and his penchant for the baroque. Rather than a means of aesthetic estrangement and what Goran Gocić sees as Kusturica's postmodern bricolage and 'toying with "magic realism"',[15] I would like to investigate this combination of representational tactics as a political statement much in line with Alejo Carpentier's theory and practice of magic realism, which he called 'the marvellous real' – *lo real maravilloso* – in the 1949 prologue to his novel, *The Kingdom of this World*.[16]

His theory of magic realism stressed the Latin American social and cultural reality as always already saturated with fantasy and excessive energy, which Carpentier defines as the baroque. His notion of the baroque has little to do with the seventeenth-century European art movement, best exemplified in Rococo and Mannerism. In his 1975 lecture devoted to the baroque and the marvellous real, Carpentier insists that the baroque is a 'human constant', a universal element of the human spirit that can evidence itself anywhere in the world and at any point in time, when diversity, multiplicity, sensuality and the coexistence of contraries culminate in a decentring of art and culture and further erosion of the Eurocentric codes of aesthetic harmony, rationality and private spirituality. The baroque eruptions of excess culminate in artistic formations that Carpentier dubs the 'proliferating nuclei' and 'proliferating foci' that can be loosely described as dynamic constellations of extravagant centrifugal representations, which somehow reflect on the historical and political excesses so common to the region of Latin America.[17] Historically, the excess here refers to both the excess of the European coloniser acting out his base desires in the colonial backwaters and, more importantly, the excess of the colonised, who continuously labour at bursting the managing categories imparted by the coloniser, the barriers and boundaries set up by the ruling master class to organise and discipline the unruly periphery. Carpentier argues that the baroque marvellous real is 'an art that moves outward and away from the center, that somehow breaks through its own borders'.[18] Unlike the confident art of European academicism, the Latin American hybrid of magic and reality 'arises where there is transformation, mutation or innovation'.[19] The cultural conditions that promote such a mode of representation, according to Carpentier, are 'symbiosis, mutations, vibrations, *mestizaje*'.[20] The baroque flight of fancy that characterises magic realism is therefore not an act of manufactured mystification but, rather, an appropriation of the surprises, absurdities and incongruities of a culture where premodernity coexists with modernity and, later, with postmodernity, as well.

It is hardly surprising, then, that, in his comments on artistic influences reflected in his cinematic work, Balkan filmmaker Kusturica cites Latin American magic realism. He recreates its exuberant energies to tell the stories of the people and the region that, much like Latin America, consists of a transcultural mix of religions, ethnicities and temporalities, where the experience of foreign domination and abuse of power created messianic ambitions that alternate with a deep sense of martyrdom. Kusturica's *Underground*, more than a realm of self-exoticising spectacle, is a screen space where temporalities coexist and their recurrent clashing leads to a certain creative exaltation of affect and perception. This space is peripheral by choice. By assuming grotesque and highly ironic dimensions, thus distancing itself from the norm, Kusturica's creation becomes intentionally peripheral and speaks of this very peripherality. Kusturica's underground and the characters that inhabit it testify to Carpentier's notion that the baroque comes with 'the awareness of being Other'.[21] Some might see this stance as defensive posturing. I see it as an admission not on the part of one European but on behalf of many, of being at home with otherness, or, to paraphrase Carpentier, of inhabiting the region where both nature and history are still untamed.[22] This otherness is very much a matter of escaping the process of 'taming', a process with a long history that dates back to the era of the Enlightenment, when Western Europe invented 'Eastern Europe' as its savage Other in need of ennoblement, cultivation and taming. I will discuss the impact of this process on the region's peripheral identity later in this chapter.

Goran Gocić comments on Kusturica's self-aware deployment of marginality:

> He completely identifies his work with this imaginary Balkan Other. Exploiting and emphasising the difference he manages to make a viewer envious of Balkan colourfulness, freedom, temperament, passion, and beauty. He thus single-handedly inverts the racist dismissal into an envy.[23]

Western audiences find in Kusturica's films a source of almost forgotten innocence and refreshing, maybe even charming, vigour, for which they might long, in much the same way that Rousseau searched for renewal and a means of re-socialisation in the pure state of nature, roughly at the same time as the natural world was being domesticated and explained away as a matter of empirical science. Local audiences, on the other hand, witness the grotesqueness and fervour of Kusturica's appropriation of otherness as a charged performance, which immediately signals a note of conflict in their own coming to terms with peripherality and its central role in their self-identity. Peripherality, it seems, can be a contestatory stance as long as it avoids becoming the centre of identification, as long as it is displaced by some form of palimpsestic doubt that both preserves and erases the European centre's prejudice.

Interestingly, *Underground* imagines the East Central European periphery both as a dystopic, very claustrophobic, subterranean inferno and as a pastoral communion set in the picturesque countryside. One tableau serves as the palimpsest version of the other, the film as a whole keeping the two visions in a dynamic tension of incongruent paradigms. I am referring here to the scene of Jovan and Jelena's wedding, which plays out twice in the course of the film. The soundtrack links these scenes via Goran Bregović's song, 'Kalašnijkov'. The first wedding scene paints the picture of a hellish carnival, where the guests drink themselves into oblivion, stuff their faces with food, fight, dance, scream, and threaten to explode the constricting space of the basement with their brio and sheer Dionysiac power. The lighting is minimal, the angles tight, and the red filter adds a surreal, almost degenerate atmosphere to the wedding celebration that turns into a *danse macabre* held in a crypt. Structurally, this lengthy sequence is chaotic and disorienting to watch. The acceleration of the musical rhythm and the frequency of cuts eventually build up to a violent climax, a

Figure 15   Emir Kusturica's *Underground* (1995) concludes with an image of floating ground.

diegetic underground explosion: Soni, the pet monkey, gets into a tank (one of the weapons manufactured underground) and starts firing shells, blasting the whole basement into a pile of rubble.

The second wedding scene is a replay of the first one, and it functions as a coda to the entire film. It is the wedding of the same couple, but it is orchestrated in a very different manner. The use of wide angle makes this scene, shot on location, stand in sharp contrast to the rest of the film. The exuberant atmosphere is still there, but the open skies, the endless horizon, the bright sunlight and the presence of nature, including a herd of cows that swim across the Danube, mark this celebration as hopeful. The expansive landscape defuses the feverish festivities. Somehow, magically, reborn under water, the characters who battled one another and died over the course of the narrative are resurrected and come to this encore wedding feast. Old enemies forgive one another. There is a sense of unification and optimism. In the closing image of the film, we see the wedding party literally take off: the piece of land where the party is being held detaches itself from the mainland and drifts off down the river like a bizarre party barge, with the dead and the living continuing their revelry, not minding the fact that they are now consigned to a tiny floating island.

In these twin wedding scenes, Kusturica's film contemplates the nature of peripherality and its two opposing incarnations: the prison and the sanctuary. As a result, two different meanings of groundedness emerge. The basement wedding shows the periphery to be a form of incarceration, a tomb where everybody lives in the past while being convinced of a steady progress. Time is a straight line. This experience of the periphery eventually turns into a suffocating, closed system that gives in to entropy, much like the Communist system did. Here, Kusturica's film asks the East Central European audience to account for their own complicity in creating the European Other during the Cold War. Mimicking the prisoners in Plato's cave, the characters who live in the basement remain grounded due to their false consciousness. The film makes it evident that, despite Marko's initial deceit that forced this group of people to remain in the basement, their continued existence among the shadows is a matter of their own moral responsibility. Their isolation in the subterranean periphery is caused by mere ignorance.

The image of the island floating down the Danube, on the other hand, illustrates the concept of the periphery as an enclosure of choice, where diverse temporalities are preserved; those from the past dance alongside those in the present. The open-endedness of this scene promises a future, despite the elected obliviousness of the participants. They agree to stay on the island, fully understanding what they are leaving behind and of what they are opting out. Visually, the underground, which engulfs 95 per cent of the prior screen time, ultimately morphs into a floating slice of ground; the sense of vertical penetration of the ground is thus replaced by a horizontal dispersion of the ground.

Being grounded in the periphery, Kusturica's film suggests, can be an experience of captivity or an act of preservation. The difference rests in the degree of consciousness involved in the act of being grounded. While the duped inhabitants of the basement follow someone else's order to remain grounded, only to be exploded into bits and pieces by a monkey, the revellers on the island can see very clearly their growing distance from the immovable mainland centre, but they keep dancing and navigating their new connection with the little scrap of floating land that is now their sole home. Allegorically, in an interpretation separate from the one where the basement stands for the Communist totalitarian state, the contrast between these two visions points towards a critique of nationalism in the postcolonial, peripheral context. The need to be grounded is not what is being questioned; the manner of groundedness is. Blind territorialism, a form of living in the ground, leads to a captive mindset and the potential destruction of a community. Navigating the ground mindfully, much in the way that the dancing revellers do in the final scene of *Underground*, is a more precarious and humble form of attachment to the land. It is focused on being respectful of the limits of your territory, while staying within the boundaries of your small world.

Although film scholars have evaluated the image of the floating island as a quintessential absent signifier, I would like to propose that it does indeed offer an accurate and quite concrete materialisation of the concept of the interstitial East Central European periphery. The floating island, at least in Kusturica's portrayal of it, is an oxymoron of a sort – a piece of solid ground that provides those who tread on it with a firm foundation, but this foundation remains always somewhat mobile and compromised; it is a hybrid formation. Luisa Rivi sees 'the happy island' as a 'nonplace' which 'makes the dissolution of the meta-narrative of history visible and marks the notion of progress as profoundly ahistorical'.[24] In her interpretation, the island signifies the impossibility of going on into a dialectically determined future. The island is a spatial metaphor for the dead end of linear time and the crisis of the Western notion of history. Also in terms of loss, Rosalind Galt sees the island – the 'fantasmatic' landscape – as the embodiment of the impossible national space.[25] She states, 'The final scene comes closest to showing what is not there, constructing an affective landscape that lays bare the logic of fantasy.'[26] Using poststructuralist and psychoanalytic tools, Rivi and Galt theorise the floating island as the negative presence of a certain absence, the absence of historical narrative and national space respectively. But this image can also evoke a positive identification. It is almost identical to the image described by another East Central European, the writer Andrzej Stasiuk, who defines his marginal European identity in the following words:

This is what it means to be Central European: to live between the East, which never existed, and the West, which existed too much. That is what it means to be 'in the middle', when this middle is really the only real land. This land, however, is never firm. It is more like an island, maybe even a floating island. Or perhaps a ship jostled by the currents and winds from east to west and back again. The cardinal directions of the world, just like the elements, come from the realm of the symbol, allegory, and inevitable concreteness. To live on this island, or this ship, is to observe every shift in the wind, constantly pacing from shore to shore, or from side to side.[27]

Instead of seeing Kusturica's image of the floating island as fantasmatic or somehow emptied out, I have always seen it as fantastically plentiful – a crowning textual elaboration, which supplements the end of the film with a magic realist correction of the dark vision that dominated the screen till those final moments and threatened to pass as the real and realistic vision of the Balkans, of the other Europe. The magic in this scene, the act of pulling the narrative out of the underground into the full sun in one quick cut, makes the previous dystopic vision of the periphery less essential. The crisp and well-lit image of the floating island, framed in a natural setting, suddenly qualifies all of the preceding scenes that took place underground as delusional, even if more realistic in terms of narrative logic. The non sequitur impetus of this final scene, along with the surprise of capturing on screen a herd of swimming cows and the mass resurrection of the dead, all contribute to appending another layer of signification to the filmic text. This unexpected magic realist layer flaunts the limitations of realistic representation and contours out the basement inferno as a single, albeit entertaining, act of visualisation.

Kusturica includes both variants of peripheral groundedness in his film as both represent active aspects of the East Central European identity: the ethnocentric marginality pushing towards the totality of a nation-state and the mosaic, multitemporal liminality with ties to indigenous folklore. The dynamic tension between the two, the creative meshing of the periphery as a claustrophobic dystopia with the periphery conceptualised as an irreverent utopia, the condemnation mixed in with the celebration, allow for Kusturica's cinematic microcosm to avoid the blind spots of choosing one stance over the other. As a text, *Underground* deals a blow to both the discourse of nationalism and the narrative of so-called Balkanisation by putting both discourses – the centripetal drive towards totality and the centrifugal dispersion of difference – side by side and letting them oscillate in what ultimately feels like baroque undulations of mounting absolutes that are held together for brief, ecstatic moments, only to be fragmented and disbanded.

Much as in other postcolonial contexts, for East Central Europeans the consciousness of inhabiting the periphery (even if only rhetorically) can become a source of productive identity reconstruction, which depends on the marginal Europeans' understanding of their essential constitutive role in enabling Europeans 'proper' to consolidate their identity so focused on centrality. This centrality can be effectively destabilised from within its own discourse through subtle alterations of balance between the subject and its constitutive object, much in the way that fantasy destabilises the discourse of realism in magic realist art. Wendy B. Faris comments on this dialectical currency of the peripheral: 'Like the frontier, like primitivism, the lure of peripheralism (more recently called by other names like the subaltern, the liminal, the marginal) dies hard, because the idea is so appealing and so central to the center's self-definition.'[28] The peripheral activated in magic realist cinema coming from East Central Europe since the early 1990s evokes the premodern elements that define the region's culture and its mosaic experience of modernity. Those premodern elements, often conflated with primitivism and backwardness in the discourse of Western modernity, are taken up by the filmmakers and used to create a cinematic tale of identity construction that is based in the objectness that is cast off by the modern European subject. This identity is unlike the illusion of autonomous and intrinsic subjectivity that dominates the tales of Eurocentrism; it is relational in ways that exceed relationships with other humans, extending to connections with spirits, animals, land and nature.

In his highly influential study on the discourse of modernity, *We Have Never Been Modern* (1993), Bruno Latour famously argues that hope for Western culture can only be found in revisiting premodern culture, and granting that culture of the past an important discursive place in our philosophical attempts to solve the impasse of (post)modernity. Latour argues that, if modernity is a project of conceptual purification of culture (society) vis-à-vis nature, the construction of the great, sterilising divide between the post-Enlightenment human and the non-human, then Western society has never been truly modern, as this project of purification has always been effectively accompanied and contested by what Latour calls the work of translation (or hybridisation). The translation project, although largely obscured in the official accounts of modernity, exists in the dialectical relationship to the work of purification. Modern processes of translation create a host of nature–culture hybrids. Many of those hybrids undermine the purity of modernity itself by showcasing its dependence on the undifferentiated, or premodern, notion of all-encompassing nature, which is, at all times, grafting connections between humans, animals, objects and spirits.

Interestingly, Latour identifies 1989, which he dubs the 'year of miracles', as the year when not only Socialism died but, arguably, capitalism, as well. It is the year, Latour argues, when the first conferences on the global deterioration of the planet were held across the capitals of the West. According to many who took part in those conferences, the capitalist dream of mastering nature turned, almost overnight, into a dystopic nightmare. Latour writes that

> nature, over which we were supposed to gain the absolute mastery, dominates us in an equally global fashion, and threatens us all. It is a strange dialectic that turns the slave into the man's owner and master, and that suddenly informs us that we have invented ecocides as well as large- scale famine.[29]

Latour sees a telling symmetry between the end of Socialism and the end of naturalism (i.e. the idea that nature is an unbridled and pure force to be harnessed), on which the capitalist economy relies. In his view, the dissolution of Socialism signals the troubles of capitalism. Both sides in the Cold War are, in fact, two elements of a hybrid formation constitutive of modernity, but the hybrid connection that links the two is usually occluded by modernity's official discourse. The acceptance of the capitalist exploitation of natural resources, which often belong to non-Western, non-capitalist societies, depends on the same 'purifying' separation between nature and society that undergirds the Communist / socialist exploitation of man by man (the ugly aftermath of the movement that sought to end man's domination of man), where the exploited masses cease to be social subjects and become the collective natural resource. On the surface of things, the difference here rests in the essence of the thing being exploited; capitalism exploits nature (non-human), while Communism exploits the human (culture). This difference, of course, relies on nothing more than a rhetorical sleight of hand – a gesture of discursive purification.

In the same way that capitalists refuse to think of themselves in continuity with Communists, the moderns cannot fathom their identity without a clear and radical break from the premoderns. In the present study, I propose to think of post-1989 East Central Europe as the territory where modern thinking and living happens in continuity with the somewhat interrupted but still very palpable premodern *Weltanschauung*, a space where things have never been fully modern but have not all simply remained premodern either. For one to understand the cultural output produced in East Central Europe after the collapse of Communism and after the introduction of advanced, carnivorous capitalism, it is necessary to tune in to the region's distinctly premodern features of being in the world: the conceptualisation of nature that coexists holistically with culture, the scrupulous, if cautious, acknowledgement of hybrid formations, where human subjects mix with non-humans (objects, divinities and beasts), where things coexist with words and symbols, and where the past is always already in the present and casting a shadow on the future. According to the premodern worldview, the ancestors accompany the living, and the belief in abundant transcendence reflects a deep distrust in human singularity and invincibility. East Central Europe becomes a hybrid of modernity and premodernity, taking advantage of what is best about the two worldviews, but it is also guilty of taking on their blind sides and prejudices. Premodernity, warns Latour, has its limits in the globalising world; it leads to ethnocentrism, territorial aggression and scapegoating practices.[30] Modernity, on the other hand, breeds colonial exploitation, homogenisation in the name of universalism, and historical amnesia. The art of the region reflects this bifurcated cultural make-up. The representational codes of realism and fantasy come together into a hybrid figuration that meets the demands of the multitemporal periphery.

Much like Emir Kusturica, though far less known to audiences outside of his native Poland, Jan Jakub Kolski brings vernacular magic realism to the screen in order to recreate the East Central European periphery imaginatively as a territory of surprising contrasts, which contribute to the region's cultural autonomy. Kolski's filmic world, like Faulkner's Yoknapatawpha County or García Márquez's Macondo, is a semi-fictional microcosm where the law of the land clashes with modernisation, where the past is challenged by the present. Most of Kolski's films are set in a generic Polish village (often shot on location in Popielawy, Poland) – a place that is clearly coded as peripheral – and filled with a perspective that paints the rural environment as being both disconcertingly harsh (witness to pogroms, denunciations and violent insurgence) and delightfully enchanting (source of communal identity).

With rare exceptions, Kolski's movies are set in the same village scenery, maintain the same raw visual / rhetorical style, and present a cast of the same actors, who speak in a dialect that is truncated, repetitive and often melodic, and which usually breaks for extensive periods of silence (filled with the folklore-inspired music of Zygmunt Konieczny). There is a common iconography that brings all of the films into one semantic space that is unique and easily identifiable as Kolski's creation. That space encompasses varied cultural codes, of which the most pronounced are nature, Christian hagiography, magic, science, history and paganism. I believe that the idiosyncrasy of Kolski's hybrid microcosm happens to be its most appealing aspect, but, at the same time, it is responsible for the fact that his films remain obscure for Western audiences. Unlike Kusturica's exuberant films that seduce audiences around the world with their raw energy and shocking excess, Kolski's work is very quiet and meditatively slow. In order to enjoy it, the viewer must enter it, as one enters a physical location.

One of the most compelling features of the cinema of Jan Jakub Kolski is its consistent *mise-en-scène*. His stories unfold in a place that remains the same from film to film. The topography makes one think of the Polish countryside of the first half of the twentieth century. Yet, upon further inspection, one realises that it is a place set apart from the Polish village as we know it. For over a decade now, in one carefully crafted scene after another, Kolski has been systematically constructing a celluloid place that attracts audiences with a mixture of seemingly incompatible elements clustered together to evoke a feeling of recognition. What we recognise in Kolski's place is a blend of reality bites, which, when placed side by side, represent the sense of place common among the inhabitants of East Central Europe. Of what does this sense consist? And how does it derive from the physical reality?

The contradictions that comprise Kolski's world unsettle the idea of 'Eastern Europe' invented in the West. Kolski imbues his place with literal and tangible provincialism, thus alluding to the Western invention of the 'shadowed lands of backwardness'. Apart from Kusturica's films, this type of ironic engagement with the dominant stereotype of East Central Europe as the armpit of the European culture has been utilised in recent commercial cinema by Sacha Baron Cohen, in his popular comedy, *Borat: Cultural Learnings of America for Make Benefit Glorious Nation of Kazakhstan* (2006). In *Borat*, it is the nation of Kazakhstan (geographically part of Central Asia, not Europe) that embodies the idea of 'Eastern Europe', somehow still conflated with the former Soviet Union, as the territory of permanent economic and cultural retardation, where people share their hovels with domestic animals, drink themselves into oblivion, and remain awestruck by the technological miracle of a TV set.

Cohen paints the eastern periphery with such exaggerated brush strokes (e.g. his Kazakh characters speak broken Polish instead of their native language) that the stereotype explodes in the salvos of the audience's hysterical laughter. But while Cohen's parody uses the stereotype of the retarded 'Eastern Europe' to expose the ridiculousness of the construct, it also reaffirms it, simply because no alternative vision is being offered, and the only consistent cultural matrix of reference is the absurd thing being parodied. Kolski taps into the same stereotype, but instead of laughing it off, he refashions it to deliver a more accurate and productive version of the East Central European provincialism. This provincialism, a bottom-up project, was under way even before the West began its dissemination of Enlightenment ideology. More importantly, it exists in a variety of cultural contexts as a source of resistance to Western expansion. In the context of postcolonial criticism, Dipesh Chakrabarty uses the figure of the peasant as the embodiment of this kind of contestatory provincialism:

> The 'peasant' acts here as a shorthand for all the seemingly nonmodern, rural, nonsecular relationships and life practices that constantly leave their imprint on the lives of even the elites in India and on their institutions of government. The peasant stands for all that is not bourgeois (in a European sense) in Indian capitalism and modernity.[31]

Ultimately Kolski's aesthetics relies on a self-conscious rhetorical gesture that re-appropriates the main discursive tropes of the Western invention of 'Eastern Europe' and is then used to reclaim the identity of East Central Europe for the project of self-representation. The attraction of his cinema lies in the fact that, with every new film, Kolski reiterates and elaborates for his viewer the portrait of a provincial place that is filled with shadow but is not at all backward. His films collectively provide a consistent and complex vision, which serves the purpose of a minor narrative for a minor people, living in a minor Europe. I use the adjective 'minor' here to follow in the footsteps of Deleuze and Guattari's literary theory, as well as Dipesh Chakrabarty's historical analysis. Chakrabarty summarises both applications as follows:

> Just as the 'minor' in literature implies 'a critique of narratives of identity' and refuses 'to represent the attainment of autonomous subjectivity that is the ultimate aim of the major narrative,' the 'minor' in my use similarly functions to cast doubt on the 'major.' For me, it describes relationships to the past that the 'rationality' of the historian's methods necessarily makes 'minor' or 'inferior,' as something 'nonrational' in the course of, and as a result of, its own operation.[32]

The appeal of this minor grand narrative rests in Kolski's brave coming to terms with the region's awareness of its provincial status. Provincialism remains a category of inferior identity (as an *unfortunate* condition of being left behind by the agents of civilisation) for only as long as it is spoken about by those who use this label to chisel out the civilised core. In the process of sculpting this core, the chips and the dust that fall off to the ground can be either swept away or saved for another project. In Kolski's hands, the by-product of building Europe retains its history as discarded matter, but, more importantly, it is reused for a new creation that gains value of its own.

To best describe Kolski's cinematic world, I once again borrow the words of Andrzej Stasiuk, another contemporary artist engaged in the project of East Central European self-representation. In his book, *Travelling to Babadag* (2005), Stasiuk delivers an account of this Europe's marginal identity through one traveller's experience of small towns and villages in Poland, Slovenia, Slovakia, Hungary, Romania, Moldova and Albania. Much like Kolski's films, this narrative heavily emphasises the place itself. Here, characters and actions are completely under the spell of the landscape and local geography. The main concern of Stasiuk's storytelling is the peculiar influence that material reality has on the mind of the inhabitant of this part of Europe:

> But on my way, I forget where I was going. As soon as I get off the main road, I'm seized by the feeling that the space surrounding me is becoming thicker and intractable, that it barely tolerates these homes, farmhouses, these miserable possessions behind fences, all that, which hardly rose off the ground, hardly emerged above the surface, and is still trying to survive. But it all endures from day to day as if devoid of hope, as if only fatalism kept it all together. Concrete, brick, steel and wood are mixed together in accidental proportions, as if growth and decline could not, once and for all, settle the argument. The old looks dilapidated, deserted, resigned and helpless; the new is arrogant and lewd, using ostentation to kill the humiliation of the past and the fear of what is to come. Nothing but the here and now, the makeshift, the present tense continuously completing itself. Everything could disappear any moment, and the space would accept it, patch up, immediately smooth over, as if nothing happened. Because it all looks like a preface to something that will never begin, like the fringes without the center, like the periphery stretching to the very horizon without the culmination of a city. Yes, the landscape will swallow it, the space will be sewn back together, because the existence of these places, these boondocks, which I pass through and desperately love, exhausts itself in the very act of being, because their sense exhausts itself in its attempt to survive. In that way they are so much like nature that on a foggy winter day they are almost indistinguishable from the land.[33]

Kolski's *mise-en-scène* visually replicates the sense of place defined here so scrupulously by Stasiuk in his literary rendition. The rural locations used in his films are far from picturesque pastoral vistas (although those can also be seen on occasion). They always seem a bit forsaken, a bit used up and always already in some aimless transition. They are a periphery completely uninterested in the affairs of the centre and totally caught up in the basic process of becoming. The fact that Kolski always shoots on location, using actual Polish villages as his sets, reinforces the authenticity of his vision. But, like Stasiuk, he transforms the encountered reality with his camera to express the complex amalgamation of feelings that rise in the mind and heart of the person destined to call this reality home.

The success of his vision depends on his ability to disclose all of the inadequacies, blemishes and flaws of this unimportant, even anachronistic, part of Europe, without eliciting in his viewers shame, anger or disappointment. On the contrary, through a masterful depiction of raw material reality and the ensuing deceleration of action, Kolski uses his camera as a discerning but loving eye, very different from the typical cinematic apparatus guided by vicarious drives to possess, regulate and consume.[34]

As a result of Kolski's contemplative mode, the viewing subject, who, according to Jean-Louis Baudry, is always a function of the ideological work of the apparatus, maintains a reciprocal relationship with the reality on screen, best defined as *invested detachment*. That relationship, between Kolski's spectator and his cinematic reality, reproduces the sense of place experienced by East Central Europeans in response to their geo-historical circumstances. This stance could be summarised as trying to deflect the horizontal tug of war between the East and the West in order not to feel *out of place* in the home that is East Central Europe. The inhabitant of this Europe has learned to be invested in the immediate physical surroundings, yet detached from the flux of global forces of domination. In the case of Kolski's spectator, this stance translates into something akin to Kristevan space of semiotic *chora*, where the spectator engages with the audio-visual rhythms and intonations, and not the symbolic progress of the narrative. In that respect, Kolski's cinema is also about the challenge to the phallocentric mode of representation.

Before proceeding to analyse the role of Kolski's art in the project of East Central European self-representation, one needs to pause and review the history of the dominant discourse of imagining the region as the constitutive Other of Western Europe: the barbaric East. Not surprisingly, this discourse was formulated by the Western outsider during the time when the ideas of development and backwardness became the key categories in appraising different cultures.

Arguably the most renowned East Central European to date, Copernicus (Mikołaj Kopernik) has been championed for formulating what came to be recognised as one of the most important scientific hypotheses in the history of humankind – the heliocentric theory of the solar system, thus propelling modern science, the paradigm behind the Western idea of progress, into existence against dogmatic thought of all kind (especially Roman Catholic Church doctrine). A Renaissance man and a member of the clergy himself, he contributed to the general confidence in human intellect, its powers of observation and logical reasoning. But another way of looking at the Copernican

Revolution is to see it as the ultimate move that deprived the Earth and its inhabitants of their central position in the universe. Although the theory that the Earth revolves around the Sun was first put forth by the Greek astronomer Aristarchus of Samos (ignored to the advantage of Ptolemy), it was Copernicus who declared that the Earth is a small and insignificant element in the complex entirety of the universe. At the time when Columbus was helping Western man to strengthen his foothold in the increasingly better-charted and knowable world, Copernicus's theory initiated the earth-shaking dispersal of a given individual's privileged position in space and time. This realisation, along with the affective reverberations accompanying the epistemological degradation – a push to the margins of the known, constitutes the underpinnings of modern science; those shadows are the humbling counterpart of modern science.

While Western Europe focused on and greatly benefited from expanding its empire of knowledge, East Central Europe represented and laboured over the simultaneous expansion of the necessary discourse of difference enforced upon it: the permanently grey cultural zone whose immediate vicinity still enables Western Europe to outline its modern contour. From Shakespeare's imaginary lands of Bohemia to the more recent depiction of the region in nature documentary *Winged Migrations* (2001), the examples of the Western European vision of East Central Europe have shrouded the region in an impenetrable grey mist; over time, the dark fog of barbaric woodlands evolved into the noxious smog of polluted post-Soviet satellite countries. This hazy visual representation continues to impress conceptual obscurity on to ambiguous but not inscrutable cultural identity. As Foucault observed, 'Western culture has constituted, under the name of man, a being who, by one and the same interplay of reasons, must be a positive domain of *knowledge* and cannot be an object of *science*.'[35] The hidden, constitutive part of this Western logic rests within the immediate outside of the 'positive domain of knowledge' – the territory that is barely visible because it is the demarcating line itself. For Western Europe that 'immediate outside' where the object of science suddenly materialised, the place where the subject whittles itself out of the object, has been the stretch of land that separates Europe from Asia (historically from the Ottoman and the Russian Empires that embodied the cultural concept of the Orient). That stretch of land has been safeguarding the standards of 'civilisation' ever since the great (and lesser) minds of the Enlightenment summoned the place into existence under the banner of 'Eastern Europe'.

In what follows, relying on Larry Wolff's 1994 seminal study, *Inventing Eastern Europe: The Map of Civilization on the Mind of the Enlightenment*, and informed by his extensive archival research, I review the formulation of the concept of 'Eastern Europe' by the key voices of the Western Enlightenment. Wolff offers a convincing argument that traces the Iron Curtain's separating curve back to the eighteenth century's political, economic and most of all imaginary divisions between Europe and Asia. To begin with Voltaire: like many Western Europeans of his time, he saw Eastern Europe as unruly and in need of discipline and domination, which ought to be exacted either by Catherine the Great or Charles XII. Painted as a land of anarchy, inhabited by the barbaric hordes prone to violence, superstition, irrational passions – the people who, according to Casanova, possessed 'souls of slaves',[36] Eastern Europe remained an imaginary location employed as the horizon of the strategic gaze of the European subject, directed from West to East, from progress to chaos. In his extended correspondence with Catherine the Great, Voltaire repeatedly encouraged the Russian monarch to 'unscramble' the mosaic of small nations littering the space between Western Europe and Catherine's empire. He advised her to use her 'genius' to disentangle 'all this chaos in which the earth is plunged, from Danzig to the mouth of the Danube'.[37] In that sense, the 'Eastern Europe' of the Enlightenment was made to function as a dividing screen, permeable only in one direction: radiating Western culture over the steppes and deserts of the continental Orient.

Another formidable voice of the Enlightenment, Jean-Jacques Rousseau, considered the topic of Eastern Europe worthy of theoretical consideration, but like Voltaire, he declined the Eastern European sovereigns' invitations to visit the region and instead proceeded to theorise about the political, economic and cultural possibilities of Eastern Europe on the basis of his imaginary vision of it. He politely turned down Catherine's invitation to come and live on a pastoral estate near St Petersburg, saying that he would visit Russia only if he were younger and Russia were 'closer to the sun'.[38] As Wolff explains, the imaginary 'Eastern Europe' of the era was constructed through a series of fictional travelogues written by Western authors who either invented 'Eastern Europe' as a dramatic setting (often a substitute for the Orient proper) for their fictional travellers, or invented Eastern European travellers, who ventured out into the West, only to attest to the utmost inferiority of their native cultures. Among the most famous of those accounts are *Polish Letters* by Jean-Paul Marat (1770s) and *The Travels and Surprising Adventures of Baron Munchausen* (1785) by Rudolf Erich Raspe. The culmination of those voyages of fantasy was Catherine the Great's actual trip from St Petersburg to the Crimea in 1787. Accompanied by Western ambassadors, she witnessed from her boat a grand spectacle prepared for her and her guests (and the international press community of the time) by her General Field Marshal, Grigori Aleksandrovich Potemkin. The riverfront along the Dnieper was temporarily transformed into a stage to host a dizzying variety of tableaus depicting pastoral scenes straight from Rousseau's *The New Heloise* and others as if lifted from the Rococo court of Madame de Pompadour. The Western ambassadors admired the illusion, but at the same time, they remained undeceived: civilisation in the East could only be a mere imitation (even if it was a dazzling performance) of the Western ideal.

Similar to Chevalier Louis de Jaucourt writing in his entries on Eastern European people and their natural resources for *Encyclopédie: ou dictionnaire raisonné des sciences, des arts et des métiers*, Rousseau sought the region's identity in its abundant natural riches and admonished its people to invest more effort into agriculture, without wasting their time on other aspects of human industry (e.g. trade, finance, goods manufacture). Through this rhetorical move, Rousseau both idealised the territory of Eastern Europe (in the spirit of sentimentalism) and, perhaps unwittingly, contributed to the exploitative economic ideology later deployed by Western Europe against its eastern neighbour.[39] From Prussian and Austro-Hungarian Empires using Eastern Europe as their granary to Hitler's planned policy of economic exploitation of the region under the Nazi occupation, the relationship of the two Europes has been that of colonisation, often paired with military occupation and cultural exploitation in the name of Orientalism.[40]

Although an imaginary construct, Kolski's cinematic village stands in contrast to Potemkin's village and its elusive romanticised splendour. It is also far from the idealised settlement that Raymond Williams identified in his study of the cultural tension between the country and the city. The idealisation of settlement, Williams argues in his Marxist critique of agrarian capitalism, began as a strategy of regulating the landless population in the countryside. The myth of the land flowing with milk and honey standing in opposition to the corrupt city, according to Williams, was appropriated by the small landowning population to idealise their access to the means of production – their share of divinely allocated countryside – and, at the same time, used to call into question those without a legitimate connection to the land, who 'loitered' around the countryside making unsubstantiated claims. Here, Williams lists 'the dispossessed and the vagrants, and the old, the sick, the disabled, the nursing mothers, the children who, unable to work in these terms, were seen as merely negative, an unwanted burden'.[41] By 'these terms' Williams refers to contracted wage labour.

Kolski's village is heavily populated with the 'unwanted burden'. Amongst his characters, most of them severely humbled by life, we meet Hanutka, the village whore (*Historia kina w Popielawach / History of Cinema in Popielawy*, 1998); the pregnant and abandoned Weronka (*Jańcio Wodnik / Johnnie the Aquarius*, 1993); the fun-loving waitress Grażynka, who one day receives the stigmata (*Cudowne miejsce / Miraculous Place*, 1994); a pair of circus freaks in love: Janka and Morka (*Grający z talerza / Playing from the Plate*, 1995); the legless Kulawik, who roams the countryside planted on a wooden cart that serves as his makeshift wheelchair (*History of Cinema in Popielawy*); the infertile Pograbek, who kills old horses for a living (*Pograbek / The Knacker*, 1992); and the amateur violinist Lunda, who reads music off the decorative patterns found on broken plates (*Playing from the Plate*). These characters, in their lack of ownership connection to the land, or to any property for that matter, remind one of the inhabitants of the city ghetto. Their cinematic presence blurs the dichotomy discussed by Williams and reminds the viewer of the complex nature of the East Central European countryside, which included a pronounced role of the Jewish *shtetl*: a semi-rural community based on farming but not on land ownership, a place where the dispossessed and the minimally 'in-possession' lived. For centuries, the *shtetl* population managed to preserve their traditional and unique modes of life precisely by circumventing both agricultural exploitation and its industrial equivalent.

Many of Kolski's characters are losers who are ready to receive each other to form an awkward but comfortable community. Some of them, like Johnny the Aquarius (in the film of the same name) or the young Andryszek (*History of Cinema in Popielawy*), are single-mindedly pursuing their dreams. Others, like Weronka or Morka, are happy to be witnesses to other people's dreams. In fact, the quiet witnesses form the majority of residents in Kolski's universe. Between the hot-headed visionaries and the mild-mannered, enduring populace, there are very few characters that could be seen as living productive and ambitious lives, at least not according to the capitalist or the Communist vision of a productive existence. Work, in the form of either private enrichment (self-improvement) or communal labour, is simply missing from Kolski's vision.

Yet, despite the general lack of aspiration and commerce, the viewer has a clear impression that the characters are living meaningful lives, and that an important part of that meaning stems from the simple, yet subtle, bond that these people maintain with the place they occupy. As Edward Casey once wrote, 'To live is to live locally, and to know is first of all to know the place one is in.'[42] It is apparent that Kolski is not afraid to send out a message about the importance of a primal sense of place in the era of global time–space compression and increasing uprootedness among the world's population. In the face of increasingly dislocated and interrupted life patterns, those who speak of the benefits of attachment to a particular place risk sounding reactionary and exclusionary. However, against some such accusations, Kolski's message is not employed in the service of ethnic rootedness and nationalism, two modes of relating to place that received severe criticism in recent years among philosophers of place.

Much of Kolski's most devoted audience is to be found among the young generations of Poles, who for various reasons are not able to leave the country to make a living abroad and thus must eke out a living at home, more often than not, unemployed. They do not participate in the time–space compression of the global market economy. More accurately, one should imagine these people's lives as decompressed and decelerated. A day in the life of a chronically unemployed person living in an economically depressed area deepens space and stretches time, sometimes to a painful extent. So the lack of characters engaged in systematised labour in Kolski's universe does not stem from a desire to depict land as perpetually fertile, thus substituting a pastoral idyll to mask over exploitative economic relations behind the prosperous enterprise of agricultural capitalism, as Raymond Williams would have it. Kolski's characters do not work not because they are graced with prelapsarian innocence – a construct of cultural and artistic sublimation of actual rural exploitation – but because there is no work to be done. If one was tempted to conduct a Marxist reading of Kolski's cinematic countryside, it would have to begin with facing the economic reality of the region. The following are the key features of economic existence in the East Central European periphery, even after its absorption into the European Union: reliance on premodern subsistence farming (low productivity, low capital endowment and low competitiveness), 10–15 per cent unemployment resulting from the dissolution of Communist, government-subsidised heavy industries, and harvesting of non-timber forest products (mushroom and berry picking, fishing, hunting and trapping) as the most popular solution to the problem of unemployment.

There is an emblematic scene in Kolski's *Pogrzeb kartofla* (*The Burial of a Potato*, 1990) that ridicules the very idea of land ownership, both as means of capitalisation and as a source of some essential heritage. The film's dramatic action is centred on the agricultural land reform initiated in Poland by the Communists in the years immediately following World War II, when large, private estates were confiscated from the Polish landed nobility to be parcelled out and handed over to local peasants, estate servants and party members. One Stefan Gorzelak (Adam Ferency) is the antagonist in the story: a cruel, greedy man who will stop at nothing to own a bigger piece of land than what the state has assigned to him. As his scheming to exclude a returning war victim, a fellow villager, from his due share of land intensifies, Gorzelak's lust for land turns literal on screen, and we see him fall to the ground and frantically inseminate the earth.

The scene is most likely a phantasm of Gorzelak's inflamed imagination. But regardless of its status within the film's narrative, the viewer is convinced that Gorzelak is precisely the kind of man who would want physically to penetrate the plot of land that came into his possession. Kolski constructs the scene as a pathetic re-enactment of the regressive search for internalised origins, the origins that Gorzelak is so desperate to acquire, because he is a singular, unattached nobody. Throughout the film, Gorzelak is portrayed as a despicable character who mistreats animals and women, and is responsible for a death of a wounded soldier, whom he refuses to help. He has no love or friendship ties with anybody in his community and has no apparent skill or profession. He seems to believe that the land grant will finally elevate his position in society, but the viewer witnesses Gorzelak's utter degradation.

The scene in question begins with Gorzelak entering a freshly ploughed field.

As he is walking in the folds of the field, a cross-cutting sequence alternates between a camera focusing on Gorzelak's body from waist down and an even row of naked male bodies, also seen only from waist down, that seem to be walking down the same field. The low camera angle suggests a viewing perspective from the ground itself, therefore animating the receiving subject of the act that is about to happen. Gorzelak first falls to his knees to fill his fists with soil. This shot, in itself an echo of a recurrent cinematic topos of human gratitude for one's place in the world, is then evacuated from the usual context and thrust into what can only be described as a grotesque imitation of a rape scene. Gorzelak hurriedly digs a hole in the ground, lowers his trousers and throws his pelvis into it. At this point the camera suddenly takes flight and gradually assumes a bird's-eye perspective. From a growing distance, we see Gorzelak's body move rhythmically against the ground, performing this bizarre intercourse. Eventually, Gorzelak is a tiny speck of dirt against the overwhelming expanse of land. What began as a menacing imitation of rape has been transformed into a laughable farce. The field of vision in which the scene culminates allows the viewer to see Gorzelak's aspiration of domination as a pitiful act of territorial onanism.

Furthermore, the scene functions as a way to activate the issue of gender with regard to land ownership. Showing Gorzelak grabbing and raping the land is a re-enactment of an earlier, much more disturbing, scene in the film, that of an actual rape of a woman. The woman violated is the daughter of a local aristocrat / landowner, who, along with the rest of his family, was murdered by the Soviet soldiers who 'liberated' Poland in 1944. The daughter is the only survivor of the bloody massacre. Deeply traumatised by what happened to her family, she barely holds on to her sanity. Gorzelak uses her as a ploy in his scheme to secure more land. He invites the land surveyor, whose job it is to parcel out the large estate, to the plundered manor house where the woman's family used to reside and she continues to live. The men drink excessively and then proceed to assault the vulnerable woman. She resists and is subsequently beaten by Gorzelak, who then throws her unconscious body on the table for the land surveyor's pleasure. The two scenes of rape are bridged by Gorzelak's role as the perpetrator of violence and the fact that they code land ownership in the language of paternal heritage. As a part of Kolski's critique of this language, we are invited to see no qualitative difference in the system of land distribution before and after the Communist reform; both are based on the usurpation of power and violence embedded in patriarchy. The two scenes differ, however, in the affect they elicit in the viewer. While the rape of the aristocrat's daughter is extremely painful to witness (one might even turn away from the screen in horror), the rape of the land evokes scorn with a dose of amusement. Kolski, thus, brings to our attention a number of observations: there is aggression involved in human affairs, no matter what the ruling political system is; the persistence of suffering that we inflict upon each other is the greatest injustice, which nature cannot equalise; the violence exacted by humans upon nature is often an extension of the dominant social ties.

Kolski shows how the notion of controlling land is a mad undertaking. There can be no such thing as possession of place. Place must arise not through exercise of power but rather through exercise of mindful cultivation of connections, a spirituality. In his influential text on the idea of place, *Topophilia*, Yi-Fu Tuan explains how human life unfolds through the experience of surroundings and the 'affective bond between people and place'.[43] Employing vernacular magic realism, which in his case is brought to screen via hyperfocus on nature, the narrative use of the miracle motif, the emphasis on the quotidian, and deceleration of camera work, Kolski puts significant effort in showing his viewer the difference between the bare fact of inhabiting a section of physical space and the place as a field of guardianship, of prudent care and attentiveness. The character of Gorzelak embodies the drive to inhabit the space and mould it in the owner's image. But most of Kolski's characters engage with their place through the practice of mindful tending. We see these people partake in ritual-like repetition of some basic exchanges with the elements of their immediate environment (actions usually omitted in cinema) – watering plants, sweeping the front yard, cooking, eating, feeding birds, caring for animals – but also talking to trees and observing the rhythms of nature. Most of this daily maintenance is performed in silence, and rather than providing the 'filler' for more important events, these rituals of caring take the centre stage of the film and are a source of magical enchantment. In this regard, Kolski's cinema offers an antidote to commercial cinema that operates through the sense of space rather than place. Kolski's world is minimally kinetic, which allows him to interrupt space, defined by Tuan as an arena of action and movement, and build a sense of place, a moment of stopping and becoming drawn into the surroundings. The fact that Kolski is labouring against the key principle of his medium – motion – and still capturing the viewer's attention is a testament to his creative imagination and extraordinary inventiveness in the realm of film form. Combined, the two ingredients result in cinema enchanted – stopped in its tracks –with the local.

East Central Europe has never rid itself of this premodern enchantment, which I like to call primary, or even primal, enchantment. This mode of viewing the world comes from being loyal to one's place in it, the small plot of land that continues to bear fruit and provide shelter against all historical odds. The sweeping horizontal upheavals of modern history, along with exploitative economic policies implemented by the imperial centres outside, taught East Central Europeans to assume a humbling, if at times territorial, attitude of looking after one's immediate surroundings, one's own back yard. The statistics support the enormous scale of this spell of gravity. East Central

Europe of the twenty-first century (especially its rural population) still relies mostly on the agrarian economy, which curiously resists industrial agriculture (which the European Union, today, and the Soviet Union, in the past, failed to implement). Subsistence farming, which stresses land stewardship and not productivity, is the dominant model of land cultivation in the area. The phenomenon of mass community gardens repeatedly stalls urban developers' ventures across the region. Most urban dwellers own tiny plots of land that sprawl just outside of city borders, which are used as gardens and places of weekend recreation. These settlements have nothing in common with the usual summerhouses owned by the more successful members of the middle class. Typically, these 'allotments' consist of a few square metres of land transformed into a vegetable and flower garden, with a tool shed occupying the central spot. Subsistence farms and community gardens are a symptom of resistance to the economic and political reforms enforced by different regimes in most East Central European nations. They attest to the need for a particular attachment to physical place, the precious strip of land dividing the East from the West. This ante-mural territory, raped and pillaged repeatedly by the hegemonies on both sides of the divide, derives much of its identity from preserving the cosmic bond between human being and nature.

In Kolski's films, the link that connects the human with the cosmos is the animal. Kolski's characters always take good care of their animals, treating them with utter respect, without, however, confusing this respect with the love reserved for another human being. When this delicate harmony between people and their beasts is disrupted by gratuitous violence in *Johnny the Aquarius*, the community has to pay the price. The film opens with a touching scene in which a village vagabond finds an old mare at the side of the road. This poor man, who has been pulling a cart filled with his meagre belongings by the strength of his own back, is now overflowing with happiness. Vagabond (the character refers to himself as such) slowly approaches the horse, while talking to it in the most endearing terms: 'Horsey, whose are you? Come here, come here. I think I might have a horse. Come here, godly little creature.' He then caresses the horse's muzzle, running his hand through its mane, but suddenly, he realises that the horse is in a very bad way. As soon as Vagabond turns away to go and get something from his cart (presumably something that would relieve the horse's suffering), the mare collapses on its side. Vagabond runs up to the animal, only to witness its quick death. While crying and petting the horse's body, Vagabond is outraged to discover that someone must have beaten the old horse and sent it away to die. Vagabond buries the animal. Disgusted with the cruel act perpetrated against a defenceless creature, he places a curse on the village, wishing a devil to be born amongst the villagers.

The mixture of heartfelt emotions (joy, sadness and anger) expressed by Vagabond, the character who, like the old mare, represents otherness expelled by the village, elicits compassion in the viewer. The scene contains the most intimate dramatisation of an animal's death, portraying the event as a fundamental and deeply unnecessary loss. After Vagabond's pronouncement of the curse, during which the camera pans across the landscape menacingly, the viewer feels that the world will never be the same. This unforgettable and devastating scene animates an important aspect of East Central European *Weltanschauung*: animals are viewed as fellow witnesses in the effort for survival, not as a means of agricultural production only. Their use value for the human is only partially based on pure consumption value. Their physical presence, good health and comfort constitute another tissue of the place as a field of care. Once again, I borrow from the beautiful prose of Andrzej Stasiuk in hope of finding a proper translation for Kolski's intense images:

> Yes, my Europe is full of animals. Huge pigs rolling in mud by the side of the road, somewhere between Tiszaörs and Nagyiván, dogs at sidewalk cafes of Bucharest, buffalos in Răşinari, horses let loose in Carnohora. I wake up at five in the morning to the chime of sheep bells. It's raining and the mooing of cows sounds muffled, flattened, it doesn't resound with an echo. I once asked a woman why she was keeping so many cows if nobody was there to buy the milk. 'What do you mean, why?' she answered as if she did not understand the question. 'One has to keep them.' It simply would not cross her mind to break this archaic bond between the human and the animal. 'What kind of people are you, if you don't have animals.' This was the sense of her response, which contained the fear of human isolation. The animal is the missing link, which ties us with the rest of the world.[44]

In terms of identity construction on screen, these ubiquitous animals are 'kept' not as mirror images of their owners, upon which human rights are thus conferred but, rather, as the embodiment of the Other, whose presence in the vicinity carries an ontological meaning. Any and every version of humanity arises through the practice of othering. While in some instances the impulse is to cover over this often-violent cognitive practice of essentialist self-aggrandisement, in Kolski's world the silent presence of the first human Other, the animal, works as an ethics of intervention.[45] It works through illuminating the axis of animal–human differentiation in order to slow down the very act of separating humanity from that which is not human. Constructing extensive screen coexistence for both products of this differentiation, Kolski infinitely suspends the final and most dangerous stage of othering: the masking over the internal fissures of that which is being defined in the process.

Just as the relationship of humans with animals is based on symbiosis, Kolski's portrayal of the peasants' attitudes towards the crops they are

Figures 16 and 17   Director Jan Jakub Kolski working with animals on the set of his films.

supposed to grow emphasises the premodern notion of the fruit of the land. In *The Saber from the Commander* (*Szabla od komendanta*, 1995), modern industrial agriculture receives a satirical dismissal. One of the main characters is an agricultural botanist, Janeczek, whose ambition is to grow healthier and hardier varieties of fruit in his father's orchard. Janeczek is the educated farmer with his own field laboratory. While Janeczek is performing his bio-experiments, his father is growing huge apples simply by fertilising the apple tree with his own excrement. He has built an outhouse in the orchard and is lovingly enriching the soil every morning. Meanwhile, Janeczek's experiments are compared to the pseudo-science of Trofim Lysenko and Ivan Michurin, two controversial figures in the history of Soviet agriculture. For decades, throughout the East Central European territory, these two figures have been associated with the Soviet effort to industrialise small-scale farming. This effort was successfully sabotaged in most of the countries of the Soviet bloc, but it irreversibly ruined agriculture across the Russian countryside.

Stalin's idea of modernising farming encompassed three disastrous programmes: the collectivisation of farms, the exile to Siberia of ten million of the most successful private farmers, and the confiscation of all available grain, including all of the seed stock (resulting in the virtual disappearance of native grain varieties). Trofim Lysenko was one of Stalin's agents authorised to facilitate the process of building the farming industry in the Soviet Union. Instead, after infiltrating the community of geneticists and sending the most progressive ones to the gulags, Lysenko put in place a series of failing farming practices based on his own dubious science of biology, which was based on Lamarckism and Darwinism.

In Kolski's film, Lysenkoism stands for the botched attempt to industrialise agriculture in Poland. It also functions as a gross caricature of land cultivation. Not unlike Communism, Lysenkoism became an absurd episode in contemporary history, best dealt with as a great source of humour. One of the characters retells the popular old joke about Michurin: 'Do you know how Michurin's wife died? . . . She fell off a strawberry.' The joke is pushed even further when human-size fruit materialises on screen. The fruit are props that Janeczek's father uses to draw his son's undivided botanist attention to women and the need to start a family. The father and his village buddies place the fake fruit in the garden of the woman they believe would make a great wife for Janeczek, in order to lure Janeczek out of his experimental orchard and into the woman's bedroom. Janeczek's father needs a grandson to pass on to him his most cherished possession, the sabre from Commander Piłsudski who led the Polish troops against the Russian invaders during the 1920 war. Here, Kolski pokes fun at Polish patriotism. The old man's single-minded drive to produce a male heir becomes equated with Lysenko's ruse to build the most successful agricultural industry in the world. Both projects are doomed because they disturb the earthly affairs of the small village community by enforcing ideological quota. Nature cannot and should not be exploited for the benefit of a few men with highfalutin ideas, Kolski seems to be saying. As the comedy intensifies, the father's scheme backfires: Janeczek breeds huge pear-flavoured plums that fall off the tree before they get a chance to ripen, and he becomes father to a baby girl who gets to use the sacred sabre as an ordinary toy.

A similar corrective vision of patriarchy appears in *The Garden* (*Záhrada*, 1995) – another great example of East Central European vernacular magic realism. This film, by the prolific Slovak director Martin Šulík, depicts the female element as a source of healing energy and Husserlian re-enchantment of man's relationship with nature. Accompanied by the beautifully minimalist score composed by Vladimír Godár, *The Garden* tells the story of one man's retreat into a simpler, even if less convenient, life in the Slovak countryside, where school-earned education proves to be useless in light of the practical wisdom required to perform such everyday chores as baking bread, fixing a leaking roof or protecting fruit trees from common pests. Before his move to the countryside, the protagonist Jakub (Roman Luknár), a teacher in his mid-thirties, is leading a dead-end existence, plagued by boredom and lack of moti-vation to act. He lives comfortably with his father and distracts himself with casual love affairs that only deepen his general sense of apathy. The character of Jakub, a teacher, therefore trained in the rational processing of life experi-ence, impersonates what Max Weber famously pronounced in 1918 about the spirit-numbing state of modernity: 'The fate of our times is characterized by rationalization and intellectualization and, above all, by the "disenchantment of the world".'[46] Most of the film's action, or rather purposeful non-action, takes place in the eponymous garden, where Jakub moves on his father's emphatic suggestion to stop moping around the flat and do something produc-tive by the end of the Summer. Ultimately, the father (Marián Labuda) wants Jakub to fix up the country estate left to him by his own father, now deceased, and sell it for whatever little profit can be had.

The said garden, along with the deserted country house, used to belong to Jakub's grandfather, who loved it for the basic pleasures it provided. Jakub's father, however, always disliked his rural inheritance. In fact, he abandoned it for the urban life of a dressmaker, embracing all of the *petit bourgeois* values associated with such a life. Therefore, when the father, fed up with Jakub's aimlessness, sends him away to the countryside, he is convinced that his son will correctly interpret this paternal gesture of discontent as punishment. Presumably, he will soon tire of the tediousness of life in the provinces and come back, begging for forgiveness. Needless to say, this paternal wish will not be granted. Jakub becomes enchanted with the garden as soon as he takes his first step into it. His senses quickly awaken and the immediate circumstances of trying to make the house, which has been severely compromised by time and

weather, once again habitable force him to mobilise all his strength and ingenuity. The place soon rewards him with unexpected treasures and small miracles that Martin Štrba, Šulík's cinematographer, brings to the screen in lyrically
subdued, yet mesmerising visuals. Shots of hands kneading bread dough or a
cider press crushing apples, a close-up of salt spilled on the wooden table, or a
scene where Jakub unearths a bottle of old slivovitz that had been buried away
by his grandfather are all excellent examples of Štrba's magic.

Štrba's eidetic photography, focused on the quotidian aspects of Jakub's new
life, conveys the sense of enchantment that he is experiencing through renewing and reactivating his investment in the world. The visuals mimic Jakub's
heightened sensory perceptions and, through the use of hyperbole, saturate the
objects depicted in them with idiosyncratic symbolism, thus transferring on to
screen Jakub's very conscious experience of the objects. Štrba uses his camera
not just to depict these objects but to meditate on them. In the course of this
careful meditation, they begin to exceed their self-containment. The meditative
lens represents the fascinated vision, which Gary Backhaus identifies for us as
the key category of enchantment. A philosopher of phenomenology, keenly
interested in theories of place and space, Backhaus insists on the experiential
structure of enchantment. He differentiates it from fantasy and links it to the
mode of consciousness that could be described as intense awareness of the
world:

> In enchantment one is reflectively aware that one's state of consciousness
> is a hyper-awareness, which is occasioned by the recognized fundamental
> change in the way one intends the environment. This provides the recep-
> tivity to a wholly different form-coherence of the overall experience.[47]

Enchantment is a state of mind, but it alters one's experience of the world
and one's being in the world. At no point, however, does enchantment cancel
the ordinary world. It is a transformative act that must occur without erasing
the fundamental reference to what Backhaus calls 'the everyday environing
world'.[48] Much as in the discourse of magic realism, in Backhaus's phenomenology of enchantment, the dichotomy of the mundane and the marvellous
must be maintained for the act of decentring, via creating a symbolic pause,
to be effected. Šulík's film documents Jakub's enchantment but also allows for
the viewer to partake in his / her own act of enchantment invited by the camera's fascination with the elements of the rediscovered East Central European
periphery. The mode of magic realism invites a new perception of the periphery. It does not exactly lift the stigma of underdevelopment, but it illustrates
the intangible advantages of slowing down. Further, its success stems from the
simultaneous deployment of the private and public experiences of periphery.
More than an escape into the confines of one's imagination, the enchantment

Figure 18   Jakub being woken up by a sheep in *The Garden* (1995).

in the periphery, as enacted through a collective cinematic experience, becomes an ethical practice of recognising the given, of wanting less rather than more, of making do, and finally, of detecting otherness in the same old back yard.

Significantly, the generational discrepancy in attitudes towards the rural in Jakub's family reflects the existing sentiments among the different generations of East Central Europeans. While the prewar generation fondly remembers the countryside as a better place, run according to the ancient, still fundamentally feudal order, and untouched by the cataclysms of war and the Industrial Revolution, the postwar generation harbours ambivalent feelings towards its quaint rural origins, which posed an uncomfortable obstacle standing in the way of Soviet industrialisation and modernisation. During the postwar decades, with the lowest urbanisation rates in Europe, the region's population laboured hard to alter its profile from rural to urban. After 1989, the post-Communist generation, unburdened by compulsory class-consciousness and ideologically enforced modernisation, was able to re-evaluate the provincial countryside as an attractive, slower-paced lifestyle option, an alternative to capitalist existence in the metropolis. For that generation of East Central Europeans, the return to the village, often a place already imbued with fond memories of Summer holidays spent with grandparents, still offers a curative meaning.

The valence of this meaning depends on reaching back in time to the relationship with the local place that predates the failed parental experiment with Communism and the parents' conflicted sentiments about roots, rural origins and the past in general, the hostile sentiments shaped by the Communist Party's propaganda, keen on promoting the vision of an egalitarian paradise unfolding in the future. In contrast to their parents' generation, which, following the party's policy, exercised caution with regard to the pre-revolutionary values and acts of memory that could be labelled as reactionary, these younger members of society are willing to explore the past and, at risk of being accused of nostalgia, to recuperate some of the premodern views on the importance of one's origins and the preservation of spatio-temporal ties with the past. Finally, this willingness on the part of the post-Communist generation to look backward signals a willingness to confront the troubled legacy of Communism. This backward gaze, therefore, contains a political potential in the mere shift towards acceptance of multitemporality.

The conflict between Jakub and his father is resolved through immersion into the family's past and a curious intervention on the part of a young woman, Helena (Zuzana Sulajová). Much like Kolski, Šulík uses his cinema to speak of the importance of groundedness through the sense of continuity with the past and immersion in nature, but without necessarily returning to the staunch rule of patriarchy. In fact, the father's conformist ambitions are ridiculed and his narrow views on Jakub's role in carrying out the father's vision of propriety and property, where property becomes the essence of propriety, become ameliorated as a result of the son's banishment into the countryside and the metamorphosis that transpires there.

What would seem, on the surface, to be the seat of patriarchal legacy, the family estate, in Šulík's film, turns out to be a heap of rubbish barely withstanding the forces of nature that have been hard at work consuming the vestiges of former glory. Significantly, however, Jakub finds in this pathetic inheritance an exit out of his existential crisis. It is by adopting this barely standing, cast-off house – a structure that has already meshed itself with the surrounding nature – that Jakub experiences enough enchantment to awaken from his stupor. When he first sees the property, the vegetation is taking over the walls of the farmhouse and the birds are making their nests in the dishevelled furniture left behind. The garden is overgrown and uncultivated. The *mise-en-scène* contributes to the general sense of loss and inevitability. As in so many of the magic realist films coming from East Central Europe, the viewer is presented with an image of peripheral space that is slowly slipping away but, at the same time, seductively promising a world of difference, a rare opportunity of a quiet entrance into a new dimension. The peripherality of this abandoned place depends not only on its remote location vis-à-vis the urban centre from which Jakub arrives but perhaps even more so on the evidence of its pastness. It is not only a hybrid of nature and culture; it is also a hybrid of the past and the present. It becomes peripheral by losing its original meaning and hovering somewhere in the semantic margins of 'house' and 'garden', in the liminal space between being and becoming, if being is to stand for shelter and becoming for the flow of nature but also history.

The enchanted presence of this place, in Jakub's and the viewer's eyes, derives from the material presentness of the physical forms of house and garden that remain on the property against all odds and despite the lack of human stewardship, but also from the traces of all that is now missing, the pastness that ascribes a spectral quality to the physical contours of reality. This imbuing of everyday material objects with ethereal character, their coming to life against their inertness, is perhaps a defining feature of vernacular magic realism. There is a similar, although visually much more emphatic, if not hyperbolic, figure of an animated house in Emir Kusturica's 1989 film *Time of the Gypsies* (*Dom za vešanje*). In one of the most astounding scenes in the film, amidst a thunderous rainstorm, we see a house suspended in mid-air, as if floating above the ground in an act of architectural levitation. This image, in an obvious way, comments on the uprootedness of the Gypsies, the marginal Europeans, whose nomadic lifestyle contradicts many of the key values of European citizenship. But, more interestingly, this cinematic vision allows for the viewer to witness, even if only as a result of a drunken trick (the house is hoisted up in the air by a spiteful character who just lost all his money in a card game), the act of transcendence that undermines all logic and common sense, the Weberian means of disenchantment. This act takes place in the European periphery where reality opens up on to a new dimension that is brought about by one foolish man's flight of fancy, in complete disregard of the key patriarchal and capitalist principle, whereupon property constitutes man's propriety. Furthermore, to an average East Central European, this image of a house floating in the air will inadvertently speak of the possibility, even necessity, of being at home in the midst of historical flux, where the borders around and the ground underneath one's home slip away and tend to shift depending on political changes.

Time of the Gypsies tells the story of matriarchy. *The Garden* likewise shows a young woman as the character equipped with wisdom and transformative powers. Helena, regarded by her own mother as near-retarded, is a teenager who pays Jakub a visit upon his arrival in the garden. Despite her lack of formal education, her knowledge of how things work in her world impresses Jakub, and so does her kindness towards her surroundings, selfless care for others and her supernatural powers. In contrast to the other visitors to Jakub's garden, Helena's is the sensible and intriguing presence. Saints and philosophers are the other visitors, yet the various wisdoms they compulsively impart on Jakub fall on deaf ears; not because Jakub wants to ignore them but because the philosophical tenets turn absurd in the world of the garden, or are simply too obscure for Jakub to understand. Jean-Jacques Rousseau, who comes to the garden to preach to Jakub on the evils of technology, turns out to be a hypocrite. After a tirade on the pitfalls of knowledge and the blessings of purity and poverty, he steals Jakub's car. Helena, on the other hand, offers her help simply by being there or enacting gestures that she knows will help, all without uttering a single unnecessary word, bringing to mind the feminist epistemology of embodied knowledge.

Figure 19   Helena embodies the ancient figure of Baba Yaga.

In her analysis of the use of female spirituality and the presence of super-natural female characters in magic realist texts, Wendy B. Faris draws on Luce Irigaray's concept of *la mystérique*, the space of radical otherness where the female is at home with her own otherness and the otherness of God, to argue that magic realism enacts a form of post-patriarchal discourse. Quoting from Irigaray, Faris comments that

> the sense of 'a *sensible transcendental* coming into being through us (women), of which *we would* be the mediators and bridges' is analogous to the way that many magical realist texts mediate and bridge different worlds and discourses, and especially, of the way they may orchestrate a presence of spirit within concrete reality.[49]

Šulík's Helena is very much the bridge for Jakub. She leads him into an alterna-tive world, but she also acts as the mediator between him and his father, there-fore preserving Jakub's existing world of familial reference. Helena is a catalyst for the integration of spirituality and corporeality. A 'sensible transcendental' of a kind, she traverses the boundary between magic and reality. The key scene that illustrates Helena's integrative power is the final scene of the film, where she, very matter-of-factly, enjoys a moment of levitation in the garden. Helena's body floats above the wooden table like a pagan Eucharist. Upon wit-nessing her peaceful state of weightlessness, Jakub and his father seem finally to be able to access a sense of great calm for themselves. The three characters participate in a bizarre act of communion. When the father, looking at the air-born girl, utters the final words of the film, 'At last everything is as it should be,' he acknowledges the gift of relief that Helena brings about by teaching the two men to see in her and her surroundings much more than physical matter.

In the context of the films that are the subject of the present study in

Figure 20   Helena as the Eucharist in *The Garden*.

vernacular magic realism, the periphery is often marked as the domain of the feminine. We can see that conflation in films as diverse as Martin Šulík's *Orbis Pictus* (1997), in which a sixteen-year-old girl uses an esoteric map to guide the viewer through a countryside awash with mysterious characters and miraculous events; Iglika Triffonova's *Letter to America* (*Pismo do Amerika*, 2001), which tells the story of a young man's search for the old Bulgarian folk song that can heal the sick, and which is still being performed by women in a remote mountain village; or Jan Jakub Kolski's *Jasminum* (2006), which portrays a set of three female characters who use their sensuality to invade an old monastery and disrupt the ancient male hierarchy. Coding the periphery as feminine helps to lift the narratives in question from the limits of regressive nostalgia, and push them instead into a more subversive register, where retreating into the periphery is an act of facing radical otherness, in opposition to the charge that such a retreat equals ensconcing oneself in the claustrophobic musings of one's fantasy-afflicted interiority. Although arguably a passive stance, this form of acquiescence towards what is given, though not yet accepted, or already discarded, calls for readiness to assimilate other worldviews. Faris explains, 'Perhaps magic serves these women as it has postcolonial literature generally, to facilitate the re-appropriation of real and imagined territories, whether bodies, lands, spirits, or discourses.'[50]

Irigaray's concept of *la mystérique* is especially helpful in thinking about the periphery as a locale of change and alternative political stance that does not manifest itself via aggressive domination, or even as much as an assertion of autonomy. *La mystérique*, according to Irigaray's theory, is a corporeal entity that is situated outside of patriarchal structures, on the periphery of logos. It is a liberating space of replenishment and creative fluidity. In it, one is happy simply to be and to await the arrival of otherness.[51] And as such, the periphery

Figure 21   Women performing magic in *Jasminum* (2006).

that the viewer encounters in magic realist films from East Central Europe, especially in those instances when it is coded as the realm of the feminine, functions as a space for bringing about transformation, as well as a discursive space for contemplating difference.

If Irigaray's feminist theory of *la mystérique* converts Freud's 'dark continent' of femininity into a space of positive subjectivity outside of the patriarchal model, into a locale of openness and readiness for change, a flesh that becomes spirit, the filmic periphery created in the works of vernacular magic realism converts Eastern Europe's 'shadowed lands of backwardness' that Larry Wolff wrote about into a mediating territory of hope for alternative citizenship in the globalising world. As a Second World legacy, this space is neither the First World nor the Third World. This fluid domain of multitemporality that is nevertheless harnessed in an image of a rural periphery is best defined in George Konrád's words:

> The existence of Central Europe is thus a given. And yet Central Europe is transitory, provisional. It is neither east nor west; it is both east and west . . . Central Europe is thus both utopia and chimera, and while some of our poets have treated it as a feverish vision, it is also a reality.[52]

NOTES

1. Larry Wolff, *Inventing Eastern Europe: The Map of Civilization on the Mind of the Enlightenment* (Stanford: Stanford University Press, 1994), p. 4.
2. Milan Kundera, *The Curtain: An Essay in Seven Parts* (New York: HarperCollins, 2005), pp. 37–8.
3. See *La Vie nouvelle* (dir. Philippe Grandrieux, 2002), *Lilja 4Ever* (dir. Lukas Moodysson, 2002), *Reservni deli* (dir. Damjan Kozole, 2003), *Masz na imie Justine* (dir. Franco de Peña, 2005), *Eastern Promises* (dir. David Cronenberg, 2007), *La sconosciuta* (dir. Giuseppe Tornatore, 2006), and the more commercial *Truands* (dir. Frédéric Schoendoerffer, 2007), *Trade* (dir. Marco Kreuzpaintner, 2007) and *Taken* (dir. Pierre Morel, 2008).
4. Dina Iordanova, 'Intercultural Cinema and Balkan Hushed Histories', *Review of Film and Television Studies*, 6:1, April 2008, pp. 5–18.
5. Wendy Faris, *Ordinary Enchantments: Magical Realism and the Remystification of Narrative* (Nashville: Vanderbilt University Press, 2004), p. 149.
6. On magic realism's conflicted relationship with modernism, see Liam Connell's 'Discarding Magic Realism: Modernism, Anthropology, and Critical Practice', in *Ariel*, 29:2, 1998, pp. 102–41; and Amaryll Chanady, 'The Territorialization of the Imaginary in Latin America: Self Affirmation and Resistance to Metropolitan Paradigms', in Lois Zamora and Wendy Faris (eds), *Magical Realism: Theory, History, Community* (Durham, NC: Duke University Press, 1995), p. 168.
7. Temenuga Trifonova, 'Stoned on Mars: Home and National Identity in Bulgarian Post-Communist Cinema', *Cineaste*, 32:3, June 2007, pp. 32–6.
8. Ibid. p. 32.
9. Ibid. p. 32.
10. '*Mila From Mars* Press Kit', n.d., at http://milafrommars.com/press/MilaMars_Press_kit.pdf (accessed 25 July 2010).
11. See Luisa Rivi, *European Cinema After 1989* (New York: Palgrave MacMillan); Dina Iordanova, 'Underground: Historical Allegory or Propaganda', *Historical Journal of Film, Radio, and Television*, 19:1, March 1999, pp. 69–87; and Slavoj Žižek, 'Multiculturalism, or, the Cultural Logic of Multinational Capitalism', *New Left Review*, no. 225, September 1997, pp. 28–52.
12. See Rosalind Galt, *The New European Cinema: Redrawing the Map* (New York: Columbia University Press, 2006).
13. Slavoj Žižek, 'Multiculturalism', p. 37.
14. Dina Iordanova, *Emir Kusturica* (London: British Film Institute, 2002); and Goran Gocić, *The Cinema of Emir Kusturica: Notes from the Underground* (London: Wallflower, 2001).
15. Goran Gocić, *The Cinema of Emir Kusturica*, pp. 172–3.
16. The original prologue was later developed into a longer essay entitled, '*De lo real maravilloso Americano*', and published in *Tientos y diferencias* (Montevideo: Arca, 1967), pp. 96–112. This essay is now available in English translation in Lois Zamora and Wendy Faris, *Magical Realism*, pp. 75–88.
17. Alejo Carpentier, 'Baroque and the Marvelous Real', in Lois Zamora and Wendy Faris, *Magical Realism*, pp. 89–108.
18. Ibid. p. 93.
19. Ibid. p. 98.
20. Ibid. p. 98.
21. Ibid. p. 100.
22. Ibid. p. 105.
23. Goran Gocić, *The Cinema of Emir Kusturica*, p. 84.

24. Luisa Rivi, *European Cinema After 1989*, pp. 102–3.
25. Rosalind Galt, *The New European Cinema*, p. 171.
26. Ibid. p. 170.
27. Jurij Andruchowycz and Andrzej Stasiuk, *Moja Europa* (Wolowiec: Wydawnictwo Czarne, 2007), p. 153.
28. Wendy Faris, 'Scheherezade's Children: Magical Realism and Postmodern Fiction', in Lois Zamora and Wendy Faris (eds), *Magical Realism*, p. 168.
29. Bruno Latour, *We Have Never Been Modern* (Cambridge, MA: Harvard University Press, 1993), p. 8.
30. Ibid. p. 133.
31. Dipesh Chakrabarty, *Provincializing Europe: Postcolonial Thought and Historical Difference* (Princeton: Princeton University Press, 2007), p. 11.
32. Ibid. p. 101.
33. Andrzej Stasiuk, *Jadąc do Babadag* (Wołowiec: Wydawnictwo Czarne, 2005), p. 249.
34. The concept of the cinematic apparatus, as theorised by Christian Metz and Jean-Louis Baudry, refers to

> the totality of interdependent operations that make up the cinema-viewing situation, including (1) the technical base (specific effects produced by the various components of the film equipment, including camera, lights, film and projector); (2) the conditions of film projection (the darkened theater, the immobility implied by the seating, the illuminated screen in front, and the light beam projected from behind the spectator's head); (3) the film itself, as a 'text' (involving various devices to represent visual continuity, the illusion of real space, and the creation of a believable impression of reality); and (4) that 'mental machinery' of the spectator (including conscious perceptual as well as unconscious and preconscious processes) that constitutes the viewer as subject of desire.

(in Robert Burgoyne, Sandy Flitterman-Lewis and Robert Stam (eds), *New Vocabularies in Film Semiotics: Structuralism, Post-structuralism, and Beyond* (London: Routledge, 1992), p. 143)
35. Michel Foucault, *The Order of Things: An Archeology of the Human Sciences* (New York: Vintage, 1994), pp. 366–7.
36. Giacomo Casanova, *History of my Life*, vol. 10 (London: Longman, 1971), p. 121.
37. William Fiddian Reddaway (ed.), *The Correspondence with Voltaire and the Instruction of 1767* (New York: Russell & Russell, 1971), p. 181.
38. William Richardson, *Anecdotes of the Russian Empire in a Series of Letters Written a Few Years Ago, from St. Petersburg* (New York: Da Capo, 1968), p. 403.
39. Rousseau took the side of Poland in the debate with Voltaire over Poland's right to independence, which accompanied the political crisis that culminated in the Partitions of Poland (1772, 1793 and 1795). While Voltaire saw in Eastern Europe nothing but chaos and desert, Rousseau, in his *Considerations on the Government of Poland*, deemed this state perfectly deserving of self-government.
40. In 1939, one of the senior Nazi officials, Hans Frank, was made Governor General of the occupied Polish territory. In an interview that took place on 3 October 1939, he described the policy he intended to put into effect by stating: 'Poland shall be treated like a colony; the Poles will become the slaves of the Greater German World Empire.' His Government General proceeded to ship all the food raised in Poland to Germany, causing mass starvation ('Nuremberg Trial Proceedings', vol.

3, The Avalon Project at Yale Law School, February 2008, at http://www.yale.edu/lawweb/avalon/imt/proc/12–14–45.htm (accessed 19 July 2010)).

41. Raymond Williams, *The Country and the City* (New York: Oxford University Press, 1973), p. 82.

42. Edward Casey, 'How to Get from Space to Place in a Fairly Short Stretch of Time', in Keith Basso and Steven Feld (eds), *Senses of Place* (Santa Fe: School of American Research, 1996), p. 18.

43. Yi-Fu Tuan, *Topophilia: A Study of Environmental Perception, Attitudes, and Values* (Englewood Cliffs: Prentice-Hall, 1974), p. 4.

44. Andrzej Stasiuk, *Jadąc do Babadag*, p. 249

45. Carol J. Adams, in *The Sexual Politics of Meat* (New York: Continuum, 1990), her feminist critique of the Western modes of food consumption, uses the term 'absent referent' for the conceptual erasure of the vitalist idea of the animal that drives mass meat production and consumption. Adams argues that patriarchy is continually reinforced through perverse human–animal relations. Those relations, in turn, inflect the treatment of women and the ethnic other.

46. Max Weber, *From Max Weber: Essays in Sociology* (London: Routledge, 2009), p. 155.

47. Gary Backhaus, 'The Phenomenology of the Experience of Enchantment', in Analecta Husserliana and Anna-Teresa Tymieniecka (eds), *The Aesthetics of Enchantment in the Fine Arts* (Dordrecht: Kluwer Academic, 2000), p. 31.

48. Ibid. p. 32.

49. Wendy Faris, *Ordinary Enchantments*, p. 212.

50. Ibid. p. 212.

51. See Luce Irigaray, *Speculum of the Other Woman* (Ithaca: Cornell University Press, 1985).

52. George Konrád, *The Melancholy of Rebirth: Essays from Post-Communist Central Europe, 1989–1994* (San Diego: Harcourt Brace, 1996), p. 157.

3. WOODEN MONSTERS, DEAD BODIES AND THINGS: EMBODYING THE OTHER

> That is, the camera eye creates an equivalence between human flesh and the flesh of things, and suggests a sanguine – and auratic – unity of transcendent being, an *ekstasis*, that has been there all the time in the flesh of the world.
>
> Vivian Sobchack[1]

A few semesters ago, when asked by my department (an English department at a large land-grant research university in rural South Carolina, USA) to teach a course on World Cinema, I decided to design my syllabus around a growing body of films that, in some way, shape or form, employ magic realism to navigate the representational antipodes of cinematic realism and fantasy. Many of the films shown in our weekly screening labs were the films that constitute the subject of the ensuing narrative, films by Kusturica, Kolski and Šulík, among others. While, on the whole, these upper-division undergraduate students found the examples of East Central European magic realism resonant with certain aspects of their own distinctly baroque Southern culture – they linked some of the magic realist tropes to the shamanism embedded in the region's native folklore, the haunting tales of Southern Gothic, and the ecstatic spirituality of the Appalachian snake handlers – they were taken aback by the abject quality of the characters and the otherness of bodies on display in the films. The non-normative, often bordering on grotesque, physicality of these characters challenged the students' own sense of embodiment in ways that are diametrically different from, although not unrelated to, the challenges posed by technological and digital interventions of their milieu.

The student reactions led me to focus on how bodies (both animate and inanimate) are represented in magic realist films and to investigate the source of discomfort that these cinematic bodies may provoke. While rereading my students' final papers submitted to me that semester, I learned that some of the discomfort was caused by 'too much realism' and 'naturalistic bodies'. Without calling it that, my students referred to the East Central European brand of miserabilism. They noted that child characters like Oskar in Schlöndorff's *The Tin Drum* (*Die Blechtrommel*, 1979) or Perhan in Kusturica's *Time of the Gypsies* (*Dom za vešanje*, 1989) seemed poor, sad and depressing. Another charge came in the form of the all-too-honest generalisation: 'The films we watched this semester were all dark and the people in them ugly.'

Intrigued by my students' reactions, I paused to acknowledge the culture's preoccupation with failed and failing elements of existence. East Central European miserabilism is a well-recognised feature of the art produced in the region. While detectable in collective attitudes towards authority, humour preferences and conversational strategies, miserabilism is, above all, an aesthetic. I like to call it the aesthetic of excessive deficiency. Perhaps best described by the Romanian writer Dan Lungu, who traces its provenance well within the boundaries of realism, miserabilism is a sensibility that 'explores everyday misery, marginal social worlds, the periphery and provinces, places with no horizons, petty lives, and larval existence, it focuses on grotesque and repulsive details'.[2] As an oppositional aesthetic that contains elements of nihilism, naturalism and the absurd, miserabilist realism positioned itself against the triumphant optimism of the Communist Party's official cultural discourse: socialist realism. Interestingly, decades after the collapse of Communism, miserabilism continues to be used by artists across East Central Europe as a way to combat the euphoria associated with free-market capitalism and the alleged myriad of lifestyle choices afforded by it. The miserabilist aesthetic stands in aggressive opposition to the utopia of the pleasurable, yet sterile, information society of the future. Many of the filmmakers who engage magic realism as their representational mode also espouse the miserabilist aesthetic. The affinity between magic realism and miserabilist realism can be found in their investment in the mundane, or to repeat after Lungu, 'petty' aspects of reality. In *The Spirit of Carnival*, David Danow analyses the notion of grotesque excess in magic realism and points out that, 'While negotiating the tortuous terrain of credibility, magical realism manages to present a view of life that exudes a sense of energy and vitality in a world that promises not only joy but a fair share of *misery* as well.'[3] Both representational modes are looking at the mundane to undermine the established codes of perception and the official value system. As Danow argues, this is often accomplished through a focus on a Bakhtinian dark netherworld.[4] In some extreme cases, often grotesque and oppressive, the miserabilist component grounds the magic within the given narrative to keep it from sliding into the escapist realms of politically and ethically divested fantasy. One might therefore argue that the miserabilism that is culturally built into the East Central European imaginary helps to qualify the variety of magic realism articulated by the artists in question in favour of social critique.

In 1956, André Breton wrote 'Away with Miserabilism', in which he called miserabilism a 'crime' of depreciating reality, and a 'plague', far worse than any act of exalting reality.[5] Breton linked miserabilist attitudes in art to capitalist decadence and the political pathologies of Fascism and Stalinism. If at all guilty of the crime of depreciation, miserabilism in East Central Europe is used to depreciate one kind of reality in order to exalt another, not always leading to cynicism and rhetorical void. One guesses that cynicism is what Breton wrote his manifesto against. Many iterations of East Central European miserabilism, however, are spirited and enthusiastic, indeed deeply caring about the portions of reality that are not narrated by the official language of the ruling authority. They are seldom only cynical about the misery they represent.

In the films of Béla Tarr, spirited miserabilism meets with the magic of the real. Frustratingly anti-fabulist, the films contemplate the material legacy of Communism found in the exhausted faces of the people who lived it, the decaying facades of the buildings that were built to house it, and the strangely depopulated public spaces that were constructed to foster collectivism. Capturing materiality – that relationship of the embodied human subject to the immediate physical reality of the object world – that resonates the forfeited past as it simultaneously speaks of the hijacked future, Tarr's images exist in the absolute and tangible present. In doing so, through the use of low light, deep focus, long take, slow pan and frame freeze, Tarr approaches the sheer intensity of the matter, and in the process questions the usual subject / object dichotomy of the perceived world. While photographing in black and white the dilapidated remnants of Communist life in Hungarian villages, Tarr imbues his cinematic microcosm with what Elzbieta Buslowska describes as

> something one can only sense, ambiguous, singular beyond individual experience; physical, concrete, and virtually present, real in a non-realistic sense; a space of 'unfixed' identity. Here the outside, the virtual nothing, opens into other outsides to infinity; embracing all: the 'negative', the pessimistic, the sad, the melancholy, the real and death.[6]

Buslowska's account of Tarr's unique vision reads almost as a paraphrase of Franz Roh's early attempt to define magic realism. In 1925, writing to explain the new creative approach to realism in the visual arts, Roh argued that magic realism in post-Expressionistic painting brought about 'the possibility of feeling existence, of making it stand out from the void'. He reminded the critics that, in the new mode of framing reality, 'a solidly modeled figure crystallizes itself, as if by miracle, emerging from the most obscure source'. As in Tarr's films, in Roh's theory of magic realism, 'the background is the last frontier, absolute nothingness, absolute death, from which something emerges and vibrates with energetic intensity'.[7]

Set in the middle of Winter, Tarr's *Werckmeister Harmonies* (*Werckmeister Harmóniák*, 2000) tells the story of an economically depressed and morally corrupt community living in a small town in a remote corner of the ice-locked Hungarian Plain. Somehow, a travelling sideshow makes its way into the main square of the town. It features the largest taxidermied whale in the world and the mysterious figure of the Prince, who boasts magnetic powers among his many talents. The presence of these outsiders incites the town's people to an apocalyptic night of terror, when they turn against each other. The Prince encourages the crowd's violent rampage, which culminates in the total destruction of the local hospital. These events are seen principally through the eyes of the protagonist, János Valuska (Lars Rudolph).

The film opens up with a scene that illustrates well how miserabilism can be used to enhance the magic realist aim of representing the miracle of the everyday existence. The evening is nearing an end at the local tavern. The proprietor, Mr Hagelmayer (Gyula Pauer), is slowly corralling the few diehard drunks toward the exit. But before the viewer catches a glimpse of the dismal characters involved, the camera focuses on the very basic spectacle of light present: the fire burning. In a black-and-white close-up, which constitutes the very first shot of the scene, one sees the thick cast-iron grid of the furnace door and a few flames of fire dancing energetically behind the door. The shot is very simple, yet it speaks volumes about the nature of the cinematic medium and the question of ontological reality. The flickering fire seen from behind the solid dark obstruction of the latticed door creates a powerful chiaroscuro effect, which operates through the tension between what is revealed and what remains concealed. For quite some time, the viewer is asked to contemplate the screen, filled with a somewhat abstract composition of light, shadow and movement. What is seen here is elemental, yet infinitely absorbing. Evoking the wonders of early silent cinema, as well as cinema's philosophical affinity with Plato's allegory of the cave, this minimalist image addresses what the remainder of the scene so wonderfully illustrates: the emergence of life from cosmic darkness, the rise of meaning.

When discussing the impact of the miniature for magic realist painting, Franz Roh reflected on the ultimate chiaroscuro spectacle found in nature:

> The extent to which the miniature can express maximum power all by itself can be explained by thinking of the greatest spectacle that nature

offers us, a sight that contains the smallest units, almost simple points placed on the prodigious surface width of the picture: *the spectacle of the starry sky, through which we experience infinity.*[8]

Tarr's miniature spectacle of light is soon crudely extinguished by Mr Hagelmayer, who pours beer dregs over the fire as he yells to his motley crew of patrons to get going. The viewer must quickly transition from contemplating a thing of transcendental beauty to taking in one of the most pathetic embodiments of humanity – a collection of drunken village riffraff. Living up to his reputation as the master miserabilist, Tarr conjures a dark vision of damned souls congregating in a damned place. His drunks are unwashed and unshaven. They wear ensembles of ragged clothes and Wellington boots. They shuffle across the floor like zombies and fall off their chairs. The space of the tavern is equally beyond salvation. Illuminated with a few bare bulbs, the place has the ambiance of an interrogation cell from the darkest days of Communism. The only food served here is diluted beer. The stains that come in all possible shades of grey uniformly adorn the walls of this establishment and the clothes of its patrons. This could only be 'Eastern Europe'.

Much like other filmmakers of his generation, Tarr deploys the stereotype of 'Eastern Europe' in order both to acknowledge the liberating potential of life in the periphery and to critique the charge of irreparable and inherent backwardness assigned to the region. Significantly, Tarr does not dismiss the fact that reactionary politics and mentality, often practised as extreme nationalism and ethnic hatred, are indeed present among the members of post-Communist society, just as they were present before.[9] Many of his characters are bigots who use violence to get ahead, and *Werckmeister Harmonies* is a loose adaptation of a Krasznahorkai's novel about the experience of the Holocaust in a small Hungarian town. In this respect, Tarr delivers a sobering account of post-Wall East Central European culture, perhaps similar to the critique offered by Kamil Turowski and Katarzyna Marciniak in *Streets of Crocodiles.*[10] Far from engaging in political or cultural commentary, however, Tarr makes his films, as Peter Hames explains, in order to 'get closer to people – "to understand everyday life" '.[11] Filming small and often trivial occurrences – for example, a man preparing and then eating a bowl of soup, or a herd of cows moving between buildings, Tarr reframes reality for his viewer and asks him or her to 're-see and re-experience the world'.[12] This world is the European periphery. In an interview with Eric Schlosser, Tarr explained that *Werckmeister Harmonies* is a film 'about what is happening in middle Europe, how we are living there, in a kind of edge of the world'.[13]

The opening scene of *Werckmeister Harmonies* is an exercise in reseeing the world from the perspective of a few very marginal characters. Before they finally leave Hagelmayer's bar, the drunks ask the village idiot, Valuska, to perform a kind of goodbye ritual. The drunks clear the floor and Valuska arranges them into a solar system. Using their bodies as illustration props, he carefully choreographs his drinking pals, first to explain the positions and movement of the stars and planets within the system, and then to stage the total eclipse of the Sun. Soon the disorderly drunken collective is dancing a bizarre cosmic dance. Their abject bodies have been transformed into planets and stars, and Valuska's measured narration returns the viewer to that initial contemplative moment, where the dancing fire spoke of light and darkness:

> All I ask is that you step with me into the boundlessness where constancy, quietude, peace, and infinite emptiness reign. And just imagine that in this infinite sonorous silence everywhere is impenetrable darkness. Here we only experience general motion and at first we don't notice the events we are witnessing . . . The brilliant Sun always sheds its heat and light on that side of the Earth which is just then turned towards it. And we stand here in its brilliance.[14]

Under Valuska's instruction, the drunken bodies are transformed into celestial bodies. The men become amused and amazed as they recreate the grand ballet of the stars and planets. Mihály Víg's spellbinding music provides a beautiful soundscape for this uncanny interlude, in what looks like the otherwise dismal daily grind of the losers who found the capitalist promise of post-1989 East Central Europe to be untrue.

While quietly funny, the scene also carries a strong spiritual impact pointing towards the connection between the collective human realm and the cosmic realm.[15] This connection slowly changes from metaphoric to metonymic with the masterful use of the long take exercised by Tarr, who shot the entire film in thirty-nine takes. At the start of the take, the viewer sees, and even admires, the drunks simulating the solar system. But there is no question of affinity here. By the end of the take, via its hyperbolised duration (10 minutes and 20 seconds) and provoked emphasis on detail, the contiguity between the drunks' bodies and the celestial bodies is patent. Buslowska points out how the director's 'long takes enable the actors to live, the landscape to breathe, and the light to persevere, rendering the film with a cosmological significance and the viewer with a space of affect and thought'.[16] In 'Magical Romance / Magical Realism', Lois Zamora states that 'magical realism's essential commitment is to universality rather than uniqueness.'[17] She argues that magic realism champions the premodern concept of selfhood over the emancipated modern self. In her opinion, the artists who employ magic realism 'refuse to remain locked into modern categories of individual psychology, insisting instead that the self is actualized by participation in communal and cosmic categories'.[18] In a tragicomic way, Tarr's drunken collective embodies this premodern subjectivity-as-constellation.

The tragedy is found in the fact that Valuska's human solar system is constructed from the survivors of the regime of collectivism: Communism. The 'communal and cosmic categories' that Zamora talks about stand in sharp contrast to the ideals of organised collectivism as practised under Socialism, Communism or Fascism. Emerging out of East Central Europe – a region immersed in the cultural and economic shift from the tyranny of collectivism into the tyranny of self-interest, Tarr's cinema may not offer a recipe for a functioning third alternative, but it dares to critique the two extremes and shows attempts at adaptable subjectivity that is at home with its objectness, or thingness, in relation to other elements within its environment. To that effect, Tarr's camera oscillates between simulating a thinking centre of consciousness and reflecting mute material presence that confronts the subject / object division.

In the scene under analysis, the viewer is guided from the mundane to the stellar perspective and vice versa a few times over, to the point where the two perspectives become fused and begin to coexist as the third perspective. As Buslowska argues, in Tarr's films 'spectacular moments give way to the most banal ones and vice versa, or tragic to comic ones'.[19] Taken from the sublime spectacle of fire to the scene of drunken chaos and again to the harmony of dancing human bodies that are re-enacting the drama of the total eclipse, then back again to the grungy scene where the bar owner is calling the human-turned-celestial bodies 'beer tubs', the viewer is exposed to what Wendy Faris, in her comprehensive study on magic realism, calls 'defocalization' – the narrative presence of 'two radically different perspectives at once'.[20] The viewer is exposed to two different dimensions of things, that of the commonplace and that of the infinite. In the first of the two dimensions, the human functions as subject, where the 'I' consolidates itself vis-à-vis the other. In the latter dimension, the human becomes an object – a pre-individual body among other bodies. Tarr's third dimension thrusts the human into a realm that 'is not reality objectively perceived and independently existing, nor a metaphysical beyond, but rather a presence, both actual and virtual, in the process of becoming'.[21] In this realm, the human being is by necessity de-centred, its autonomy questioned and its mastery of vision disturbed. Neither subject nor object, and at times a hybrid of subject and object, Tarr's human, his character and his inscribed viewer, gets incorporated into the fabric of the world where self meets alterity, and conversely alterity is endowed with intentionality and autonomy. Both are embodied and materially fleshed out.

Faris elaborates her concept as follows,

> defocalization creates a narrative space of the ineffable in-between because its perspective cannot be explained, only experienced. Within it, one does not know quite where one is, what one is seeing, or what kind

of voice one is hearing. It is therefore a space that figures a sense of the mysterious within the ordinary.[22]

The dislocation that comes with the defocalised perspective is pervasive in Tarr and responsible for the demanding, often emotionally taxing, viewing experience. However, the sense of dislocation is ameliorated by the director's careful efforts to bring into our view the material fabric of photographed things – landscape, weather, objects, bodies and, paradoxically, time – in order to signal the continuity and coexistence of humans and space. While refused any sort of linear sequence of events, the viewer is offered a sense of groundedness through the monochromatic images of a small town. In the words of John Orr, these images show 'a visceral fascination with its topography of rain- and wind-lashed streets and squares, run-down smoky bars and dancehalls'.[23] Orr also talks about 'presentness', 'a being-there' and 'sheer weight' that characterise Tarr's images and transfer 'a sense of terror lurking in the material world'.[24] Similarly, in his Heideggerian reading of Tarr's metaphysics of the void, Steven Marchant observes that 'Tarr is dedicated to the concrete aspects of beings existing in the world'.[25] Tarr's camera works hard to take hold of physical reality. As a result, a strong sense of the concrete emerges from the screen. The well-worn surfaces of buildings, bodies, roads and furniture emit what Franz Roh called 'the thickness and density of all cosmic relationships'.[26]

One of the cosmic relationships that Tarr explores is that of the human body as an embodied object that is always embroiled in a web of complex engagement with other bodies and things in the world. In *Carnal Thoughts: Embodiment and Moving Image Culture*, Vivian Sobchack contemplates cinema as both a viewing agent with intentionality and a viewed object, a mode of visual culture that is uniquely equipped to address the dual and reversible nature of 'our existence as "objective subjects" and "subjective objects"'.[27] In her analysis of another East Central European director's cinematic vision, Sobchack admires Krzysztof Kieślowski's tendency to endow his characters with an ability 'to admit something *within* existence that is always potentially both awful and awesome in its obdurate materiality, its nonanthropocentric presence, and its assertion of the *existential equality* of all things, human and animate or otherwise'.[28] While Kieślowski excelled at endowing, somewhat animistically, inanimate objects with agency in order to arrive at this 'existential equality', Béla Tarr, in a much darker demiurgic gesture, reveals the thingness of his humans.

Werckmeister Harmonies contains an image that is burnt into the viewer's mind and refuses to leave, on par with the slashed eyeball of Luis Buñuel's *An Andalusian Dog* (*Un Chien andalou*, 1929). A part of the image's shocking impact stems from confrontation with the frailty and mortality of the human body delivered by the camera. The image appears at the very end of the longest take within the film, the one that documents the attack of the mob on the town's hospital. Usually, Tarr's scenes of violence are unaffected and unglamorous. This is no exception; once again, the director makes sure that the evil portrayed is banal. Armed with sticks, and with no apparent rationale, the attackers demolish the old hospital. Going from room to room and methodically wrecking the furniture and brutalising the patients, the motley crew does not seem to differentiate between the things and the people. This is amplified by the fact that the patients remain mute in the face of the assault. All that is audible throughout the sequence shots are the sounds of the commotion caused by objects, both animate and inanimate, being aggressively manipulated in their space. The patients refuse to resist. Passive, some of them inert, these ailing bodies of the hospital patients represent what Sobchack calls the 'radical materiality', which is a sense of material embodiment that is aware and inclusive of the universality of matter, its infinite alterity and expansiveness that speaks of equivalence and reciprocity among the world's subjects and objects.[29] These bodies are not merely reduced to objects, since Tarr's objects are always already subjective objects, shown with great care in their interrelatedness and intentionality. Because they speak of matter, these bodies attest to human mortality, eventual dissipation of the edifice of subjectivity, and the final return to what Sobchack refers to as the 'flesh' of the world, quoting Maurice Merleau-Ponty.[30] Finding philosophical support in existential phenomenology, Sobchack carefully avoids talking about magic and metaphysics. Instead, she insists on the notion of the 'secular and empirical mystery (or transcendence)' that emerges from what is immanently real: bodies and things captured by the camera eye in their concreteness and thereness.[31] This 'mystery' of worldly matter comes very close to magic realist investment in the aura of the commonplace. The difference rests in the ideological underpinnings of the thought. While phenomenology assumes a strictly materialist approach, magic realism allows for premodern spiritualism.

To address, finally, the memorable image that concludes the scene at the hospital, I must try to translate its apparent immanence into words. As the mob makes its way deeper and deeper into the dreary and dimly lit labyrinth of the hospital building, wreaking havoc on anything that comes into its path, the camera tracks behind the attackers. The viewer sees how two of them enter yet another room, ravage it, and then turn to see a luminous side room behind a set of heavy plastic curtains. Quickly, with a forceful tug, the curtains come down; bright, white light pours in and fills the screen. The two men suddenly freeze and stare at something that the viewer cannot yet see. Soon the camera enters their field of vision and reveals an old man standing in a bathtub, his body completely naked, emaciated and shrivelled up. The man stands motionless and unperturbed. He is extremely frail and vulnerable, but also fearless and somehow monstrous in his bare and completely static demeanour. The

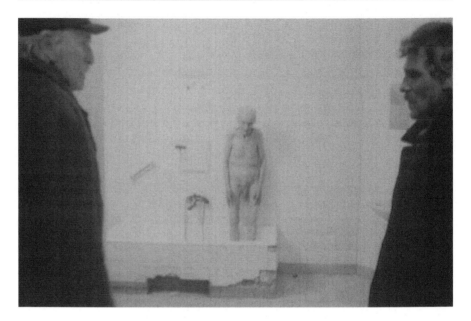

Figure 22   The old man as the flesh of the world in *Werckmeister Harmonies* (2000).

image is dramatic because of yet another instance of Tarr's masterful use of chiaroscuro. The dark contours of the intruders' bodies flank the washed-out interior of the bathroom on both sides. The central image framed in this manner, blinding in its bright simplicity, leaps out at the viewer, arresting the gaze. While all action ceases at this point – the men, sobered up by this harrowing apparition, walk out of the hospital – a new energy altogether is introduced through the soundtrack. The blunt sounds of violence cease at last, and are now replaced by Mihály Víg's melancholy tune, along with an unabashedly large dose of pathos. An unanticipated sense of reverence follows.

The image of the old man, in its capacity to signify *thing* and *nothing*, paradoxically, speaks of both immanence and transcendence. The ageing human body appears here to be merged with the dilapidated interior: the withered genitals enmeshed with the cracked floor and the broken tiles of the walls. There is no question that we are looking at decomposing matter. At first, matter is all the viewer sees. The intense light that makes the body of the old man as white as the tiles of the bathroom in which he is standing suggests an equivalence of matter between the man and his surroundings, at moments making it difficult for the eye to pick out the contours of the body. The lack of animation or expression in the body narrates its status as object. At the same time, the washed-out effect imbues both the body and the walls with a glow that defies the finitude of matter and promises inexorable continuity that reaches beyond the frightening assault and beyond the compromised existence of the hospital structure, the town and this particular community. In its intense radiance, the image teeters on the border of the visible. Thus suggestive of much that is invisible, this grotesque body speaks of both death and Bakhtin's notion of eternal renewal. According to this paradigm, the individual body must cease at some point, but every individual body, beyond its immediate contour, always also partakes in the timeless existence of all matter that constitutes the flesh of the world.

Traversing the boundary between life and death, animate and inanimate, subject and object is very much the central focus for many magic realists. In *The Porcelain Doll* (*A porcelánbaba*, 2005), the Hungarian filmmaker Péter Gárdos offers three tales that poetically contemplate the idea of resurrection. Based on novellas by Ervin Lázár (*Csillagmajor*, 1996), *The Porcelain Doll* has an episodic structure, which is pulled into focus by the same village setting and the ensemble of amateur actors who comprise the fictitious peasant community of Lázár's titular 'Star Farm'. Set in times of political turmoil, between the 1930s and 1950s, the stories address the presence of the delicate spiritual balance within the sheltered, provincial community, which seems to regulate the affairs of the living and the dead. The film gains its narrative momentum when this tenuous equilibrium is breached by the intrusion of ignorant and aggressive outsiders.

In the first episode, a boy named Hötöle (Bálint Péntek) is introduced to the viewer as an aspiring village athlete. Although modestly endowed with a gangly and awkward body, the boy is relentlessly testing his strength and increasing his body's dexterity and endurance through day-and-night practice. One of the opening scenes shows him sitting in a tree and peeking into the garden of a rich, aristocratic family, whose children are competing against each other in high jump and hammer throw. Hötöle is envious of the rich children's' improvised Olympic field, so he steals his way there in the middle of the night to practise. Through sheer perseverance, it seems, he breaks the children's highest records. When a troop of soldiers arrives at the village to search for illegal arms and contraband, Hötöle gets roped into a competition with the soldiers. Expecting the wimpy boy to lose instantly to his brawny men, the troop leader becomes incensed as Hötöle outperforms all of his best athletes. He pumps the boy's chest full of bullets as Hötöle, once again, outruns the fastest soldier to the finish line. Just as Hötöle's extraordinary performance seems to be fuelled by some supernatural power (perhaps summoned by his steadfast determination and the collective will of the village people), what comes next in the film confronts the familiar notion of bodily existence. Namely, Hötöle's lifeless body is brought back to life.

In a stylised overhead shot, the viewer sees the boy's nude form submerged in water in what looks like a drinking trough for cattle. Brought together by

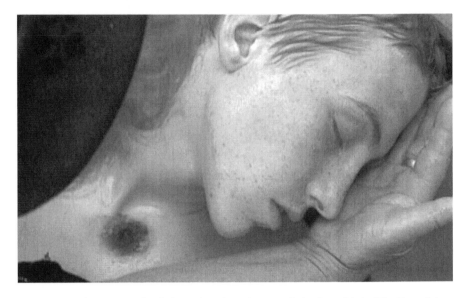

Figure 23   The matriarch's helping hand guides Hötöle back to life in *The Porcelain Doll* (2005).

their joint intention to resurrect the young life, the villagers gather around the trough as the village matriarch proceeds slowly to wash away the wounds from Hötöle's chest. Her movements are caring and tender. She begins by washing his face the way a mother would wash her baby's face. Then she moves down to the gruesome evidence of violence. In close-up, her ageing, toil-worn hand glides over the bullet holes, wiping them clean. The camera alternates here between shots of the healing hand and those of the witnesses gathered around. Visually, there is a connection suggested between the work of the hand and the work of the collective mind. The music score emphasises the unison. As soon as the woman has finished healing the last wound, Hötöle comes back to life, spitting the bullets out one by one. The crowd disperses without much astonishment, as if the task of bringing the boy back to life was a common farm chore. Life in the village is back in balance, and the violence dealt by the agents of power, who represent the political forces at play at the time, has been undone. As Christina Stojanova argues in her discussion of the use of magic realism in recent Bulgarian cinema, specifically in films by young female directors Iglika Triffonova and Zornitsa Sophia, the village offers a compensatory vision of an authentic community for viewers whose own sense of local community might be fading due to the various traumas of modern life. Stojanova points out that the films draw on local folklore in their construction of the old villagers as 'wise helpers offering much-needed miraculous resolutions'.[32] Stojanova suggests that, with their curative powers and strong investment in

collective responsibility, the villagers are 'cast as a canny symbol of the cer-
tainty and comfort of the "here" and "near"'.[33]

Much of the popularity surrounding magic realist texts stems from the
compensatory vision that the texts frequently offer in response to the dismal
actuality encountered in the mimetic process of representing reality. Theorists
of magic realism have commented on this feature at length and championed
its political potential, which extends well beyond the nostalgic pleasure typically found in artistic visions that use a corrective lens. In his seminal work
on magic realism, *Magic Realism Rediscovered*, Seymour Menton remarks on
the polemical stance of magic realism directed against the contemporary discourses of technology, history and international politics. Conceptualising it as
a cultural movement, Menton sees magic realism as aligned with the 'Western
world's search for an alternative to the limitations of an overtly rational and
technological society'.[34] Additionally, Menton argues that magic realism came
into being as a compensatory response to the interwar and postwar fatigue
of European society: 'magic realism has provided one alternative to the exis-
tentialist anguish caused by the cold war and the constant possibility of an
atomic holocaust'.[35] Thinking of it as a form of restorative discourse, Menton
attributes its later proliferation in postcolonial cultures and across East Central
Europe to the extreme socio-historical circumstances experienced by these
societies throughout much of the twentieth century.[36] María Ruth Noriega
Sánchez, in her study of gender politics within magic realism, comes to the
conclusion that magic realism 'makes use of magic as a cultural corrective,
requiring readers to scrutinise accepted realistic conventions and is, therefore,
invested with political potential'.[37] In his analysis of D. M. Thomas's *The
White Hotel* (1981), John Burt Foster Jr links magic realism's tendency to
correct history with Jungian theory of art as expressive of the collective uncon-
scious, which works to heal and elevate modern man, who is drowning in neu-
rosis and living in an increasingly mechanised and disconnected society.[38] In
the words of Ewa Mazierska, 'The magic is frequently a means to facilitate an
imaginary overcoming of discrepancies and inequalities, bringing justice and
prosperity to those who are harmed and marginalized, or just allowing them to
find a place in an unknown or hostile universe.'[39] These scholars agree in their
appraisal of magic realism as a productive artistic mode, well utilised to cope
with different degrees of radical otherness delivered as part of the experience
of modern life.

The scene of Hötöle's resurrection found in *The Porcelain Doll* is an example
of the corrective vision in question. The frivolous act of violence perpetrated
against his body is an attack on the entire village collective and all the values
that the collective stands for: self-reliance, perseverance, pride and blind faith.
Most of all, however, this act of violence, in its shocking absurdity, stands for
the traumatic experience of modern history. Synonymous with technological

warfare, the rule of terror and mass victimisation of civilians, this painful experience frequently obliterates the delicate networks of give-and-take, contracted with nature and the native place, which traditional societies establish in an effort to demonstrate gratitude for what is given and to ensure renewal of the gift. The image of mother's hand using water, one of nature's most overlooked yet most wondrous resources, to undo the damage of a senseless crime committed by a military aggressor becomes a statement with political resonance, but also clear gender implications. In Gárdos's film, where men, young and old, brutally compete in silly contests and women work to mend their brutalised bodies afterwards, modern history, with its concomitant bouts of unwarranted violence, is confronted as a dumb patriarchal death machine. The reversal of a technological assault on the integrity of the human body, delivered via a series of rifle shots, is all the more stunning here because it is performed manually and so minimally, simply by repeating one of the most commonplace tasks imaginable, that of washing.

Teetering between life and death, Hötöle's young body, although performing according to the fit and invincible athletic ideal of normative masculinity, is very much a site of transgression and boundary dispersal. Pale and effeminate, this body is trapped between genders. Both active and passive, beautiful yet incomplete, it invites the notion of queerness with its connotations of hybridity. In line with other aspects of the oxymoronic world of magic realism, where opposites and incongruent elements come to coexist in what Homi Bhabha calls the 'third space', this body is a transitory zone.[40] Its translucent, fragile physicality stands in defiant contrast to its own masterful athletic performance. This body's experiential incongruity – hybrid impurity – provokes the soldiers' bewilderment and eventual aggression. But its most radical area of conceptual mutability stems from the body's comfortable habitation in the space of the abject, which Julia Kristeva defines as in between the subject and the object, being 'neither subject nor object'.[41] Hötöle's body, which oscillates between life and death, immobility and hyper-motion, like Kristeva's abject, 'disturbs identity, system, order'; like the abject, it is 'death infecting life',[42] but also, in its resurrection, it is life infecting death. This oscillation, similar to other boundary crossings envisioned in magic realist art, brings the viewer face to face with otherness. It is the otherness of the object, Hötöle's human body turned into a thing in death, and then manipulated out of its thingness back into human subjectivity, that marks this encounter as quintessentially magical. For magic, against its popular misconception as the realm of irrational prejudice, has always been focused on pragmatic aspects of life, on the objective aspects of the existing world, and the ways in which these aspects can be manipulated towards humans' advantage.

Magic has been used to manage and domesticate the Other, which should be defined here as the autonomous and obdurate strangeness of the material –

and objective – reality that confronts individual human existence. Both James Frazer and Bronislaw Malinowski differentiate magic from religion. While religious belief assumes a certain measure of human impotence in the face of divine agency, magic invests in acquisition of knowledge and practical skill. Magical thinking puts faith in the human ability to reshape the adverse living conditions that humans encounter in nature. Akin to science, equally methodical and based in the knowledge of certain basic laws and fundamental assumptions, magic seeks to improve those conditions and, in doing so, it should be recognised as 'an entirely sober, prosaic, even clumsy art, enacted for purely practical reasons, governed by crude and shallow beliefs, carried out in a simple and monotonous technique'.[43] Prosaic, yet essential in its ultimate goal to cope with adversity, magic has been theorised by modern anthropology as practice, 'a special mode of behavior',[44] that is singularly focused on the immediate circumstances of life, rather than some idealised hereafter. Magic, at its origin, was used (and is still used in premodern tribal societies) as a craft passed on from generation to generation, devised as a strategy to optimise man's ability to sustain life (via efficient hunting, fishing and crop cultivation skills), rather than to communicate with the divine for the sheer purpose of mystical communion. Its tools are ordinary objects that gain ritual value over time. Magic is an action that is performed in real time and space with the use of objects that represent aspects of the phenomenal universe. The ordinary object becomes the talisman through the act of ceremonial estrangement. Interestingly, summoned into a hyperbolic presence, the talisman is there to ensure that the ordinary world remains 'ordinary': namely, safe and predictable. The act of magic, via the measured repetition of the ritual, reveals the ordinary object as extraordinary and impacts its meaning within the objective fabric of reality. Paradoxically, in magic, the object speaks of both familiarity and otherness, revitalising man's awareness of the uniqueness of his surroundings, but also pointing out the continuity between the human subject and the phenomenal object. This focus on the objective and palpable world has been the defining feature of magic realism, and a feature that separates it from fantasy art.

When Franz Roh wrote his magic realist manifesto in 1925, he devoted extensive thought to the issue of objectivity. Arising as a reaction against the 'fiery exaltation' of Expressionism, the movement of *Magischer Realismus* that Roh theorised and promoted in the pictorial arts was better known as New Objectivity (*Neue Sachlichkeit* in German).[45] In the words of Sergiusz Michalski, '*Neue Sachlichkeit* was interested first and foremost in the world of objects, irrespective of whether the items depicted belonged to technology or not.'[46] Roh also stresses magic realism's 'insatiable love for terrestrial things and a delight in their fragmented and limited nature'.[47] From the start, however, the ambiguity of the concept of objectivity is brought to the forefront by Roh. He talks about the objective world's 'coldness and apparent sobriety', its quality of being 'civil, metallic, restrained', at the same time as he evokes the 'radiation of magic, that spirituality, that lugubrious quality throbbing' in the objects represented in magic realist paintings.[48] Although theorists and practitioners of literary magic realism who embraced Alejo Carpentier's more socially aware and politically invested version of magic realism (the Marvellous Real) have since distanced themselves from Roh's highly aesthetic and object-centred vision of magic realism, I would argue that, in the definitional conflation of sober verisimilitude with representational animism, Roh's theory may be more useful when analysing cinema's use of magic realism to represent worldly objects and the quality of thingness found in these objects. Magic realist cinema's distinctive discourse on things, as the argument advanced in the remaining portion of the chapter suggests, is not without its own socially and culturally relevant message.

As an apparatus that combines the mechanical eye of the camera with the consciousness and intention of the filmmaker, cinema has always been a medium aware of its interstitial status as a phenomenon that arose from a complex relationship between humans and things. In 1922, expressing the modernising and revolutionary potential of cinema, resonant in the tone of the Bolshevik Revolution, Dziga Vertov wrote the following statement:

> I am kino-eye, I am a mechanical eye. I, a machine, show you the world as only I can see it. Now and forever, I free myself from human immobility, I am in constant motion, I draw near, then away from objects, I crawl under. I climb onto them. I move space with the muzzle of a galloping horse. I plunge full speed into a crowd, I outstrip running soldiers, I fall on my back, I ascend with an airplane, I plunge and soar together with plunging and soaring bodies. Now I, a camera, fling myself along their resultant, maneuvering in the chaos of movement, recording movement, starting with movements composed of the most complex combinations.[49]

Vertov's kino-eye is a techno-organic construction, the human eye enhanced by the mechanical eye, trained to explore the objective world in ways that human vision allegedly never could. In its unabashedly ecstatic goal to penetrate, dominate and conquer space and the objects found in space, the kino-eye reflects modernity's rather aggressive model of spatio-corporeal existence. Kino-eye sees the world anew as it engages in the practice of *ostranenie,* the artistic technique of defamiliarisation theorised by the Formalist Viktor Shklovsky, Vertov's contemporary. In its attention devoted to the world of ordinary objects, the kino-eye, as well as Russian Formalism, certainly resembles magic realism. However, in a violent revolutionary gesture, Vertov forsakes the old and the commonplace. Vertov's formally manipulated and artfully estranged object parts ways with the habitual and repetitive way of being in the world. Differently so, the magic realist object is singular in its new, estranged guise, but it speaks of tradition, as all magical practice does.[50] This object's synthetic nature as both old and new is best described by Franz Roh, when he talks about magic realism's tendency to address simultaneously being and becoming, tradition and revolution: 'Out of that flux, that constant appearance and disappearance of material, permanent objects somehow appear: in short, the marvel by which a variable commotion crystallizes into a clear set of constants.' Roh sees the magic realist object as a 'miracle of an apparent persistence and duration', also an 'enigma of total quietude in the midst of general becoming'.[51]

Cinema is by no means limited to, or inherently invested in, movement and expansive visual supremacy over the objective world. In opposition to Vertov's visual revolution (and much of today's hyper-kinetic, fast-cut cinema), which he rallied against 'the weakness of the human eye',[52] I would like to propose the existence of cinematic magic realist vision, which, while embracing the enhancements of technological vision, is also utterly devoted to human vision, 'unsophisticated' yet concretely situated in material phenomena. Capable of speed, but also of complete stasis, the magic realist cinematic vision allows for the objective world to come to the embodied human subject, both the subject represented in the diegesis and the viewer, in its alterity and strangeness, without Vertov's compulsion always to 'decipher in a new way a world unknown to you'.[53] This vision, I like to think, is fond of approaching objects, rather than capturing and explaining them away. In this, it documents the premodern subject's wonder and respect for the world of objects, which somehow remain external and even threatening to the subject's immediate domain of knowledge. The magic realist cinematic vision frequently operates through what the scholar of imaging arts and performance technologies, Barbara Maria Stafford, calls the 'slow conscious look' and the film critic Matthew Flanagan dubs 'an aesthetic of slow'.[54] Through its methodically slower pace and contemplative approach, this vision observes and represents reality in greater detail and with sustained focus on the rich fabric of material existence.

Taking in profilmic reality without parsing it through frenetic cuts and jagged montage technique, the magic realist vision, through its process of representation, preserves the Bazinian continuum of the object world, respecting and 'mummifying' objects in their duration and interconnected coexistence in a specific time, space and place.[55] Not looking to revolutionise, not invested in building a new hierarchy of the visible, magic realist vision makes room within the frame for the less important worldly objects, the old and the worn-out that endure despite any change. They simply are. They are stunning because they are familiar to the point of seeming trite, yet they appear in their objective strangeness to the viewing and knowing consciousness of the subject. Some of that strangeness comes from the clash of the old materiality with the 'newness' of cinematic technology. In 'On Magic Realism in Film', Fredric Jameson focuses on this 'proximity to the bodies and solids' that dominate the filmic text in magic realist cinema.[56] He argues that the intensities of the object world become amplified in this kind of cinema – the colours and textures of bodies and things – as a way to indicate overlapping, often conflicting, modes of production. Different from nostalgia films that tend to fetishise the object world represented on screen, magic realist films, 'which irritate and intensify' the gaze, Jameson explains, operate through bringing to the foreground the 'historical raw material' – visual figurations that expose conflicting materialities found in Second World contexts.[57] Relying on Marxist thought, with its unique focus on the relationship that modern man has with things, Jameson's theory posits that 'magic realism depends on a content which betrays the overlap or the coexistence of precapitalist with nascent capitalist or technological features'.[58] The represented object world comes into focus in its often-disturbing otherness due to a temporal paradox: 'the articulated superposition of whole layers of the past within the present'.[59] In reference to García Márquez's fiction, Salman Rushdie observes that magic realism resides in the world where 'the impossibly old struggles against the appallingly new'.[60] In terms of cultural objects – that is, objects transformed by human work, one might want to think here about the differences that set the artisanal, handprint-bearing, pre-industrial object apart from the mechanically produced 'mass' object of the capitalist era. And, then, moving into the postmodern milieu, one encounters the cultural object that loses its material substance altogether and becomes software. Jameson claims that magic realist film is uniquely intentioned to represent the co-presence of these different object formations in economies and cultures that foster such co-presence.

In the cinema analysed in this volume, there are countless examples of this kind of 'historical raw material'; it attests to the varied materialities that reflect the East Central European mosaic of different modes and means of production, found in coexistence in the region where cultural and economic transformations from premodernity to postmodernity continue to take place. Among those examples one stands out for its formal and diegetic attention to things physical. Piotr Trzaskalski, in his film *Eddie* (*Edi*, 2002), frequently and almost compulsively features Jamesonian 'historical raw material' that speaks of the disjunction between what constituted human attachments to things (and surroundings) in the precapitalist past (yet still very much present in the East Central European context today), and what constitutes those attachments in the era of post-1989 capitalism with its attendant symptoms of commodity reification, planned obsolescence and atomisation of daily experience. His film constitutes a perfect example of the Jamesonian definition of magic realism because it focuses directly on issues of labour, ownership and commodity value. Although the film tells a private tale that has little regard for the histori-

Figure 24   The protagonists of Trzaskalski's *Eddie* (2002), Edi and Jureczek, push
their cart of valuable junk.

cal and political situation in contemporary Poland (this is where the film's narrative is situated), it manages to comment on that very situation through the
characters' relationship with the object world.

In this sense, Trzaskalski's film moves beyond the escapism associated
with magic realism by scholars like Barbara Klonowska. In her analysis of
magic realism in Polish cinema, which focuses on the movement's nostalgic backward glance and the lack of direct engagement with the politics of
present-day Poland, Klonowska finds that 'The exclusion, or reduction, of the
socio-political aspects of reality, present only implicitly, contradicts Frederic
Jameson's definition of magical realism as a politically-engaged aesthetic
mode.'[61] In response to this criticism, it must be noted that Jameson never
mentions political discourse as being constitutive of magic realism. His definition is heavily based in the aesthetics of the mode: colours, textures and composition within a filmic frame. Technically, Jameson's notion of magic realism
engages politically, only implicitly, in the process of depicting the possibility
of varied material existences, dependent on different economic systems, coex-
isting in one society. It is necessary to observe, then, that while indeed magic
realism in Polish cinema is less directly political than the Cinema of Moral
Concern (popularised through the works of Andrzej Wajda), it musters a
vision of the world with a distinct socio-economic valence. It might not argue
for or against Communism or capitalism; instead, it does its best to articulate
a form of ideological dissent by holding on to a hybrid reality that preserves
the old in the times when this act became unfashionable and easily dismissed

as regressive nostalgia. Qualified by an element of East Central European irony and / or grotesque, magic realism invests in the 'old' as a reaction against the risks of the compulsive 'new' characteristic of the late capitalist milieu, especially within the realm of material culture. In that sense, magic realists express what Cristina Sandru calls the 'sceptical imagination'.[62] On the other hand, magic realism's loyalty to the 'old' is simply mimetic of the premodern aspects of the unevenly developing, and historically peripheral, region of East Central Europe.

Trzaskalski's film tells a story of Edi (Henryk Gołębiewski) and his pal Jureczek (Jacek Braciak), two vagrant scrap-metal pickers who become involved with the local mafia bosses in a scheme that soon turns tragic. When they are not working, the two men spend their days discussing philosophy, reading highbrow literature and drinking cheap wine. Their life, despite the abject poverty, is constructed as an ideal of good living. In her study of the film, Ewa Mazierska focuses on Trzaskalski's text as part of a larger discourse on the post-1989 transition from Communism to capitalism. She points out that, ultimately, Trzaskalski's world is an escapist dream of men who selflessly and stubbornly refuse the temptations of capitalism in order to continue their existence of moral edification in material privation. As a whole, Mazierska argues, the film expresses 'disdain of capitalist values', as well as a 'tendency to ridicule spaces, objects, and activities associated with consumerism'.[63] Mazierska is absolutely correct when she observes that much of the narratorial force in the film pushes against the capitalist present or future. In the end, Trzaskalski's capitalism is a scheme that ensnares and corrupts. Rather predictably, the director and his text side with the disenfranchised. The strength of the film, however, does not stem from this simple didactic message. *Eddie*'s impact on the contemporary viewer rests in the film's ability to visualise cultural, political and economic change through one's embodied encounter with the immediate material reality of the change. The first two shots (also the last two shots of the film) of Trzaskalski's film accomplish just that; they illustrate one man's ability to navigate his way between precapitalist and capitalist material cultures. Compositionally, these two shots establish the synthesis discussed by Jameson and stamp the remainder of the film with energising tension. In terms of a political and ideological message, this film (as well as other magic realist films) does not attempt to pit the precapitalist against capitalist. Rather, in its investment in material culture (whether artisanal or mass-produced), the film challenges the immaterial culture of post-capitalism, characterised by the atrophied material object and the growing importance of information transfers. Never mentioned or visualised, this immaterial culture of the pure information society of the future, where machines and immigrant labour do all the work, becomes a spectre haunting magic realist cinema. Through its gravity, sense of groundedness and ability to materialise objects on screen, magic realist cinema is challenging the disembodied culture of 'play'. Trzaskalski's *Eddie* champions the clunky weight of material world over the kind of fantastic lightness of being imagined in films like James Cameron's *Avatar* (2009).

Trzaskalski's film opens with an image of raindrop ripples colliding on the steel blue surface of a lake. Soon the rain dies down and the camera zooms out into an overhead shot of an old wooden pier jutting out into the lake. The mirror of the lake is now reflecting the sun, which is slowly making its way out from underneath the cloud cover. At the very end of the pier, a young boy is lying, his pale naked body accentuated by a pair of dark swimming trunks. He is resting, whiling away the time. His relaxed body stance suggests that he feels very much at home within this particular space and time. The boy's actions are minimal – he is playing with a stick, first banging it against the wooden surface of the pier, then letting the stick float away on the pristine surface of the lake.

The camera constructs a solid structural and conceptual bridge between the boy and his natural surroundings. The overhead shot shows the boy's body as being woven into the fabric of the lake shore. He is one element in an ensemble of many. The bird's-eye view, as opposed to the linear anthropocentric perspective of the human eye, reveals a degree of equivalence among the different elements, animate and inanimate, human and non-human, within the frame. From an overhead shot, the camera lowers down to the boy's perspective, just as he is setting the stick afloat, but then quickly zooms in on the water surface. At this point, the camera leaves the boy's side and frames the floating stick, which is now moving very languidly across the screen from left to right. Beautifully abstract, at the same time as it is emphatically organic, the shot is a perfect example of the 'calm attenuation' that Matthew Flanagan finds to be one of the defining features of the 'aesthetic of slow'. In his words, the camera's choice to linger on a less central aspect of the *mise-en-scène*, not the agent of the narrative, before it cuts to the next shot, 'opens a space for reflection on events, encouraging a contemplation of presence, gesture and material detail'.[64] That very first shot of Trzaskalski's film operates in its entirety through that 'contemplation of presence, gesture and material detail' that Flanagan evokes. It portrays a human being safely ensconced in his material environment. While static, almost inert, the embodied human subject is busy drawing up subtle sensory connections with the surrounding nature, and by extension the entirety of cosmic matter. Trzaskalski's camera (in the hands of the unrivalled Krzysztof Ptak) seduces the viewer to take a similar contemplative pause. One might point out that Trzaskalski does not have to try hard since the theme of the scene is leisure – therefore, a time of contemplation. The very next shot, however, pairs this scene of quiet with a scene of intense labour, yet manages to preserve the same contemplative mood and the same sense of harmony between man and his surroundings.

In the second shot, the viewer sees the continuation of that slow horizontal

Figure 25   Edi's childhood memory of playing at the lake.

movement across the screen, initiated only a moment ago in the previous shot, but otherwise the scene could not be more different. The stick has been replaced by a pushcart that is casually navigated in the middle of a very busy highway, a sea of cars and motorcycles speeding around the slow-moving, non-motorised vehicle. The camera has moved back to its overhead vantage point and is now looking down at the film's two central characters, Edi and Jureczek, as they precariously traverse the urban space, from left to right, pushing their primitive means of transportation, and means of (re)production (they use the cart to collect scrap metal), towards the collection point. The great distance of the camera from street level works to diminish the two human figures, who begin to look like tiny ants in the midst of a bustling, industrial anthill. As in the first shot, the overhead framing contributes to a holistic vision. Although an obvious nuisance for the other drivers on the highway, the two men bizarrely belong there, just as today, horse-drawn wagons and shrines celebrating folk saints seem still to belong to the material culture of metropolitan East Central Europe.

These two shots constitute a sequence stitched together through a clever montage of movement. There is simultaneous unity and discord between the two shots as they comment on the uncanny, Jameson would argue 'magical realist', coexistence of the precapitalist and capitalist materialities within the same cultural and economic context. In a charming, if puzzling, act of symbiosis, the pushcart coexists with the cars and motorcycles, the surface of the lake morphs into the surface of the highway, the movement of technology imitates the movement of nature. The boy who used to play at the side of a lake grows up to be a denizen of a big city. Instead of sticks, he now carries across the city the discarded remnants of technology. This apparent symbiosis is not free of tension, however. The soundtrack reveals the concerned voices of the two men traversing the highway on foot, lamenting their slim scrap-metal pickings of the day. The highway itself is shown to be riddled with deep, threatening cracks in its surface. The overhead camera chooses one of these cracks as a compositional axis for the shot, vertically dividing the screen in half and showing the horizontal flow of traffic over the gaping crevice in the road to be a near-miracle.

Trzaskalski's highway is hardly a symbol of a technologically enhanced conduit of mass transportation, smoothly advancing metropolitan subjects into the future. Rather, it speaks of stumbling and faltering progress, where the future is weighed down by the past and triumphs of technology are frequently sabotaged by forces of nature. Unlike the utopic highway of the road movie, or the information superhighway of digital communication, for that matter, this highway does not deliver liberation or salvation. In fact, it struggles against nature to connect two points in space. Similarly, Trzaskalski's vision of technology – a pushcart filled with scrap metal – is stripped of its commodity gloss and reduced to junk, mere things that testify to their basic physical and chemical properties, outside of their former use value. In his gesture of expos-ing the commodity, Trzaskalski inspires his viewer to contemplate what Henri Lefebvre calls the 'social space' – the space of everyday life that is shaped by the dominant modes of production. The problematic relationship that Trzaskalski constructs between nature and technology, between man and material reality, discloses the capitalist investment in the mystique of the object, and warns against the death of the object in the postcapitalist information society. In *The Production of Space*, Lefebvre argues that 'Things lie, and when, having become commodities, they lie in order to conceal their origin, namely social labour, they tend to set themselves up as absolutes.'[65] Capitalism, curiously, relies on its own practice of 'magic', if magic is defined as the stereotypical notion of communal obscurantism. By showing things as failing commodi-ties, and his protagonists as those who have to deal with the consequences of things losing their commodity aura, Trzaskalski partakes in the 'unmasking of *things*' – the project that Lefebvre hails to be 'the most durable accomplish-ment of Marxist thought'.[66] In the spirit of such commodity 'unmasking', Edi, the physical labourer, repurposes an old refrigerator to store his impressive library of found books. While this act of repurposing does not exactly expose the social relations of labour and the politics of the market connected with the existence of the refrigerator as commodity, it symbolically reworks the social reality of this object. Edi renews the meaning of the refrigerator and grants it a new existence within material culture. On screen, Edi's refrigerator stuffed with books becomes a miniature spectacle of conceptual defamiliarisation.

Edi's practical ingenuity defeats the obscurity of this discarded mass-produced object and grants it a new intensity and individuality. This refrigerator-turned-bookshelf surprises the viewer with its 'miracle of an apparent persistence and duration' of all matter that Franz Roh so admired in the objects painted by the early magic realists. In its new guise, the refrigerator speaks of its thingness, its essence as a sturdy container still perfectly fitted to store and protect books, well beyond its assigned commodity value.

Importantly, when the opportunity arises, Trzaskalski's protagonists do not choose to escape their meagre urban existence for the pastoral life in the countryside. After a brief sojourn there, Edi and Jureczek find themselves back on the cracked streets pushing scrap metal. The film suggests that the junk will keep piling up, but if more people, like Edi and Jureczek, saw treasures in junk, the economic system responsible for the inundation of the environment with disposable goods would need to change. Although Edi's beautiful flashbacks to his childhood at the lake shore might be reminiscent in tone of Lefebvre's notion of nature that 'does not seek to deceive' and 'never lies',[67] the film as a whole does not pretend to argue that nature offers salvation while technology leads to damnation. After all, Edi and Jureczek make a decent living collecting the remnants of technology. Their occupation affords them basic sustenance, while leaving them with plenty of unregimented leisure time, when they read and watch television. But their attitude to the things they live with, and live off, has much to do with Edi's boyhood encounters with nature (the filmic text uses montage to suggest that link). In those brief childhood flashbacks, the raindrops and the stick floating on the lake provide the young Edi with palpable, sensory pleasure. They are means of learning about the world and the boy's connection with the world. These basic elements of material reality are free of the duplicitous simulations of commodity objects that 'tout the satisfactions they can supply and the needs they can meet' to human subjects.[68] The raindrops and the stick never become objects as such, or if they do, a certain amount of subjectivity is retained and detectable in Trzaskalski's portrayal of those objects, as a young child might perceive them. These elements of physical matter are shown by Trzaskalski, and seen by his child character, as fragments of cosmic matter, which links humans with things in material coexistence.

Much as in the discourse of magic, in Trzaskalski's film the exact ontological affinity between humans and things might not be empirically evident, but it is sensed and felt as a form of intersubjectivity (and interobjectivity) between the human subjects that are attuned to the subjective autonomy of things (and the human subjects who are aware of their own objectness with regard to things). Writing in 1956, the French philosopher and sociologist Edgar Morin pronounced cinema to be supremely equipped to represent the unceasing metamorphosis of 'a *fluid universe* where things are not hardened in their identity, but participate in a great cosmic unity that is in motion. This fluidity explains and accounts for the reciprocity between the microcosm man and the macrocosm.'[69] Morin's theory of cinema pays tribute to what magic realist filmmakers attempt to capture in their films: the coexistence of physical matter that reaches beyond hierarchical divisions between the human and the non-human. Morin sees cinema as 'the greatest apostle of animism', which documents the perpetual change and continuity of matter.[70] For him, cinema is nothing less than life-giving:

> Certainly in real life, glass menageries, knickknacks, handkerchiefs, pieces of furniture charged with memories, are already like little presences watching over us, and we admire landscapes sprinkled with soul. The cinema goes further still: it takes hold of things scorned in everyday life, handled as tools, used out of habit, and it kindles new life in them.[71]

In *Little Otik* (*Otesánek*, 2000), Jan Švankmajer stages an extreme, and rather grotesque, spectacle of the cinematic transfiguration described by Morin, where an inanimate object – a wooden log – morphs into a baby; Little Otik is summoned to life by the willpower of a young woman who is desperate to have a child. Following the Czech folk tale that the film is based on, the wooden baby develops a monstrous appetite and begins to grow at an alarming rate. Soon he is devouring members of the local community one by one, until an angry matriarch intervenes. Although technically a work of surrealism – Švankmajer, a member of the Czechoslovak Surrealist Group, identifies his art as surrealist – *Little Otik* showcases what magic realism and surrealism have in common: the energising process of defamiliarisation of the commonplace aspects of reality.[72] Both surrealism and magic realism tend to disrupt the perceived and codified boundaries and borders that guide our material existence in an effort to point out the fluid nature of physical matter – the unceasing metamorphosis of worldly stuff that is responsible for the shocking, often threateningly other, encounter that the human subject might experience when engaging with the object world. This kind of premodern shock (even horror) in response to encounters with physical matter stands in opposition to modern modes of consumption, where matter is owned, possessed and manipulated by the consuming subject in his or her effort to increase their sense of comfort and mastery over the world.

Švankmajer's wooden monster, in his insatiable hunger and bursting physical might, is only scary because he embodies the autonomy and agency of physical matter that modern man, with the assistance of science, media and technology, is continuously trying to deflect. In an interview with Peter Hames, Švankmajer describes his film as 'a topical version of the Faust myth: a rebellion against nature and the tragic dimension of that rebellion'.[73] The filmmaker explains that his version of the folk tale represents modern man's learnt reluctance to possess matter and control nature after a long history of failure to do so:

> The Marquis de Sade invoked nature in his early texts, but in later works he condemned it, calling it a whore and a murderess, rebelling against it. But between de Sade and the present, there's a history of shocking experiences in human civilization. Without that terrible ambivalence we are unable to face anything, certainly not nature. That's why we end our rebellions on our knees.[74]

The wooden monster takes on the identity of the human subject only to emerge, through a series of uncanny cannibalistic scenes that hyperbolise its horrific physical alterity, as another failure of the civilising project.

The technique of stop-motion animation used by Švankmajer to breathe life into Little Otik, in the otherwise live-action film, underscores, and self-referentially comments on, cinema's own hesitation in terms of the civilising project. Does cinema rebel against nature, or does it somehow enhance nature's animistic agency? The somewhat clumsy and slightly stroboscopic movement within the stop-motion sequences, set at counterpoint with the fluid live-action movement of the majority of the film, draws the viewer's attention to the role of speed in the medium's work of representation. Within a single text, Švankmajer juxtaposes two kinds of cinematically mediated velocity and two very different aesthetics, that of the slow and the rapid. Capable of both, cinema has been contracted in many ways to embrace the rapid at the expense of the slow. A technologically enhanced sense of greater speed has been considered cinema's most defining feature since its dawn as a product of the same Industrial Revolution that led to the increased mechanisation of daily life, Europe's colonial expansion, and the ongoing exploitation of the natural world. Writing in 1911, Ricciotto Canudo, one of the earliest theorists of cinema, discussed the medium's tendency to employ the 'excess' and 'precipitation of movement' in order to civilise the unknown through visually consuming it. The speed would somehow annihilate the distance between the viewing consciousness and the unknown. Canudo's cinema would deliver to the spectator 'the farthest countries, the most unknown people, the least known of human customs, moving, shaking, throbbing before the spectator transported by the extreme rapidity of the representation'.[75] In *Little Otik*, Švankmajer contrasts accelerated movement with slow movement in order to disclose the Faustian mission as a rather foolish project. The awkward movement that animates the organic monster in stop-motion is pre-industrial, made possible by careful manipulation of the animator's hand. Cinematic technology is used here by the filmmaker to lead the viewer beyond the technological vision, into the slow optics that intentionally fails to master the unknown, instead preserving its horrifying alterity. Eventually, the stop-motion wooden monster symbolically takes over the live-action diegetic world by simply absorbing it.

In her reading of *Little Otik* as a comment on the conditions of late capitalism, Anikó Imre observes that the film uses a 'resurrection of the folktale pattern of cannibalism to critique modern consumption'.[76] In her interpretation, the monstrous Otik, allegorically, represents the compulsive consumption of the modern era, and the filmic world offers an allegory of 'a dystopian global consumer society'.[77] Summoned to life by a woman and fostered by a girl, the wooden monster, Imre argues, is a grotesque caricature that mimics the rhetorical feminisation of late capitalism's gluttonous consumption detectable in recent cultural discourses. But if one chooses to view Švankmajer's images in their palpable, multisensory richness, the allegorical perspective becomes harder to grasp. In fact, the narrative itself (the characters, events, dialogue) becomes secondary to the emphatic presence of the object.

The material texture, so important in all of the filmmaker's works, short-circuits the allegory. In his study on the role of objects and their tactile aspect in Švankmajer's animation, Michael O'Pray comments on the filmmaker's inclination to 'allow the very materiality of objects and natural matter to express the torment and horror' of the characters in his films.[78] O'Pray also points out that there is an important industrial / natural distinction among Švankmajer's objects. He uses outdated and trashed cultural artifacts to enact a resurrection of 'objects that have been marginalized and rendered useless by consumerist capitalism (and communism)'.[79] Natural objects, on the other hand, such as stone, dirt or wood, figure in Švankmajer's films as self-renewing matter – O'Pray calls it the 'primeval mud' – that absorbs the refuse generated by mechanical reproduction and commodity consumption.[80] Little Otik belongs to the second category of objects.

At some point, the viewer cannot help but see Otik, the monster, as nature overgrown – a jumble of roots and branches that cannot be trained, pruned or cultivated. Otik's fast-growing body shoots through clothes, furniture and walls that have been put up to contain him. The horror that the wooden monster evokes is the horror of Kristeva's abject, whose border-crushing power rebels against the civilising instinct. Otik is the rampant, engulfing vegetation that grows over man's best and man's worst experiments in cultivation – the physical ordering of matter, as well as the symbolic efforts at meaning-making. Ironically, while Otik's cannibalism goes unpunished, his ravishment of the matriarch's perfectly neat cabbage garden (a space of cultivation) is a transgression that will not be overlooked by the gardener. The wooden monster, if viewed in the context of material transfiguration, illustrates nature fighting its way back to some form of equilibrium. This fight can only be perceived as cataclysmic by the postindustrial human subject.

When writing about the magic realist cinema of Jan Jakub Kolski, Ewa

Mazierska talks about the 'ecological' message that these films espouse: 'Every film by Kolski contains a message that can be described as "ecological": human beings are only one of the many inhabitants of the Earth and have no right to behave in a superior manner towards animals and plants.'[81] This ecological message of egalitarian coexistence in space with animals and plants can be extended to the relationship of the human being with technology, and especially products of technology that, over time, become undesirable as commodities. It seems that ecological existence today requires not only respect for the natural environment but also a mindful attitude towards mass-produced consumer goods. Through its emphasis on material reality, magic realism does a great job envisioning agency ('the soul') not only in plants and animals, but also in old refrigerators and bicycles.

Having emerged from decades of grim Communist legacy, which left the environment littered with the failed infrastructures of heavy industries and Soviet-style collective farming, and having encountered the sudden deluge of mass-produced consumer goods that flooded the landscape in the wake of the 1989 revolution, East Central European filmmakers developed a unique critical discourse on technology, mechanical reproduction and consumer mentality. Akin to steampunk's preoccupation with anachronistic technology, many magic realist films depict dated technology and / or modified technology that is being salvaged and re-used in unpredictable new ways by both set designers and characters within the diegetic world. Much of the *mise-en-scène,* as well as the dramatic action in these films, highlights the stubborn continuation of mass-produced goods, which continue to last against, and in spite of, the destructive forces of history and the built-in obsolescence. Apart from the refrigerator in Trzaskalski's *Eddie,* one might want to recall the tank in Emir Kusturica's *Underground* (*Bila jednom jedna zemlja,* 1995), the clocks and watches in Martin Šulík's *Landscape* (*Krajinka,* 2000), the abandoned funicular in his *Orbis Pictus* (1997), the old cinematograph in Jan Jakub Kolski's *History of Cinema in Popielawy* (*Historia kina w Popielawach,* 1998), the hand-cranked camera in his *Afonia and the Bees* (*Afonia i pszczoly,* 2009) or the early model of Warszawa car in his *Johnny the Aquarius* (*Jańcio Wodnik,* 1993). These various objects of technology punctuate the filmic space with Jamesonian 'historical raw material', foregrounding different modes of production, but also different modes of material preservation. The ecological message is to be found in how the films imaginatively repurpose the often dilapidated and cast-off products of technology. These clanky objects' perseverance in filmic time and space challenges the disposable attitude that comes with the mechanically produced goods. Far from a Luddite rejection of the idea of technology, the films in question offer an inspired critique of the ways in which technology has been advancing in the economy of the modern world, whether capitalist or Communist. The films contest this economy's race towards ultimate efficiency

Figure 26   Afonia with her hand-cranked camera in Kolski's *Afonia and the Bees*
(2009).

and homogeneity through the artful, unpredictable and often ridiculously impractical uses invented for these common objects of consumption.

One of the exemplary films to contain this kind of critique is Emir Kusturica's *Black Cat, White Cat* (*Crna mačka, beli mačor*, 1998). Set on the banks of the Danube, the film tells the story of small-town hustlers who smuggle washing machines and fuel from Russia. To settle an old debt, these provincial gangsters agree on a marriage deal that will push the sleepy place into a spectacle of Rabelaisian chaos. As smugglers and aspiring capitalists, Kusturica's characters are supposed to be connoisseurs of consumer goods, yet ironically their attitude towards these goods is perfectly blasé. Brand-new washing machines are dropped into the river and cheaply made cars are left for pigs to feed on, in a film whose plot unabashedly champions love at first sight and family loyalty. The desire and reverence that would accompany a sought-after commodity become displaced and ridiculed, as in the wedding scene, where the young couple are receiving their wedding gifts. The screen provides the stage for a parodic procession of assorted commercial goods; each gift – an unpackaged and heavily used household appliance – is lifted into the air and collectively appraised in its shoddy glory.

While new things are damaged with nonchalance, old things are kept in working order through an endless cycle of repair. A woman at the local café waters her telegraph pole every time she needs to make a phone call to improve her reception. There is no doubt that technology in this far corner of Europe is falling apart, but Kusturica takes pride in showing how, through sheer ingenuity, people extend the life of obsolete technology both out of need and for the fun of it. The practice of finding new ways to use old things is not only ecological,

Figure 27   Smuggling Russian washing machines down the Danube in *Black Cat, White Cat* (1998).

but also magical in its transformative, pragmatic intention. Kusturica's characters deploy their ingenuity for profit, but also curiously to make their lives more comfortable as well as pleasurable. From the very first scene, the viewer is confronted with Kusturica's bizarre repurposed contraptions – down the Danube floats a raft carrying an old truck that has been converted into a little red house, fitted with a flower-adorned balcony. From Matko's (Bajram Severdžan) mechanised fan, made with a rat-propelled bicycle wheel, to Uncle Grga's (Jašar Destani) whimsical, multifunctional conveyances, these recycled inventions represent the imagination and conceptual unpredictability that stand in contrast to mechanical mass production but none the less foreground the spirit of technology as such. Passionate enough about their gadgets, the characters are rather nonchalant in their attitude towards material possessions. Unapologetically and brazenly, Kusturica ridicules the attachment to things so characteristic of *nouveau riche* mentality, as well as the understated fetishisation of vintage objects that is typical of postmodern nostalgia.

Offering a unique way of seeing, recording and showing the represented swatch of reality, of manipulating that portion of reality in ways different from our unmediated sense of the world, cinema models a certain investment in our material surroundings, our attachments to one another, the place we live in, but more importantly for this argument, our attachments to things. For a subject representing late capitalist society, those attachments are diametrically different from the attachments formed by a Second World subject, whose circumstances are shaped by the hybrid socio-economic formation that is simultaneously premodern, modern and postmodern. Informed by Frederic Jameson's theory of cinematic magic realism as optics attuned to colliding modes of production, where the 'mode of production' stands for the material circumstances

Figure 28   Kusturica contemplates technology's re-absorption into nature via one
hungry pig.

of human life, one begins to see how the magic realist films from East Central
Europe offer a vision of social change simply by imagining a space where man
is capable of seeing things as both objects and subjects, and where the material
affinity between the human and the non-human is not obscured or sanitised by
science or philosophy. Rather, equality of all matter is brought to the surface
and contemplated as both a creative and a productive endeavour. The human
subject manipulates the object world; in turn, objects always manipulate the
subject's humanity.

When Marx explained his concepts of production and consumption, he
implied a reciprocal relationship of man with things: 'In production the person
is embodied in things, in [consumption] things are embodied in persons.'[82]
This very relationship, rarely as easily definable as Marx would have it, is what
magic realism sets out to illustrate. And it is not a coincidence that East Central
European filmmakers, whose audiences are in the midst of renegotiating their
own modes of production and consumption, would engage magic realism to
produce a cinema that calls for a new pace of consumption.

Notes

1. Vivian Sobchack, *Carnal Thoughts: Embodiment and Moving Image Culture*
   (Berkeley: University of California Press, 2004), p. 301.
2. Dan Lungu, '"Miserabilism" or Post-Traumatic Realism (in Romania)', *Writer's
   Notebook,* February 2010, at http://www.facebook.com/note.php?note_id=
   339756166627 (accessed 2 June 2010).
3. David Danow, *The Spirit of Carnival* (Lexington: University Press of Kentucky,
   1995), p. 67. My emphasis.

4. Ibid. p. 104.
5. André Breton, *Surrealism and Painting*, trans. Simon Watson Taylor (New York: Harper & Row, 1972), pp. 347–8.
6. Elzbieta Buslowska, 'Cinema as Art and Philosophy in Béla Tarr's Creative Exploration of Reality', in *Acta Univ. Sapientia, Film and Media Studies* (2009), pp. 113–14 (pp. 107–16 inclusive).
7. Franz Roh, 'Magic Realism: Post-Expressionism', in Lois Zamora and Wendy Faris (eds), *Magical Realism: Theory, History, Community* (Durham, NC: Duke University Press, 1995), p. 20.
8. Ibid. p. 29. Author's emphasis.
9. The première and distribution of Tarr's film *The Turin Horse* were postponed in Spring 2011 under pressure from the right-wing Hungarian Government, after Tarr expressed his criticism of the Government's lack of support for Hungarian intellectuals and the arts in an interview for the German daily *Der Tagesspiegel*.
10. Katarzyna Marciniak and Kamil Turowski, *Streets of Crocodiles: Photography, Media, and Postsocialist Landscapes in Poland* (Chicago: University of Chicago Press, 2011).
11. Peter Hames, 'The Melancholy of Resistance: The Films of Béla Tarr', at http://www.kinoeye.org/01/01/hames01.php (accessed 5 June 2011).
12. Ibid.
13. Interview at http://www.brightlightsfilm.com/30/belatarr1.php (accessed 5 June 2011).
14. Reference the film *Werckmeister Harmonies / Werckmeister harmóniák*, directed by Béla Tarr. Hungary / France / Germany / Switzerland: Mikoos Szita, Franz Goess, Joachim von Vietinghoff, Paul Saadoun, 2001.
15. In interviews, Tarr frequently talks about the cosmic dimension of his work. For example, in 2004, in an interview with Phil Ballard, the director explains his preoccupation with poverty as a problem that is 'not only social but ontological, then afterwards cosmic'. 'In Search of Truth: Béla Tarr Interviewed', *Kinoeye*, 4:2, March 2004, http://www.kinoeye.org/04/02ballard02.php (accessed 5 June 2011).
16. Elzbieta Buslowska, 'Cinema as Art and Philosophy in Béla Tarr's Creative Exploration of Reality', p. 110.
17. Lois Zamora, 'Magical Romance / Magical Realism', in Lois Zamora and Wendy Faris (eds), *Magical Realism: Theory, History, Community*, p. 544.
18. Ibid.
19. Elzbieta Buslowska, 'Cinema as Art and Philosophy in Béla Tarr's Creative Exploration of Reality', p. 111.
20. Wendy Faris, *Ordinary Enchantments: Magical Realism and the Remystification of Narrative* (Nashville: Vanderbilt University Press, 2004), p. 43.
21. Elzbieta Buslowska, 'Cinema as Art and Philosophy in Béla Tarr's Creative Exploration of Reality', p. 109.
22. Wendy Faris, *Ordinary Enchantments*, p. 46.
23. John Orr, 'Béla Tarr Circling the Whale', *Sight and Sound*, 11:4, 2001, pp. 22–4.
24. Ibid. p. 23.
25. Steven Marchant, 'Nothing Counts: Shots and Event in *Werckmeister Harmonies*', *New Cinemas: Journal of Contemporary Film*, 7:2, 2009, p. 145 (pp. 137–54 inclusive).
26. Franz Roh, 'Magic Realism: Post-Expressionism', p. 30.
27. Vivian Sobchack, *Carnal Thoughts*, p. 4.
28. Ibid. p. 91.
29. Ibid. p. 302.

30. Ibid. p. 99.
31. Ibid. p. 298.
32. Christina Stojanova, 'Fragmented Discourses: Young Cinema from Central and Eastern Europe', in Anikó Imre (ed.), *East European Cinemas* (New York: Routledge, 2005), p. 216 (pp. 213–27 inclusive).
33. Ibid. p. 217.
34. Seymour Menton, *Magical Realism Rediscovered, 1918–1981* (Philadelphia: Art Alliance, 1983), pp. 9–10.
35. Ibid. p. 10.
36. Ibid.
37. María Ruth Noriega Sánchez, *Challenging Realities: Magic Realism in Contemporary American Women's Fiction* (Valencia, Spain: Universitat de València, 2002), p. 190.
38. John Burt Foster Jr, 'Magical Realism, Compensatory Vision and Felt History: Classical Realism Transformed in *The White Hotel*', in Lois Zamora and Wendy Faris (eds), *Magical Realism: Theory, History, Community*, pp. 270–1.
39. Ewa Mazierska, 'Post-Communist Estonian Cinema as Transnational Cinema', *KinoCultura*, Special Issue 10, 2010, http://kinokultura.com/specials/10/mazierska.shtml (accessed 15 August 2011).
40. Homi Bhabha, 'The Third Space: Interview with Homi Bhabha', in J. Rutherford (ed.), *Identity, Community, Culture, Difference* (London: Lawrence & Wishart, 1990), pp. 207–21.
41. Julia Kristeva, *Powers of Horror* (New York: Columbia University Press, 1982), p. 1.
42. Ibid. p. 4.
43. Bronislaw Malinowski, *Magic, Science, and Religion, and Other Essays* (Garden City, NY: Doubleday Anchor, 1954), p. 70.
44. Ibid. p. 24.
45. Franz Roh, 'Magical Realism: Post-Expressionism', p. 22.
46. Sergiusz Michalski, *New Objectivity: Painting, Graphic Art and Photography in Weimar Germany* (Cologne: Benedikt Taschen, 1994), p. 178.
47. Franz Roh, 'Magical Realism: Post-Expressionism', p. 17.
48. Ibid. pp. 18, 20.
49. Dziga Vertov, 'Kinoks: A Revolution', in Philip Simpson, Andrew Utterson and K. J. Shepherdson (eds), *Film Theory: Critical Concepts in Media and Cultural Studies: Volume I* (London and New York: Routledge, 2004), p. 233.
50. On that subject, Bronislaw Malinowski comments 'Magic is thus not derived from an observation of nature or knowledge of its laws, it is a primeval possession of man to be known only through tradition and affirming man's autonomous power of creating desired ends' (*Magic, Science, and Religion*, p. 76).
51. Franz Roh, 'Magical Realism: Post-Expressionism', p. 22.
52. Dziga Vertov, 'Kinoks: A Revolution', p. 232.
53. Ibid. p. 233.
54. This is a reference to Stafford's unpublished lecture entitled 'The Slow Conscious Look: Toward a Pedagogy of Attentiveness', delivered on 14 April 2009 at Rice University, part of the Biennial Menil / Rice Lecture Series, 'Museums and the Medical Humanities: The Art of Transformation'. Matthew Flanagan, 'Towards an Aesthetic of Slow in Contemporary Cinema', *16:9*, 6:29, November 2008, http://www.16-9.dk/2008-11/side11_inenglish.htm (accessed 27 July 2011).
55. See 'The Ontology of the Photographic Image' for Bazin's concept of photographic mummification. André Bazin, *What is Cinema? Volume I* (Berkeley: University of California Press, 2005), pp. 9–16.

56. Frederic Jameson, 'On Magic Realism in Film', *Critical Inquiry*, 12:2, Winter 1986, pp. 301–25.
57. Ibid. pp. 305, 311.
58. Ibid. p. 311.
59. Ibid.
60. Salman Rushdie, *Imaginary Homelands: Essays and Criticism 1981–1991* (Harmondsworth: Granta, 1992), p. 301.
61. Barbara Klonowska, 'Far Away From the Present: Magical Realism in Polish Film', *Studies in Eastern European Cinema*, 1:2, p. 193 (pp. 183–96 inclusive).
62. Cristina Sandru, 'A Poetics of the Liminal: Magical Realism and its Horizons of Escape', *American, British and Canadian Studies*, vol. 5, December 2004, http://abcjournal.ulbsibiu.ro/Cristina%0Sandru.html (accessed 11 August 2011).
63. Ewa Mazierska, *Polish Postcommunist Cinema: From Pavement Level* (Oxford: Peter Lang, 2007), p. 169.
64. Matthew Flanagan, 'Towards an Aesthetic of Slow in Contemporary Cinema'.
65. Henri Lefebvre, *The Production of Space*, trans. Donald Nicholson-Smith (Oxford: Blackwell, 1991), p. 81.
66. Ibid.
67. Ibid.
68. Ibid. p. 80.
69. Edgar Morin, *The Cinema, or The Imaginary Man* (Minneapolis: University of Minnesota Press, 2005), p. 72.
70. Ibid. p. 68.
71. Ibid. p. 65.
72. On the shared genesis as well as the aesthetic and philosophical parallels of surrealism and magic realism, see Jean-Pierre Durix, *Mimesis, Genres and Post-Colonial Discourse: Deconstructing Magic Realism* (Houndmills: Palgrave Macmillan, 1998); Shannin Schroeder, *Rediscovering Magical Realism in the Americas* (Westport: Praeger, Greenwood, 2004); and Maggie Ann Bowers, *Magic(al) Realism* (London and New York: Routledge, 2004).
73. Peter Hames, 'Bringing up Baby: An Interview with Jan Švankmajer', *Sight and Sound*, 11:10, October 2001, pp. 26–8.
74. Ibid. p. 28.
75. Ricciotto Canudo, 'The Birth of the Sixth Art', in Philip Simpson, Andrew Utterson and K. J. Shepherdon (eds), *Film Theory*, pp. 26–7 (pp. 25–33 inclusive).
76. Anikó Imre, *Identity Games: Globalization and the Transformation of Media Cultures in the New Europe* (Cambridge, MA: MIT Press, 2009), p. 201.
77. Ibid. p. 208.
78. Michael O'Pray, 'Jan Švankmajer: A Mannerist Surrealist', in Peter Hames (ed.), *The Cinema of Jan Švankmajer: Dark Alchemy* (London: Wallflower, 2008), p. 58.
79. Ibid. p. 56.
80. Ibid. p. 58.
81. Ewa Mazierska, *Polish Postcommunist Cinema*, p. 238.
82. Friedrich Engels and Karl Marx, *The German Ideology, including Theses on Feuerback* (New York: Prometheus, 1998), p. 6.

4. BETWEEN FANTASY AND MIMESIS: CARNIVAL, CHILDREN AND CINEMA

I would even go so far as to say that the cinema is polytheistic and theo-gonic. Those lives it creates, by summoning objects out of the shadows of indifference into the light of dramatic concern, have little in common with human life. These lives are like the life in charms and amulets, the ominous, tabooed objects of certain primitive religions.

Jean Epstein[1]

In order to begin approaching the theory of cinematic magic realism, one has to consider the old question of cinematic specificity. Is film uniquely committed to realism or illusionism, to science or art? Much of the existing theory of the medium seems to agree that film, especially in comparison with other media, offers an exceptional space for representational realism that is somehow intensified by cinema's hybrid investment in both art and science. Writing in the 1920s and 1930s, as one of the earliest contributors to the budding field of film theory, Jean Epstein used the word *photogénie* to refer to film's quintessential ability to represent reality with unprecedented visual insight, therefore intensifying the viewer's perception of it. As a result, Epstein argued, an unfamiliar world emerges in film – the world without boundaries between spirit and matter, life and death, the 'world in its overall, continuous mobility', which is populated by 'individual beings we thought invisible and inaudible'.[2] Epstein's concept, based in the process of representation and simultaneous intensification, has a cultural and an aesthetic dimension to it, and in that way, it offers the best theoretical approximation of what the magic realist filmmakers try to accomplish in their films when they show reality mobilised for transformation.

Some theorists – most famously, André Bazin in his metaphor of cinematic mummification – argued that film not only represents reality but also, in fact, preserves it. The photographic image, which is the basis of film for Bazin, 'embalms' reality in ways that other modes of representation fail to do.[3] Walter Benjamin believed that film technology produced, through artifice, a perfect recreation of reality: 'the sight of immediate reality has become an orchid in the land of technology'.[4] Stressing the mechanical aspect of photographic reproduction, which minimises the subjective input from the filmmaker, theorists like Siegfried Kracauer or Cesare Zavattini, writing in the wake of World War II (arguably a result of Hitler's perverse creative vision), thought of cinematic realism as potentially curative and democratising, allowing us to document the 'ordinary business of living' in contrast to symbolic and propagandistic aims. 'It might tentatively be said', argued Kracauer, 'that films favor life in the form of everyday life – an assumption which finds some support in the medium's primordial concern for actuality.'[5] Finally, phenomenologists, like Maurice Merleau-Ponty, viewed film as the glue that brings together appearance and embodiment: 'a movie has meaning in the same way that a thing does: neither of them speaks to an isolated understanding; rather, both appeal to our power tacitly to decipher the world or men and to coexist with them'. Furthermore, Merleau-Ponty argued that 'the movies are peculiarly suited to make manifest the union of mind and body, mind and the world, and the expression of one in the other'.[6] Whether film's realistic impulse is attributed to the representational objectivity inherent in the medium's technology, the verisimilitude derived from the photochemical process, or the spatio-temporal unity preserved in a single shot, the theorists agree on cinema's power to impress upon the viewer, if not reality itself, at the very least a strong sense of what Roland Barthes called the 'reality effect'.[7]

Film's capacity for illusionism is a more contentious area of theory because filmic illusionism has been caught between the discursive antipodes of experimental, socially engaged art and cinema for the masses (employed in the service of political propaganda or escapist entertainment). While art cinema might offer an illusion of an alternative world to explore the artist's creative mission, entertainment cinema will strive to construct a perfect illusion of the viewer's experiential world as its means to maximise escapist pleasure. Soviet Montage theory valued film's openness to manipulating the vision of reality for greater revolutionary impact. Sergei Eisenstein's constructivist approach championed film's potential for ideological interrogation and political change. The French movement of *cinéma pur*, inspired by Germaine Dulac's vision of 'pure cinema', emphasised film's ability to move beyond the narrative conventions of other arts and accomplish its artistic mission through experiments in light, rhythm and movement. Rudolf Arnheim, the author of *Film as Art*, insisted on film's limitations with regard to recreating the real. However, he embraced those limitations as the seat of film's artistic potentiality that elevates film above the mere mechanical reproduction of reality. Similarly, Béla Balázs saw film as an art that could move away from naïve realism. He credited film for its unique capacity to defamiliarise and estrange our routine perceptions of the world: 'a good film with its close-ups reveals the most hidden parts in our polyphonous life, and teaches us to see the intricate visual details of life'.[8]

In their 1944 critique of film as mass entertainment, Theodor Adorno and Max Horkheimer focused on film's compulsion to equate its constructed world with reality. In their famous essay, 'The Culture Industry: Enlightenment as Mass Deception', Adorno and Horkheimer argue the following about film: 'The more densely and completely its techniques duplicate empirical objects, the more easily it creates the illusion that the world outside is a seamless extension of the one which has been revealed in the cinema.'[9] Important in this critique is the direction in which the imitation proceeds. Adorno and Horkheimer do not find the cinematic illusion problematic as such. The problem arises when the cinematic illusion permeates the viewer's sense of the real, paradoxically 'repressing the powers of imagination'.[10] Film as a means of mass entertainment crushes individual consciousness through the grand illusion, with its concomitant dematerialisation, that has been fashioned for optimal profit to the film industry. Within this theoretical framework, film's mimetic capacity is seen as perilous precisely because it can be easily exploited in the service of ideological phantasmagoria.

In the midst of this energetic and contentious theoretical conversation on film's relationship to reality, one notices that the many voices seem to agree on one thing – film can both reveal and transform. Cinematic magic realism is a mode of representation that *emphasises* this dual function of cinema. It is used to represent *simultaneously* the inevitability of the real – the ontological firmness found in the material fabric of the experiential world and captured in the photographic image – and the unceasing dissolution of that inevitability via the medium's kinetic valence, a feature perfectly suited to explore the perpetual transformation of matter that, in time, turns any existence into a mere illusion. Such use of film, which I will designate here as cinematic magic realism, works to replace every instance of meticulously established ontological presence with a 'ghost' of presence, to use Jacques Derrida's convenient term. In Ken McMullen's 1983 improvisational film *Ghost Dance*, Jacques Derrida discusses cinema as 'the art of letting ghosts come back', suggesting that cinema's nature allows for the radical otherness of the extratextual reality to appear before the spectator.[11] Derrida's elaboration of his thinking on the spectral presence – the concept of 'hauntology', which he summons to interrogate ontology's apparent fullness of being – has been used to theorise cinema by film scholars who focus on the medium's inherent liminality.[12]

By juxtaposing presence with absence, ontology with Derridean hauntology, being with becoming, cinematic magic realism utilises cinema's inherent representational duality – a drive to document and preserve the profilmic reality and the concurrent process of radical dematerialisation, which pushes the represented reality into an endless cycle of metamorphosis. The theory of literary magic realism identifies a similar duality, where the reader experiences productive tension by being exposed to the initial 'evocation and subsequent transgression of the narrative conventions of literary realism'; the critic Anne C. Hegerfeldt calls it the 'bidimensionality' of magic realism.[13] While both cinema and literature are capable of staging the conflict between the realist mode of representation and the immediate rejection of the hegemony of this mode, cinema seems to accomplish this much more easily on the level of form alone. The cinematic image, like a ghost, can push for both appearance and simultaneous disappearance. Most typically, literature accomplishes the same by contrasting realist form with supernatural content for the transgression to become apparent. The source of transgression dealt to the realist convention in works of literary magic realism is almost never the material of language itself. The important exception is the technique of literalisation, when a figure of speech, a metaphor, is rendered real in violation of linguistic conventions. But even then, paradoxically, the materialising metaphor, in its logic of increased ontology, becomes a hyperbole of the realist mimetic effort (transgressing through excess of the real).

Magic realism in both cinema and literature depends on an act of sparring between the literal and the figurative. Since, in cinema, this sparring always already happens on the level of form, within the image itself, it is harder to discern and dramatise it. Arguably, cinema is more 'at home' within the literal, since it operates primarily through what Charles Sanders Peirce defined as iconic and indexical signification, where the visual signifier corresponds to the represented signified via resemblance or an actual connection.[14] This foundation in icon and index is responsible for the perceived realist bias of cinema. In turn, that might explain why, despite the self-proclaimed magic realist practice of so many contemporary filmmakers, there is an awkward scarcity of critical writing on magic realism in film. It is as if the perceived realist weight of film preempts any considerations of how this weight can be removed. In her attempt to theorise magic realism in Polish cinema, Barbara Klonowska notes that

> the pressure of the realistic convention is ubiquitous in movies and much more difficult to neutralize than in literature, where huge parts of the presented world can simply be left undefined, leaving room for the reader's imagination and creation of separate imaginary worlds.[15]

While it might be true that the anti-realist mode is harder to dramatise in cinema, I believe that when the filmmaker does successfully transgress the realist confines, it is all the more stunning, precisely because of the sense of the all-pervading realist norm within the medium.

The situation is reversed in the case of literature, which consists of mainly symbolic signification. In Peirce's classification of signs, language in general, as well as its literary variety, signifies through symbolic convention, where a given signifier stands arbitrarily for the signified, without any connection existing or intimated between the two. Therefore, one might argue that literature is more 'at home' within the symbolic or figurative register. It proceeds from figurative to literal; the words pre-exist the things. If magic realism is defined as the spectacle of first evoking and then transgressing reality, then cinematic magic realism has to work harder to stage the figurative transgression dealt to its literal 'home'. Literary magic realism, meanwhile, works harder at the initial process of constructing the literal, the all-encompassing illusion of experiential reality, so that the anti-realist thrust, native to the house of fiction, has the desired effect. Magic realism in both literature and cinema calls attention to the constructed and fictive nature of the narrative it tells. The impulse of magic realism is not to cover up the workshop of the magician so that his illusion may mesmerise the viewer / reader, but rather it is to unveil the sleight of hand that is involved in the act, yet still admire the transformation. Unlike stage magic, with its exotic paraphernalia and highly constructed performative space, magic realism is invested in identifying the possibility of transcendence in the midst of the mundane plane of existence. Maggie Ann Bowers defines the difference as follows: 'Conjuring "magic" is brought about by tricks that give the illusion that something extraordinary has happened, whereas in magic(al) realism it is assumed that something extraordinary *really* has happened.'[16]

The history of magic realism points towards an interesting cross-fertilisation between cinema and literature. This process, largely overlooked by existing theories of magic realism within literary studies, yet of key importance in the ensuing effort of defining the cinematic application of magic realism, is cinema's role in shaping the imaginations of the writers who popularised magic realism as a literary genre. In his volume devoted to exploring how cinema adapts the novel, Robert Stam points out that 'magic realism was linked to the cinema long before it was adapted in films'.[17] Stam provides a meticulous account of the genealogy of Latin American magic realism and notes that the key figures within the movement were often involved with film, through personal connections with the film industry, the choice of *auteur* cinema as artistic inspiration, or writing film scripts and film reviews. Significantly, Stam's analysis discloses the magic realism of Gabriel García Márquez as being shaped by the author's admiration and close study of Italian neo-realism. In his reaction to Vittorio de Sica's *Miracle in Milan* (1951), Márquez reportedly observed,

'The story of *Miracle in Milan* is a fairy tale, but one realized in a surprising milieu, mingling in a brilliant way the real and the fantastic, to the point that, in many cases, it is impossible to know where one ends and the other begins.'[18] The formative impact of the young and energising medium of cinema on the earliest practitioners of magic realism (the painters and writers of interwar Europe) must be contemplated, even if the exact extent of this influence cannot be verified within the scope of research completed for the present study.

In terms of film history, cinematic magic realism must be seen in the context of cinema's inception within the lowly and popular art of the sideshow and carnival spectacle. Many theorists point out that cinema has always been closely related to the art of visual illusion and vaudevillian magic. Arguably, the evolution of stage magic led to the birth of cinema.[19] On a certain level, both stage magic and cinema commodify the human interest in transcendence. Often, the artists who created early cinema – Georges Méliès, Félicien Trewey and John Stuart Blackton, among others – were also stage magicians, who used the technology of cinema to advance their craft. Magic realist cinema picks up, in a sense, where these magician filmmakers left off. In the tradition of the early sideshow cinema, which Tom Gunning dubbed as the 'cinema of attractions', magic realist cinema once again activates the viewer's curiosity in transitions between the material and the ethereal.[20] In order to satisfy this curiosity, magic realist texts will frequently situate the action within the world of a circus, a carnival or a folk festival, where spectacular transformations unsettle the usual divisions between realist norm and fantastic transgression.

The affinity between the world of the carnivalesque and the world of magic realism has been observed by a number of literary critics. Anne Hegerfeldt argues that the frequent choice of a circus, or any of the many carnivalesque spaces that invert the norms of the everyday world, for a setting in a magic realist text 'facilitates the endorsement of an alternative worldview' and anti-canonical culture.[21] David Danow, who considers magic realism to be the positive, 'life-affirming' modality of carnivalesque literature, talks about its 'transformations, reversals, and inversions of fate and fortune that reveal in turn a resultant, necessarily dualistic view of the world'.[22] This creative pairing of the worlds of carnival and magic realism, and their philosophical kinship, become even more pronounced in the case of magic realist cinema, since it is reinforced by the history of early cinema that brought together carnival's investment in the performance of visual excess and cinematic technology's readiness to spectacularise that excess.

Furthermore, for the sake of the ensuing narrative, it is important to note that carnival culture has been studied as an influential factor in determining certain trends within the body of East Central European art. Specifically, it is Mikhail Bakhtin's account of the premodern carnivalesque tradition of the folk festival (with its attendant practice of excess, chaos and hierarchy reversals) that has informed scholarly enquiry.[23] In the area of humour studies, Marta Dynel discusses the carnivalesque as an important feature of East Central European literature and its frequent ironic stance.[24] The historian Padraic Kenney discusses the role that carnivalesque rhetoric played in the streets of East Central Europe during the anti-communist protests.[25] In her analysis of the cultural changes in post-Communist society, Denise Roman observes: 'Thus, from an aesthetic perspective, postcommunism can be apprehended as a fragmented, flamboyant, and eclectic new artistic sensibility – as carnivalesque.'[26] Finally, Anikó Imre, in her critique of consumption discourse in post-Wall cultures, explains how Bakhtin's concept of the carnivalesque is indeed useful to analyse the new cultural formations from East Central Europe.[27]

In Ildikó Enyedi's 1989 film, *My Twentieth Century* (*Az én XX. századom*), magic realism, the carnivalesque, the birth of cinema, and the identity of East Central Europe interestingly converge. In this debut feature, Enyedi, a Hungarian female director, spins a tale of twin girls, Dóra and Lili, who are born in Budapest on the same day that Thomas Edison presents his electric light bulb to the excited public in Menlo Park, New Jersey. The year is 1880. The transatlantic perspective that pairs Budapest and New Jersey soon gives way to a global one, now set exactly at the turn of the century, and moving at a dizzying pace amid places such as Budapest, Hamburg, Burma, Austria, Paris, Siberia and New York. But the initial dichotomy between the West as modernity's progressive centre, where the male twins of science and technology are born, and the East as modernity's feminised Other, where women give birth to women, is preserved by the filmmaker throughout the narrative, although interesting reversals and gestures of mirroring frequently unsettle the dichotomy, commenting on the role of East Central Europe as one of modernity's othered peripheries.

The narrative focuses on the adventurous lives of the two girls, who become orphaned and separated early in their childhood. The background to this main plot is constructed via documentary and fictional documentary footage from the turn of the century. These inserts fragment the main narrative with vignettes of historical events, scientific discoveries, advancements in technology and political upheavals. While Dóra grows up to be a sensualist, who seeks pleasure and financial security in her relationships with men, Lili barely ekes out a living in search of her next political mission and suffragette emancipation. Both women, unbeknownst to one another, become intimately involved with the same man, a character called 'Z' (played by the Russian actor Oleg Ivanovich Yankovsky). In their performance of femininity, the two sister characters (both played by the Polish actress Dorota Segda) duplicate the West / East dialectic and literally embody the two faces of modernity. Dóra, who relies on the art of seduction to secure the means for her upmarket lifestyle, stands for the rational and pragmatic force of capitalist progress. Lili, whose hopeless romanticism and naïveté lead her to anarchy and terrorism, portrays the Communist revolution. Such symbolic pairings and doublings push the film into the realm of magic realism, where the identity of things is often questioned in this very way, by exposing the doppelgänger presence or the shadowy residue that unsettles the appearance of stable reality. Splintering the fictitious story line with inserts of documentary-like footage amplifies this effect. Fiction mirrors reality, and reality imitates fiction. Just as 'Z' cannot tell the difference between the twins, the viewer cannot tell fact from fiction in this film that cleverly fuses actual documentary footage, mock documentary passages and fiction sequences, which are shot in grainy black and white.

The doubling of identity that the twins represent is emphasised in the doubling of their voices in the film's unique sound design. Within the complex narrative structure of the film, the twins have been assigned their celestial counterparts, two stars twinkling in the firmament and in voice-over commenting on the story from above. These talking stars are part omniscient narrator, part disembodied female agency somehow related to the twins. Their privileged perspective allows them to witness but also manipulate events. They look after the twins, but also at times they simply channel the thoughts and desires of the twins. This defamiliarising conceit contributes to the film's general polyvocality, a feature of the carnivalesque, where authority's voice is always mocked by the impostor's voice. Mikhail Bakhtin referred to this discursive strategy as polyphony or heteroglossia, defined as the layering of different, often conflicting, voices within a single utterance. Bakhtin's theory of polyphony evolved from his philosophical and political convictions, which always made room for the role of the 'Other' in the process of identity formation. On the very basic level, polyphony is one's dialogue with the constitutive 'Other'.[28] Linking Bakhtin's concept with the idea of the subaltern discourse (feminist and postcolonial), which creatively appropriates the master voice of patriarchy and imperialism, Wendy Faris thinks of polyvocality as an important feature of magic realism. The doubling of voices, Faris argues, works to 'disrupt the mimetic program of realism'.[29]

In *My Twentieth Century*, the talking stars offer a discursive alternative to history. The way they are introduced into the story as characters and narrators is striking. The film opens with recreated documentary footage of Thomas Edison's first light show. The initial image on the screen is an abstract composition of light and shadow: a number of bright light points pierce through the sheet of total darkness. For a brief moment, the viewer sees what could be a constellation of stars in the night sky; but quickly, this understated and intimate spectacle turns into something very different. As the sources of light become brighter and brighter, the viewer begins to see an elaborate network of electric lights that are arranged in the trees, much like a display of Christmas lights, for the amusement and amazement of the curious crowd. People gawk and gasp in disbelief. This spectacle of illumination is soon displaced by nature's equivalent of it. The camera looks up at the sky and focuses on the flickering stars. Unlike Edison's bulbs, the stars are animated; they have souls and voices to express those souls. At the same time, it is blatantly obvious to the viewer that this 'natural' celestial spectacle is, in fact, completely artificial, a feat of cinematic special effects indebted to Edison's important contributions to the development of early cinematographic technology. The stars, endowed with female voices, begin to call on Edison, who seems to be utterly bored with his miracle of electricity. He hears the call from the stars and is visibly moved. The voices ask him to redirect his gaze and look to the East. A spectacle of an entirely different sort is about to unfold there.

The talking stars relocate the action of the film to a hovel in Budapest, where a poor woman is giving birth to twins, unassisted, with a Cheshire-like cat as her sole companion. Along with Edison, the viewer is invited to abandon the space of modernity, with its vibrant lights and crowds, and immerse herself in an utterly premodern, if not primordial, scene. A female body contorts in labour; the camera pans over the woman's dark and cramped quarters. Vats of boiling water and the roaring fire provide a semblance of comfort, but not enough to 'civilise' the scene. Technology and the advancements of science have not reached Budapest yet, the filmic text mockingly insinuates. In fact, Budapest might be so out of time that its status as a real place comes into question. Later in the film, Enyedi comments on the perceived peripherality of Hungary and the rest of East Central Europe within the discourse of modernity, when she stages a conversation between 'Z' and his English colleague, also a scientist, during which the Englishman becomes amazed that 'Z' actually comes from Hungary, because he was convinced that countries like Hungary, Bohemia or Romania were fictitious places invented by Shakespeare. This definition of the East of Europe as a lack is subsequently echoed by another scientific authority. This time, the verdict about non-existence is directed against East Central European woman.

In one of the film's many humorous scenes, the viewer accompanies Lili to a meeting of Hungarian suffragettes, where Otto Weininger, the controversial Austrian philosopher (who, like the twin protagonists of Enyedi's film, was born in 1880), is delivering a lecture based on his notoriously misogynistic and anti-semitic book *Sex and Character: An Investigation of Fundamental Principles*. Through a shot / counter-shot scene set-up, Weininger ends up addressing his vitriolic speech to Lili, who is visibly affected by his 'scientific' diagnosis of her female flaws. Frequently zooming in on Lili's face, the camera frames her as the 'face' that stands in for all the women gathered in the auditorium. After a lengthy tirade on the countless deficiencies of woman, which reiterates Freudian psychoanalysis's tendency to position the female as lack, Weininger confronts Lili one last time by informing her that 'She simply doesn't exist.' While Weininger's absurd pronouncement, and his pronoun 'she', refer to woman in general, in Enyedi's fictitious staging of the encounter between this Austrian man of science and his Hungarian audience, it is the collective body of feminised East Central Europe that is portrayed as a site of his attempt at forceful rhetorical dematerialisation. For a moment, as if witnessing a magic trick gone wrong, the viewer stares at the incongruity of Weininger, the magician, saying 'Poof! East Central Europe simply doesn't exist,' on one hand, and Lili's face in close-up, bolstered by the sounds of gregarious Hungarian suffragettes loudly protesting Weininger's efforts to erase them, on the other hand. Not surprisingly, Weininger's magic fails; the film goes on embodying the story of East Central European women, which, as Anikó Imre argues, 'requires luring Man into an artificial and magical space created by the female camera, where he may understand what he failed to understand before'.[30]

Weininger's lecture brings to mind Georges Méliès's 1896 magic film *The Vanishing Lady* (*Escamotage d'une dame chez Robert-Houdin*), which features the act of a disappearing woman performed by a male magician. Elsewhere in the film, Enyedi directly references Méliès. Her star narrators, who, apart from talking, are also capable of making films, are a nod to the name of Méliès's production unit, Star Film Company. The frequent iris shots of the surface of the moon quote Méliès's 1902 film *A Trip to the Moon* (*Le Voyage dans la Lune*). These references become important because Enyedi stages a concerted effort to critique the practice of conjuring up the marginalised subjects and making them vanish, whether they are women or colonised people, that typifies the patriarchal discourse of stage magic, but also the discourses of history, science and cinema. Lucy Fischer, who analyses the treatment that the female body receives at the hands of the magician in the early films by Méliès and Edison, argues that 'the act of conjuring and "vanishing" ladies tends to dematerialize and decorporealize the female sex – to relegate woman to the level of "spirit" '. In Fischer's interpretation of stage magic's sexual politics, 'magical practice literalizes the notion of woman as "Other," as unfathomable "mystery" '.[31] By opening her film with the scene of birth, and then throughout the film consistently framing images of female carnal pleasure, Enyedi gives woman her body back, therefore challenging her cinematic forefathers, Edison and Méliès.

Apart from substantiating the female subject, *My Twentieth Century*, a film released in 1989, East Central Europe's *annus mirabilis*, performs another kind of materialisation in the face of a curious act of discursive disappearance. It offers a lasting testimony to the existence of the Second World and the cultural difference that it signifies. Unlike many films produced on the eve of, or soon after, the collapse of the Communist world, which symbolically tend to send off the territory of East Central Europe westward and away from its often-shameful Soviet legacy, Enyedi's film revels in the in-between status of the region. By directly acknowledging its provincial and interstitial status, the filmmaker challenges the collective push of post-Wall society, on both sides of the Atlantic, to dissolve the figure of the Second World that has been tainted by Communist bankruptcy. Katarzyna Marciniak contemplates the symptomatic denial of Second Worldness, and its legacy, in postcolonial and transnational studies as a sign of the compulsive discursive polarisation of cultural space into the extremes of the First World and the Third World, which paradoxically mimics the growing geo-political distance between the West and the non-West. Marciniak argues that the 'murky territory of the post-socialist-communist second world' challenges scholars to pause and consider alternatives to the First / Third World binary that tends to simplify discussions of the recent global and local transformations.[32] Enyedi's film visualises the 'murky territory' of East Central Europe at the very same time that the world was celebrating its dissolution. Significantly, she conjures the Second World as the legacy embraced by women.[33]

Catherine Portuges sees the two opening scenes of the film as complementary:

> Together, the birth sequence and the Edison scene create the film's ambiance of joyful admiration for the mysteries of the universe, without neglecting the image of poverty and despair from which they cannot be separated. The twin – yet dichotomous – miracles of life-giving maternity and male scientific achievement are inseparable.[34]

In her reading, Portuges suggests, although indirectly, an almost organic dependence of the technological progress of Edison's world on the poverty and despair of the twins' world. It is important to note that, far beyond the 'ambiance of joyful admiration', the two scenes create a narratorial discord that pushes the rest of the film into a heated dialogue, whereupon the disembodied female voices, which represent the peripheral and the premodern, tell a story that erodes the triumphant account of the birth of the twentieth century, as the century of the West. More than just a testament to poverty and despair, that alternative story speaks of colonisation and exploitation that assisted modernity's advancement. The colonised in *My Twentieth Century* is Europe's internal periphery – East Central Europe. More specifically, the colonised appears here as the doubly colonised East Central European woman, who is marginalised not only by the imperial coloniser, but also by her native system of patriarchy.

In this respect, Anikó Imre's evaluation of the film's duality seems more precise. She states:

> *My Twentieth Century*'s spectatorial pleasures may primarily come from the visibility of the effort to create a self-subverting, double coherence: from the ongoing tension between celebrating modernity's masculine

scientific triumph, particularly the invention of electricity and cinematography, and the simultaneous satirical distance that Enyedi keeps from Edison's and Weininger's scientific hubris and from Z's irritating confidence. While both efforts appear equally serious, the latter prevails in the sense that making the film itself is a deliberate effort to appropriate cinematography to create a distinctly female address.[35]

When she talks about 'double coherence', Imre highlights the film's tendency to preserve its irreducible polyvocality as a productive way of retelling official history. Wendy Faris writes about the use of doubling in magic realism as a way to 'suggest the existence of parallel and converging realities'.[36] Doubling and doubles suggest the possibility of an alternative to the status quo, to the visible and the normative. In that way, doubling splits open the one identity and reinforces the likelihood of a transition from one world to another. This signals a liberating vitality in envisioning the alternative.

The alternative in Enyedi's film is not limited to the twins and the talking stars. There are also animals that contribute another voice to the conversation, and another perspective to this alternative account of modern history. At the Budapest zoo, where Dóra (or Lili – at this point the viewer has a hard time distinguishing between the two women mirroring one another) has a rendezvous with 'Z', a caged chimpanzee addresses the couple, and by extension the viewer, to tell his sad story of captivity. A flashback narrated by the animal relocates the action of the film to the heart of the African jungle and illustrates the exchange between the chimpanzee and the white explorer. The encounter begins as a friendly one, where animal and human are simply curious about each other. The chimpanzee amuses the intruder and is amused by the 'strange furless animal', until it becomes obvious that the human came with hostile intentions and will not leave the jungle without the exotic animal as his living bounty. As a last resort, the chimpanzee tries to charm the white man into mercy by being extra-playful. Needless to say, the animal fails and ends up spending its entire life behind bars.

The account delivered by the chimpanzee frames the preceding exchange between Dóra and 'Z', during which the two discuss the purpose of the 'cinematograph'. 'Z' mentions a failed assassination attempt that took place in the cinema earlier that day. Outraged, Dóra wonders aloud, 'What's the point in going to such stupid places?' She is clearly sceptical about the new invention, and she shrugs off 'Z's' enthusiasm for it by declaring that 'Curiosity killed the cat.' This proverb is then picked up by the chimpanzee as the cue for his story about curiosity that had perilous results. Interestingly, the chimpanzee asserts his agency by stating that it was his curiosity about the 'strange furless animal' that led to his confinement. In an important way, the two stories link the space of the zoological exhibition to the space of cinematic exhibition,

Figure 29   The talking chimpanzee narrates his life story to Dóra and 'Z' in Enyedi's
My Twentieth Century (1989).

and the exploitation of the colonised territories to technological advancement. This pairing allows the viewer to contemplate cinema as modern man's self-imposed site of maximum visibility and minimum freedom, akin to the zoo. Together, these two scenes displace the canonical interpretation of modernity's *Weltanschauung* as always informed by territorial aggression, biological essentialism, the violence of symbolic representation, and mastery over nature.

In Enyedi's film, women and animals form a chorus, which expresses a collective investment in the intuitive and unmediated understanding of the world, which challenges the values of Western individualism and what Imre calls the 'masculine scientific conceit'.[37] This solidarity between women and animals as bodies contained and exploited during the colonising project of modernity is touchingly explored in the most magical sequence in the film, which contemplates the life of one of Edison's experimental dogs. During the so-called 'War of Currents', Edison had thousands of animals electrocuted to prove that Nikola Tesla's invention of alternating current (AC – now an international standard in electric power systems) was deadly. In her discussion of the scene in question, Katherine Gyékényesi Gatto quotes the filmmaker's explicit interview statement, in which Enyedi is concerned with 'the dangers of our over-technical and soulless age' and worried about the fact 'that science has lost its moral basis'. Gatto further remarks that *My Twentieth Century*

> attempts to drive home the point once again, that twentieth-century science, like the dog with electrodes on his head, can be tied up in the confines of the laboratory and yet know nothing about the world. Thus it can be used for any purpose, good or bad.[38]

The sequence begins with a close-up of a dog's head wired full of electrodes; dimly lit, this shot points to the dog's misery as an experimental animal, isolated and contained in a laboratory. Its lone and sad existence is noticed by the two talking stars, who decide to alleviate its suffering. Since the dog has lived in captivity all its life and is completely unaware of the arrival of the new century, the stars decide to show it some movies of the brand new world. As if to question modernity's race into the future, and its simultaneous disavowal of the past, of the provincial and the unfashionable, the montage of images that the stars assemble for the viewing pleasure of the dog resorts to anachronism and temporal play. Along with the dog, the viewer sees a bizarre collage of time-lapse footage of growing plants, high-speed images of a bumble bee, actual footage of Leo Tolstoy at Yasnaya Polyana, images of helicopters and the Holocaust. These images speak of past, present and future, but without much of a timeline. Time slows down or speeds up, creating an impression of flexible chronology. Images from the future penetrate the present and make it seem always already obsolete, while contemporary images show the archaic life forms that speak of the past despite their presentness. This vision of the world complicates modernity's anthropocentric investment in linear, cause-and-effect time, and instead offers a perspective that might be closer to the cosmic and micro-cosmic concept of time–space that better reflects the holistic view of reality, which makes room for stars, dogs, machines and humans.

Edison's dog watches this unique version of Eisenstein's montage of attractions and is moved to flee his scientific prison cell. What follows is a joyful getaway indeed. In extreme long shot, the viewer sees the dog traversing grassy fields and beautiful beaches. At some point, the dog runs on to a railway line and into the path of a moving train. Just as the viewer is expecting the worst, the dog bravely stops in its tracks and meets the steam locomotive head-on. In a shot / counter-shot face-off between the machine (framed in low angle to imitate the dog's perspective) and the animal (dwarfed in high angle), it becomes obvious that this time technology will be tamed. The locomotive brakes, just inches away from the dog's nose.

In the process of telling her peripheral story, Enyedi does not straightforwardly dismiss progress and technology, or the agents that made those possible. Neither is she championing the East over the West. After all, she is using Edison's invention to make herself seen and heard. Rather, through an intricate play of doubling and reversal, Enyedi undoes the usual thinking about the winners and losers of modernity. Her dichotomies are twins, not opposites. Unlike binary opposition, where each element is hierarchically defined by what it is not, the twin figure suggests identity gained through correspondence. But this correspondence, or sameness, is always already questioned through the *mise-en-abyme* mirroring of the twin elements, which splinters the sameness into an endless chain of difference. Enyedi's twins of nature and culture, celestial and terrestrial, male and female, human and bestial, Eastern and Western provide for a more complete, but also more dizzyingly absurd account of modernity. Here Faris's words offer a felicitous description of the effects of the film's mirroring strategy: 'Like the theme of unpredictability, these patterns of reversal implicitly figure lack of human control over events and erode distinctions between discrete events and individuals.'[39] *My Twentieth Century* strives to compose a multifarious picture of modernity's project, making sure to signal its unfinished, deferred outcome that escapes the controlling human agency that initiated the project.

In his review, Steven Shaviro frames Enyedi's film within the category of magic realism, but also points out that '*My Twentieth Century*'s fantasmagoria is altogether more spectral, more hauntological, than that with which we are so familiar from South American fiction'.[40] Shaviro explains that the film shows the scene of turn-of-the-century modernity as being haunted by the 'ghosts of old Europe', the ghosts that presumably represent the victims of Europe's imperial aggression, as well as the ghosts of future victims of the mass genocide facilitated by technologically enhanced modern warfare. The spectral atmosphere that brings together cosy Victorian spiritualism and twentieth-century nightmare is brought to screen by Tibor Máthé, the acclaimed Hungarian cinematographer, who also shot *The Porcelain Doll*, the film discussed in the previous chapter.

Máthé uses dramatic chiaroscuro to contrast different depths of darkness with a variety of light intensities, which are used both to illuminate and to obscure. Cinematography thus becomes the playing field for Enyedi's main theme, the confrontation of the old with the new. Imitating many of the visual effects of early silent film, Máthé's camera becomes self-aware in its mission of bringing the twentieth century out of the smog and steam of the Industrial Revolution and ushering it into the electrically illuminated dawn of late modernity, with its global Information Revolution just about to happen. The latter is shown to have been launched by Edison, who, in one of the final scenes of the film, connects the world with his quadruplex telegraph. Of course, this contrast between the dark ages and radiant modernity receives a satirical treatment. It is used to engage playfully with the much-entrenched stereotype of East Central Europe as the 'shadowed lands of backwardness'.[41] Máthé uses his camera to conjure that shadow of barbarism and appropriate its dark undertones to aid Enyedi in her mission of recasting the face of modernity from a radically peripheral vantage point.

Using minimal lighting and night-for-night photography, Máthé creates the thick noir shadow that seems to steep the filmic world in almost medieval darkness. From that darkness, the light emerges dramatically, either with exuberance, when it is Edison's incandescent light bulb or the early cinematograph's projection beam, or with quiet resignation, when it is steam warming up the third-class train carriage where the poor travel huddled together or when it is a tiny flicker of matchstick light. The two opening scenes polarise the source and distribution of light into the electric light that shines from the West, standing for the Western idea of progress, and the natural light (starlight, moonlight or fire) that keeps the East in semi-darkness. This binary opposition is then quickly scrambled, and the viewer is immersed in the vision of Budapest, and other parts of East Central Europe, as a place where the antiquated lives on with the modern in hybrid formation. This is reflected in some of Enyedi's more idiosyncratic choices of set design. For example, in one scene large candles are used as streetlights; in another, an early cinematograph theatre features an endless array of separate screens, an imagined prototype for the postmodern space of multiplex cinema.

Máthé and Enyedi construct a vision of the East Central European periphery that is haunting and spectral. It portrays the Western fears and prejudices about the unspoken 'other' Europe, which has been swallowed by the Communist horde (a close cousin of the yellow horde). But it also, less directly, represents East Central Europe's own dark prejudices and shameful compromises. Throughout most of the film, there is no doubt that the space of the filmmaker's visual enunciation, the semiotic shadow, is what Homi Bhabha calls the 'split-space' or the 'third space'.[42] In Bhabha's theory, the third space allows for cultural difference to emerge and testify of 'the others of our selves'.[43] In this ambivalent space, the structures of law and language, along with a set of given socio-historical conditions, inflect one's utterance, filtering it through the discourse of the Other. The third space of enunciation is therefore the space of the uncanny – the repressed elements of the cultural dominant. It is from here that Ildikó Enyedi addresses her 1989 audience, which is expecting to see their culture, liberated and returned to the West and to Europe proper, with a vision of East Central Europe as a projection of the Enlightenment's European Other, a spectre of Marx but also a spectre of the Holocaust.

Using magic realism, Enyedi co-opts the technology of cinema to engage in her practice of hauntology, which in turn hijacks cinematic technology from its celebrated seat within the metropolitan centre of the developed world and takes it back to the space where progress is not always a positive word. Very different from the controversial tradition of the early ethnographic film, this kind of appropriation of cinema, and the ensuing interrogation of its history as a modernising medium, to tell the tale of the shadowed periphery, or to visualise the invisible, is common to other magic realist filmmakers. In a more intensely self-aware manner, Jan Jakub Kolski, in his film *The History of Cinema in Popielawy* (*Historia kina w Popielawach*, 1998), explores the official account of the origins of cinema and envisions an exciting alternative.

Set in 1960s Poland and presented from the perspective of ten-year-old Staszek (Tomasz Krysiak), a boy who grew up in the cinematic city of Łódź, but who is temporarily living with his grandparents in the nearby village of Popielawy, the film tells the story of a local family of blacksmiths, the Andryszeks, whose forefather, Józef Andryszek the First (Bartosz Opania), built a horse-powered 'kino-machine' a hundred years earlier. Staszek learns about the fascinating history of the village inventor and his prototype of cinema from Józef's youngest successor, Józef Andryszek the Sixth (Michał Jasiński), who goes by the nickname Szustek – the 'sixth little one'. Quickly becoming Staszek's best friend, Szustek is also a fellow student in the village school. Just as Szustek's own father, a hard-drinking blacksmith, is absolutely indifferent to the legacy of the inventor, Szustek is obsessed with it. He dreams of one day recreating the 'kino-machine', which burnt down in a revenge arson fire. To this end, he sketches out endless blueprints and constructs models of the device, which fuels his passion for cinema and the family chronicle. When not working on his project of reconstruction, Szustek, accompanied by Staszek, attends the screenings brought to town by Uncle Janek (Franciszek Pieczka) via his travelling cinema. Uncle Janek teaches the boys to operate his projector and allows them to assist him in the village screenings. However, Szustek's passion is thwarted by his father, who wants his son to learn his blacksmith trade and inherit his business. An unhappy widower drinking his sorrows away, Andryszek the Fifth discourages his son's preoccupation and, in an angry fit, destroys all of his designs. He then decides to sober Szustek up from his obsession by stripping him naked in the yard and dousing him in freezing water. The already sickly child contracts tuberculosis and is sent away for specialised treatment at a sanatorium. It is not until Szustek is on the brink of death that his father finally accepts his son's dream. Seeking forgiveness, Andryszek the Fifth reproduces the precious drawings from memory. Soon enough, Szustek recovers from his illness, claiming the power of cinema as his cure.

Kolski's gesture of provincialising cinema is best encapsulated in one of the most charming scenes in the filmmaker's entire œuvre – the scene of unfreezing Uncle Janek's travelling cinema. Shot at nighttime, the scene is set in a stunning winter landscape, and combines the aura of nature with that of technology. It is film time in the village of Popielawy, yet to everybody's surprise, Uncle Janek's dependable horse-drawn wagon that carries his mobile cinema is nowhere in sight. While the boys are wondering what happened, the viewer

Figure 30   Andryszek the First consults a saint on his cinematographic invention in *History of Cinema in Popielawy* (1998).

Figure 31   Andryszek constructs a wooden frame for his 'kino-machine'.

already knows the reason for the delay. In the preceding scene, the village cripple Kulawik (Mariusz Saniternik) becomes the laughing stock of a group of drunken, rowdy men. They mercilessly taunt Kulawik about his love life. Insulted and angry, he decides to put a curse on the whole village in the form of bitter frost that is going to prevent the cinema from reaching Popielawy that night. Disappointed, Staszek and Szustek run out of the village and in the direction of Uncle Janek's usual arrival route.

Soon enough, they come upon a bizarre tableau on the outskirts of the forest. Uncle Janek (frosty vodka bottle in hand), his horse and his wagon are caught in mid-step and frozen into a morbid ice sculpture. After the initial shock, the boys quickly find the solution. There is a reel of film marked with the word 'Spring' on the tin in Uncle Janek's collection. Without wasting much time, the boys hang up the projection screen on a tree and start up the equipment. The projection beam softly illuminates the forest, attracting a bevy of deer out of the darkness, who then become the unwitting audience in Staszek and Szustek's outdoor cinema. The scenes and sounds of springtime – birds hatching, trees blossoming, little creatures scouring around – begin to thaw the ice. In long shot, the camera frames the astonishing scene of two huddled boys watching animals watch other animals on screen. When Uncle Janek's bottle slips out of his thawed hand, the boys know that their trick has worked. Moments later, having regained his chutzpah, the old man is cursing Staszek and Szustek for messing with his gear. In his voice-over, Staszek comments that this event taught him that cinema's magic can revive people and tame wild animals. This scene in a way contributes to what Rachel O. Moore recognises as the long tradition of conceptualising cinema as a curative ritual, which began with the early film theorists, who as modernists were deeply preoccupied with the primitive and its magic. Moore argues that 'Early theorists' dependence on primitive beliefs in animism, the sacred, ritual sacrifice, idol worship, and sympathetic and homeopathic magic to interpret the cinema's power for a modern audience suggest that technology did not lay the irrational to rest for good.'[44] Since then, according to Moore, this faith in cinema's primitive magic and its ability to cure the 'modern fatigued subject' has been cultivated by many experimental filmmakers.[45] While not directly informed by the discourse of modernism, which conceived of primitivism as its constitutive other, Kolski's film reactivates this tired dichotomy from the perspective of the imagined primitive – the other Europe. Within Kolski's rural territory, cinema that is suggested to exist outside of modernity (and its discourses) performs its magic as an expression of genuine enchantment and not as a primitive or naïve rite fetishised by Moore's theorist, filmmaker and the modern subject. An invention of a blacksmith, Kolski's cinema stands closer to alchemy, with its highly spiritual proto-scientific method, than modern technology.

In all his films, Kolski uses cinema – the technology energised by the capitalist

Figure 32   Staszek and Szustek on their way to see a movie in *History of Cinema in Popielawy*.

city – to tell tales of rural communities without the patronising or exoticising focus. The conflict between the acknowledged urban provenance of cinema and the need to employ this inherently metropolitan medium to represent the periphery lies at the centre of Kolski's project. In *The History of Cinema in Popielawy*, Kolski re-imagines the origins of cinema and depicts the birth of the cinematic apparatus as having taken place in a Polish village, invented by a creative blacksmith, only then to be sold in design to the Lumière brothers. Kolski's revisionism comments on early cinema's relationship to colonialism, and the fact that both the history of cinema and cinematic versions of history were told from the perspective of the imperial colonising subject. Few accounts visualised those who were exploited or dispossessed in the process of colonisation, and even fewer explored the role of those subjugated people in 'fuelling' the technological advancement credited solely to Western Europe and North America. By moving the scene of the birth of cinema to an East Central European village, Kolski forces the viewer to consider the discursive erasure of the 'other' Europe from the annals of film history. On a smaller scale, Kolski uses the film to recreate his own family history, very much intertwined with the history of the birth of cinema in Poland. At the start of the twentieth century, his Jewish great-grandparents owned one of the first cinemas in the country, Théâtre Optique Parisien. Later, Kolski's grandfather was a film producer and distributor, representing Fox, MGM and Paramount in Poland.[46] Although, obviously, cinema was not invented by a Polish blacksmith, the camera that predates the Lumière brothers' invention, called the Paleograph, was invented by Polish inventor Kazimierz Prószynski, a fact rarely mentioned by early film historians. Furthermore, in many of his films, Kolski references the booming interwar period within Polish cinematography, when Polish and Yiddish film productions successfully competed with Hollywood and Western imports. Kolski evokes these films and filmmakers with a simultaneous reminder that most of them, both the creators and their work, perished during the Holocaust and the mass destruction of the East Central European cultural heritage during World War II. Many of those early films exist only as subjects of brief film reviews printed in the newspapers of the day. The surviving journalistic accounts exist as a memory of what once was, but also as a textual spectre of a visual culture that can never be recovered.

Kolski's meta-cinematic narrative, which paradoxically showcases cinema as both the skilled magician that can make objects appear and disappear, and the object itself that is conjured or vanished by the magician depending on historical circumstances, seems to be employed in a critical effort to disclose cinema as a mode supremely equipped to enhance the work of mimesis, but also a mode that is capable of accommodating the loss of reality, or its attenuation. In her analysis of the film, Ewa Mazierska focuses on this ambiguity of the medium: '*The History of Cinema in Popielawy* is neither about simple remembering nor forgetting, but about their interplay, their dialectic. Similarly, cinema in Kolski's film is both an agent of immortalizing and destroying history.'[47] As such, Kolski's vision of cinema approaches Bazin's theory of film as a unique process of mummifying reality, which relies on the preservation of life in death. Central to this vision is the recognition of a certain amount of loss that accompanies the acknowledgement of a certain advantage. Cinema is therefore contemplated as a powerful technology of reproduction that creates spectres of reality. These spectres testify to the passing of reality, yet they also guarantee a version of its immortality.

Invested in a different, yet related, kind of paradox, there is a burgeoning trend within the cinema of East Central Europe that has to be addressed in the ensuing study on magic realism – these are films about children that use the perspective of a child to focalise the act of representation in accordance with the enchantment and animism commonly ascribed to the child's perception of the world. The films most emblematic of the trend that I will presently discuss are *The Crows* (*Wrony*, dir. Dorota Kędzierzawska, 1994), *Jasminum* (*Jaśminum*, dir. Jan Jakub Kolski, 2006), *Tricks* (*Sztuczki*, dir. Andrzej Jakimowski, 2007) and *Time of the Gypsies* (*Dom za vešanje*, dir. Emir Kusturica, 1989). These films flesh out an important aspect of magic realism by expressing, via a 'child's-eye' focalisation, a contradictory combination of wonder at the small things continuously rediscovered in the object world, and the attendant lack of amazement at the grand socio-historical dramas of the community of adults. Privileging revelation over reason, the child's intuitive way of acquiring knowledge stands in opposition to science and history, two discourses that push the small things, along with the small people enchanted by them, completely outside of the official epistemological realms. This split reaction to the world – a mixture of wonder and stoicism – represents a coping mechanism of the marginalised subject, a child, a woman, a colonised people, in the face of discursive and physical aggression. In this way, the films provide a platform to interrogate patriarchal and imperial interests.

In her analysis of the child's viewpoint in contemporary British magic realist fiction, Anne C. Hegerfeldt lists the following features of the child's worldview that correspond and enhance the magic realist mode of representation: 'an intrinsic belief in magic and the supernatural', a tendency not to 'distinguish between reality and fantasy', 'an attitude of naïve wonder' at the world, and the unique ability to encounter the Other with ease, in ways inaccessible to adults.[48] Pointing out a similar link between magic realism and the child's manner of perceiving the world, David Danow argues that 'Magical realism's most far-reaching origin is perhaps rooted in the remembrance of childhood, with its attendant wonder at the splendor of the world, whose multitudinous variety of actual and potential manifestations within it engenders extraordinary corresponding flights of the human imagination.'[49] Maggie Ann Bowers recognises the influence of magic realism on children's fiction. Bowers points out the safe and reassuring environment that the combination of magic and realism promotes for the benefit of the child reader. She writes, 'Magical realist children's fiction offers the opportunity for children to explore disruptions in their ordinary world secure in the knowledge that such magic and extraordinariness can be contained.'[50] In his work on the fantastic, a close cousin to magic realism, Tzvetan Todorov catalogues themes such as 'the fragility of the limit between matter and mind' and 'the collapse of the limit between subject and object' as being common to both the infant's world and the category of the fantastic.[51] Finally, Wendy Faris talks about the 'childlike tone of wonder in magical realism'.[52]

Aside from the list of above-mentioned affinities, I would like to add a number of other features that bring together the child's magical worldview and the specifically cinematic mode of figuration. There seems to be a correlation between a child's intense narcissism and a sense of omnipotence, on one hand, and cinema's magnifying quality – the larger-than-life, compensatory reflection of the spectator's self on screen – on the other hand. There is, also, the fluidity that characterises the child's understanding of world relations, a reason for the child's incredible adaptability in the face of change, which is mimicked in the kinetic valence of cinema and its ease in exacting metamorphosis. Furthermore, the child's perception denies death and resides in the immortal, constant present. In her inability to recognise the boundary between life and death, the child compulsively attempts to resurrect what has been pronounced dead, much like cinema that reanimates, in perpetuity, figures long gone. Speaking of how cinema, in its ability to conjure a phantom image, encompasses magical vision as a certain state of the human mind, Edgar Morin explains that 'death–renaissance is a universal of archaic consciousness . . . a universal of oneiric consciousness, a universal of poetic consciousness, a universal of infantile consciousness'.[53] This strong correlation between the child's vision and the cinematic vision is explored and utilised by the filmmakers who work within the magic realist mode. When allowed to coexist in a symbiotic rapport, these two visions yield refreshing and powerful results. The films about to be discussed deliver what Morin would call a magic that, in its image form, is now 'interiorized, nascent, subjectivized'.[54]

The film that constitutes perhaps the most famous early example of East Central European cinematic magic realism focalised through a child's eye is *The Tin Drum* (*Die Blechtrommel*, dir. Volker Schlöndorff, 1979), based on the magic realist novel by Günter Grass. Set between the 1920s and 1940s, the film tells the story of a little boy, Oskar Matzerath (David Bennent), who lives with his family in the war-torn city of Gdańsk (then the Free City of Danzig), where the rise of Nazism is quickly antagonising the multicultural and multilingual community that consists of Germans, Poles, Dutchmen, Jews and Kashubians. As if in revolt against what he witnesses among his adult relatives and friends, Oskar decides never to grow up. With that goal in mind, and to provide his parents with a logical explanation for his absolutely irrational decision, he hurls himself down a flight of stairs and stops growing. It is clear, in both the novel and the film, that Oskar's lack of growth after the fall is due to his omnipotence, which allows him to arrest the workings of time, and not the physiological damage of the head wound that his body suffers during the fall. His further rebellion is carried out through the use of a toy drum, which he impulsively beats on to drown out the hypocritical and contentious language that surrounds him. His telekinetic powers enable him to use his voice (through screaming) to shatter glass and therefore control the adults, who are continuously fighting, cheating or scheming around him.

Historical and private events mingle in the boy's narrative, which challenges the discourse of realism with mystification – the steady reformulation of realist representation enabled by introducing the irreducible and ineffable elements. Through Oskar's child perspective, the viewer sees the war as a banal and boring series of events. His critique of both his bourgeois family and the society engaged in carrying out the projects of World War II and the Holocaust leads him to join a troupe of travelling circus performers. The carnival in which Oskar partakes allows him to distance himself from the grand dramas of history and playfully manipulate the world around him. In this itinerant marginal community, Oskar finds happiness and a semblance of stability. Rather than portraying Oskar's arrested development as a caprice of the infantile mind, the film positions it as a critical strategy. In his review of the film, Vincent Canby argues that the film's narrator, although unchanging in his body, goes through a stunning transformation: 'It's the kind of transformation that makes you believe in the occult.'[55]

The Crows, directed by Polish filmmaker Dorota Kędzierzawska, who has consistently employed child focalisation in her work, stages another scene of youthful rebellion. Like Oskar, Kędzierzawska's protagonist narrator has quite a misanthropic attitude, which contributes to the film's decidedly unnostalgic atmosphere. A nine-year-old girl nicknamed Crow (Karolina Ostrożna) is unhappy in her rather lonely life as a child who is bullied in school and neglected by her mother, who is always too busy working. A girl with a rich imagination, yet forced to endure the emotional void of her situation, she spends her time pretending to be a bird, strolling tirelessly about town, talking to strangers and animals, and looking into the lives of others. During her peregrinations, Crow takes risks and tests the boundaries erected by society to prevent precisely the kind of existence that she has already embarked on, where familial attachments and institutional regimentation have been displaced to the advantage of an unbridled exploration of the object world. Balancing between the opulence of image and the minimal *mise-en-scène*, the filmic text elaborates on Crow's flights of the imagination, at the same time as it works towards a very tangible and accurate portrayal of the girl's modest circumstances. Tracking behind the girl, or on her side, the camera covers a lot of ground, visualising Crow's uninhibited movement and fluid traversal of space. However, this intensified feeling of mobility and navigational freedom is always curbed by the crumbling and dilapidated surfaces of the buildings, alleyways and interior spaces that the girl comes to occupy briefly. There are frequent excursions into nature, but nature is portrayed as untamed and potentially hostile. Still, Crow's exploration of those spaces is visualised as impassioned and enviably uncharted.

There are a few scenes that showcase the girl's magical thinking, while, at the same time, operating well within the coordinates of experiential reality. One of these scenes takes place in a bakery, where the hungry Crow offers a live frog in payment for a loaf of bread. When Crow categorically deposits the frog on the counter, the woman selling the bread yells out in terror and gives up the bread. Although Crow is precocious enough to know that one needs money to buy things, she tests that knowledge against a different value system, where frogs can be bartered for bread and where little girls can go exploring the wide world on their own. The viewer knows that Crow knows that she is stealing the bread, yet the viewer is rooting for her since it is obvious that the system that configures her as a thief is also responsible for the child's experience of neglect and premature loss of innocence. The magical logic is used in the scene in its archaic tradition – as a practice used by humans to circumvent dangers and obstacles on their way to safety and comfort.

Figure 33   Crow spends long hours alone, while her mother is working shifts in
Crows (1994)

At some point, Crow decides to locate a companion for her journey of discovery, a companion who will also serve as a person to love and care for. In one of the houses that she peeks into during her spree about town, she sees a picture of happy family life, where a very young daughter is doted on by two loving parents. Once again, ignoring the conventions of society, Crow decides to take the little girl as her own child, presumably in order to absorb some of the happiness by mere proximity to the loved girl. While concealing herself in front of the happy family's house, she begins to count in the hope of willing the little three-year-old Maleństwo (Kasia Szczepanik) to come outside. This is a perfect example of what Jean Piaget calls 'magic by practice', a feature of child's epistemology that echoes premodern magical thinking. Piaget observes,

> Firstly, there is magic by participation between actions and things. The child performs some action or mental operation (counting, etc.), and believes that this action or operation exercises, through participation, an influence on a particular event he either desires or fears.[56]

The power of Crow's intention is effortlessly realised by the camera, which transports Crow's intention straight into the family's house, from which Maleństwo runs out soon after. The three-year-old spontaneously accepts Crow's declaration that she is her new mother. The two girls, holding hands, set out for a day of adventure.

Figure 34   Kędzierzawska's child protagonists take good care of each other in the absence of the parents in *Crows*.

In what follows the viewer is confronted with a tension between the reality focalised by the children, which is wonderfully free of any constraints or fears, and where miraculously the two little girls carry on without a single external intervention, and the conventional sense of reality, which every so often makes itself painfully felt. The tension becomes difficult to tolerate, in the scene when Maleństwo wets her underwear because Crow ignores her repeated plea to use the bathroom. Also, later in the film, the realist perspective becomes palpable when the two girls are fighting and Maleństwo falls overboard, off an old boat that Crow wants to use to travel the world. The film intensifies this perceptual and epistemological tension by contrasting poetic shots – long shots of the girls' silhouettes safely ensconced in a landscape presented as open and welcoming – with tight, claustrophobic shots, which suggest a vague presence of danger, always lurking in the vicinity of the girls. The viewer cannot decide whether the girls' adventures are carefree or careless. This disconcerting hesitation, which cannot be reduced to any single narrative event, but rather is experienced throughout the film, stems from the state of being arrested between worlds and worldviews, a quintessential quality of magic realism. Interestingly, the film begins and ends with an abstract image that encapsulates this in-betweenness, experienced as an ongoing state of transition. In this shot, the camera focuses on the grey sky and Crow, who is jumping up and down, flapping her arms and playfully pretending to be a bird. As she jumps up, Crow appears within the frame, her dynamic body erupting upwards into the centre of the screen, only to disappear into the off-screen space below as her body suddenly drops down with the force of gravity. This movement of soaring and coming down replicates the rhythm of magic realism's dual interest in enchantment and the concomitant trivialisation of reality.

The similar clash of worlds and worldviews receives a gendered inflection in Jan Jakub Kolski's *Jasminum*. Without the consistency and commitment of Dorota Kędzierzawska, who has only made films about children and narrated from the child's point of view, Kolski uses child focalisers in some of his films. As discussed earlier, in *The History of Cinema in Popielawy*, the boy narrator, Staszek, tells the intriguing story of his best friend's ancestors, who invented the first 'kino-machine' in the world. The filmmaker's most recent film, *Venice* (*Wenecja*, 2010), features an eleven-year-old narrator, Marek, who is trying to cope with the horrors of World War II by inventing a simulacrum of Venice on his parents' flooded country estate. In *Jasminum*, Kolski's cinematic response to Patrick Süskind's 1985 novel *Perfume: The Story of the Murderer*, it is the five-year-old Gienia (Wiktoria Gąsiewska), who arrives at the ancient monastery with her mother Natasza (Grażyna Błęcka-Kolska), an art conservator, who has been commissioned to restore an altar painting at the monks' church. The mother and the daughter will spend a substantial amount of time living and interacting with the brothers, which is a source of anxiety for the Prior and a source of great anticipation for the child. Word has it that the monastery is home to three monks who have taken vows of silence and who live in complete isolation within their dark cells. Quite mysteriously, these three monks emit the smell of fruit trees, a phenomenon known as the 'odour of sanctity' within Christian hagiographies. One of the three sweet-smelling monks is anticipated to become a saint in the near future. Life at the monastery is guided by strict rules of asceticism and solitary confinement. The order and harmony in which the monks live is substantially revised upon Gienia's arrival. The girl gifts the monks with some of the most profane gestures and ideas they have ever encountered. She expresses her wishes, opinions and questions with deadpan delivery and expects the same from her hosts. In one of the first scenes, which depicts the very moment of the female visitors' entry into the monks' world, Gienia unceremoniously announces that she is hungry. The Prior calls on Brother Sanitas (Janusz Gajos), who is the cook in residence, to take care of the hungry child, but Brother Sanitas is so flabbergasted at the sight of a little girl that he turns to flee. It takes the Prior's assurance that the little person is simply a girl who needs some food for Brother Sanitas to conquer his apprehension.

Back in the kitchen, Gienia instructs Brother Sanitas on the thickness of the slice of bread and the proper layer of butter that she requires, making him cut the bread three times before she deems it acceptable. After she has had her snack, she shows the brother how to burp, an act that is announced

Figure 35   Gienia's kitchen conversations with the nurturing Brother Sanitas in
Kolski's *Jasminum* (2006).

and performed as if it was an amazing trick of magic. From then on, the two
become best friends, whose interactions, many of them involving feeding
themselves and the monastery's livestock, provide the film's most enchanting
moments of everyday routine, more magical than the host of other mysterious
occurrences within the narrative. Of those there are many: there are ducks
levitating in a monk's cell, there is a saint materialising to complain about his
statue being soiled with bird shit, and there is a ghost of a lovelorn girl, whose
affair with a monk has troubled the collective memory of the community for
four hundred years.

These events are all part of the story that is narrated by Gienia, often in an
off-screen voice-over. Filtered through her child perspective and recounted in
her unruffled voice, these otherwise quite unbelievable phenomena become
rather commonplace as a result. And if one were surprised at any point within
her story, Gienia would undoubtedly reprimand the viewer, the same way
she reprimands Brother Sanitas whenever he wants explanations for Gienia's
statements or requests. Gienia's knowledge and practical knowhow seem to
exceed that of anyone else at the monastery, including her own mother, who is
both an artist and a scientist. The girl's omniscience allows her to solve quite
a few earthly intrigues that take place in and around the monastery, as well
as to illuminate a saint on the basic facts of life. When, one day, Saint Roch
(Franciszek Pieczka) appears before Brother Sanitas, it is Gienia who explains

to him that Brother Sanitas's daily ritual of picking up pigs and holding them up in his arms is not a crazy whim. Because of their short necks, Gienia informs the puzzled saint, the pigs cannot turn their heads up to see the sky. The benevolent monk spares no effort to help the animals enjoy the small pleasures in life. The kitchen conversations that Gienia holds with Brother Sanitas, exemplified by one in which they discuss why ducks shit so much, are juxtaposed with the lofty conversations that her mother conducts with the Prior, Father Kleofas (Adam Ferency). Those latter conversations, sprinkled with Latin and chemistry jargon, are about the old competition between science and religion, knowledge and belief, sex and love. They take place in the quiet, dark space of the Prior's study or in the hall where Natasza is restoring the altar painting. Those spaces are filled with books, religious art and antique furniture to evoke the sacred register, which is obviously lost on our five-year-old narrator and therefore displaced for the viewer.

As is the case in other films by Kolski, the most significant communication takes place at the messy kitchen table. At this domestic altar, the slice of bread and butter is dispensed to Gienia as profane Eucharist. The girl's presence at the monastery challenges its sacred order from the perspective of a child and a female. While her mother contests the head of the monastery in a somewhat futile debate, during which various discourses compete for the viewer's attention, Gienia imparts her influence on the monks (and the viewer) through being disarmingly honest and direct in her approach to people and things. She circumvents religious doctrine and authority by being patently pragmatic and inquisitive. Gienia's simple philosophy of life is summed up in the proverb, 'One good turn deserves another.' She repays Brother Sanitas's kindness with a pair of new shoes that she buys with the help of her mother. Much like Brother Sanitas, who is observant enough to provide everybody with the necessary creature comforts, Gienia is perceptive enough to see that the caregiver needs care: his shoes are falling apart. She is also the only person to find out that Brother Sanitas, who has been relegated by Father Kleofas to perform the menial tasks in the monastery's kitchen, is more erudite than any other brother and his knowledge of Latin exceeds that of the Prior. Subtly, then, the film posits Gienia and the motherly Brother Sanitas as two figures whose wisdom confronts the institution of patriarchy.

The film ends with Brother Sanitas waking up to see the bleeding stigmata on his hands. He is quite alarmed at this discovery and asks God for some explanation as to why he has been singled out in this way. Concerned about his daily chores, the monk looks at his bleeding hands and wonders how to start the fire in the kitchen stove that very morning. At this point, we hear Gienia in voice-over clarifying the situation as to why Brother Sanitas gets to be the saint and not the pious Brother Birdcherry (Krzysztof Pieczyński), whom everyone else expected to be chosen for that honour. There is no doubt in the viewer's

Figure 36   Patriarchy is at Gienia's service when monks break their contemplation of God to plait her hair.

mind that Gienia had something to do with this decision, and in turn that decision was influenced by the perfect thickness of the slice of bread that Brother Sanitas learned to cut for her. Brother Sanitas's domestic work and nurturing skills are rewarded with sainthood, yet the film does not fail to express its scepticism as to this dubious honour for someone who, like Brother Sanitas, enjoys earthly affairs, along with the most mundane minutiae of life. It is quite telling to find out, towards the end of Gienia's narration, why Brother Birdcherry might have been denied sainthood. It turns out that he used to be romantically involved with Natasza. Instead of marrying her, however, he sought solitude and the path of enlightenment at the monastery. Thus, the story's moral rests in the difference between the two monks and their attachments to others. The man who is compassionate and knows how to love and care for others in the domestic sphere is rewarded over the man who refuses love, instead devoting himself to strict monastic practice and theological study.

While I would argue that most of the magic realist films question the patriarchal politics of gender, there are also films that offer a rather conservative vision of gender dynamics. One such film, which uses a child character to teach the benefits of patriarchy – in this case, the institution of the nuclear family – is Andrzej Jakimowski's *Tricks*. The film is set in contemporary Poland, at the heart of the mining district of Silesia, a region once prosperous but today

Figure 37   Ghost of a saint in conversation with ducks in *Jasminum*.

largely struggling to survive. The minimalist plot, which spans only a few Summer days, takes place in a provincial town, where people lead sleepy lives not because they choose to do so, but because they have been made redundant by the collapsed mining industry. The lack of commerce, the empty streets and the squalid building facades function as subtle reminders of the complicated history of the place and the ongoing crisis. This sobering setting stands in semiotic tension with Adam Bajerski's seductive, sun-saturated photography, which introduces a note of warm buoyancy into the otherwise very honest depiction of a disadvantaged post-Soviet community. The viewer is not confronted with the stereotypical darkness of the East Central European periphery. The filmmaker's vision, although quite austere, is also strategically enhanced to show a source of hope identified in the repaired family structure and healed father–son relationship. Jakimowski is not afraid to show the poverty, aimlessness and isolation experienced by the inhabitants of his fictitious town. His choice of costumes, props and locations contributes to an almost neo-realist sense of authenticity. It is therefore very surprising that Jakimowski manages to lift his characters – two young siblings – out of their difficult material circumstances and place them in a magic realist narrative, where they shape their unlucky lives with the use of elaborate rituals that are designed to tempt fate to their advantage. The surprise diminishes as the narrative progresses and it becomes evident that the filmmaker is pushing the masculinist ideal of the penitent father returning to his family and restoring the balance, thus lifting the family (and, by extension, the town) out of its moral and economic crisis.

The premise of Jakimowski's film is rather minimal. The eight-year-old Stefek (Damian Ul) and his teenage sister Elka (Ewelina Walendziak) live with their mother, who works long hours at a grocery store to support her family. The mother is so overworked that we barely see her in the film. She shows up in three very brief scenes. The children's father abandoned them when Stefek was born and left town in search of a more comfortable life with another woman. Stefek is very attached to his sister, who becomes a substitute mother and father for the boy. Sentimental in tone, the film is largely focused on the tender relationship between the siblings, their daily routines and the games they play together to kill time. Partly autobiographical, *Tricks* is dedicated to the director's own older sister, who, as the dedication suggests, used to make him sit on top of the wardrobe to keep him out of trouble. The siblings' attempt to persuade the father to give their family a second chance becomes the motivation for the action in the film. Slowly but surely, the balance tilts towards the father, whose return implies the happiness and stability that Stefek misses and, as the film suggests, needs, as a boy stepping into adolescence. The matriarchal, substitute family structure that Stefek has known for most of his childhood life is disclosed in the course of the film as necessarily pathological.

An attractive and independent girl on the cusp of womanhood, Elka is trying very hard not to share her mother's miserable lot in life. She is diligently learning Italian and takes motivational courses to be able to land a secretarial job at a newly opened, local branch of a big Italian corporation. When she is not studying, Elka is washing dishes at a beer garden and taking care of Stefek. Her boyfriend Jerzy (Rafał Guźniczak) is a car mechanic, who rides a motorbike. Frequently, we see the three characters, in different combinations, riding the motorbike in pleasurable abandon. Lacking in other action, perhaps even idling at times, the film creates a sense of comfort whenever showing Stefek engage with Jerzy in 'manly' activities, whether it is racing a train on the motorbike, fixing an old car or flirting with Violka (Joanna Liszowska), the sexy neighbourhood strumpet. In these scenes, Jerzy's character stands in for the missing father and reminds the viewer of the 'proper', man-modelled family that little Stefek deserves. If it were not for the film's thinly veiled chauvinist agenda, expressed in the promotional tagline 'Film about cars, women, and love', it would be very easy for the viewer to mistake the scenes featuring the boys' adventures as the filmmaker's anti-capitalist manifesto about the need to enjoy the simple pleasures in life in the face of economic disadvantage. To be fair to Jakimowski, there are plenty of other scenes in his film (outside of the heterosexist assignment) that do carry that very message. Whether it is enjoying a slice of watermelon, admiring the sight of the homing pigeons soaring high in

Figure 38   Left to his own devices, Stefek watches trains and awaits his father's return in Jakimowski's *Tricks* (2007).

the sky, or watching trains, Stefek is frequently shown in the act of genuinely admiring what he can observe and experience around him. He is a child, and as such, he has much to teach the adults around him and the viewer. In this way, Jakimowski issues an unmistaken statement about the quality of life that is affordable to all, even those in economically depressed areas with the highest unemployment rates, simply through developing a certain level of sensitivity.

While Stefek does not have Elka's ambition or work ethic (he is seen wandering about town without a specific errand to direct him), he is busy trying to understand how human relationships work and how one can influence one's surroundings. His understanding is enhanced by Elka's set of 'tricks', which are the mental machinations, akin to what Piaget identified in child psychology as 'magic by practice', that she successfully employs in her negotiations with reality. Thanks to Jakimowski's clever storytelling, the viewer never finds out whether Elka's tricks are indeed acts of conjuring or simple coincidences, leading to that moment of hesitation between magic and reality that characterises the best of magic realist narratives. This epistemological nuance contributes to the film's message that it never hurts to be earnest in trying to see one's intentions realised. Conjuring reality must begin with heartened anticipation, and the film delivers plenty of it. It is this very message that pushes the film from the realm of existential neo-realism to magic realism, even if at the expense of the female characters in the story.

As someone who has mastered magical thinking, Elka teaches her brother, a receptive student, how to re-order playfully the circumstances of their immediate reality. It is significant that Elka performs her small miracles to have fun, rather than to reshape reality to benefit from it. As someone who is entering adulthood, Elka knows that her intentions should be modest and based on the rules of probability if she is to avoid disappointment. Her philosophy involves bribing destiny with a small sacrifice and then allowing things simply to happen, all the time trusting in the efficacy of the sacrifice and the wisdom of destiny, although not without first accurately assessing the potential outcome. She shows Stefek how her magic works by remotely depositing a piece of rubbish, a hamburger wrapper, in a dustbin. The sacrifice this time is a piece of burger that Elka leaves inside the crumpled paper, which she simply places on the ground. With the help of a dog, a woman with an infant, and a homeless person, the wrapper eventually makes it to the dustbin. Elka's intention materialises, without much effort, albeit without any meaningful change in her reality. Stefek quickly becomes obsessed with his sister's tricks and begins to perform his own bargains with fate. Unlike his sister, however, his determination has no limits and the risks he takes are very real (at some point he faces off with an oncoming train). Also, his tricks concern the thing that matters most to Stefek: the happiness of what he (as the alter ego of the filmmaker) sees as his incomplete, damaged family. This happiness can apparently only be secured by restoring Stefek's father as the head of the family. Elka's carefully calculated tricks are those of a stage magician. Stefek's impassioned rituals resemble shamanic practice that is deployed in the service of the patriarchy.

One day, Stefek's attention is drawn by a commuter at the town's train station. The well-dressed man spends a few minutes waiting on the platform of Stefek's provincial town, as he changes trains on his daily trip to the big city, identified later as Wrocław. In this man, Stefek recognises his father (Tomasz Sapryk) and decides to redirect his journey, so that the father may end up in the grocery shop with the mother, hopefully in a reconciliatory conversation. Single-mindedly hoping for his parents' reunion, the boy devises an elaborate magical ritual, which involves perfect timing and carefully selected magical objects. He places coins of very specific denominations on the railway track to regulate arrivals and departures, so that the father does not make his usual smooth transfer between trains. After the father misses his connection and decides to wait for the next one in a bar, Stefek leaves his tin soldiers as 'guards' to watch over the father, as he runs across town to arrange for his next trick that will lead the father away from the train station and closer to the mother. Jakimowski uses parallel editing to show the viewer the intricate web of connections that Stefek choreographs in order to manipulate the father's slow but steady progression towards the grocery store. In cross-cut scenes, we see all four family members converging on Stefek's intended site

Figure 39   As substitute parents, Elka and Jerzy take Stefek on rides about town in *Tricks*.

for the reunion. Both Elka and Jerzy are in on Stefek's plan and they implicitly agree to help the boy. The film intimates a happy ending for Stefek. His father manages to miss several trains and fails to leave the town. He acknowledges his son in a touching finale. Without any definite resolution – the scene of parental reunion is never visualised – the viewer is left with a sense of heartened anticipation, arrested in the state of mind that mimics what Stefek must have felt as he advanced his magic.

Tricks, much like Jakimowski's first feature, *Squint Your Eyes* (*Zmruż oczy*, 2002), explores the child's unhappiness with the malfunctioning family, but also, indirectly, a certain dissatisfaction with the state of society, where both the rich and the poor are so busy making a living that they forget about their children. In *Squint Your Eyes*, a young girl, Mała (Ola Prószyńska), runs away from her *nouveau riche* parents, who are too obsessed with their careers and social ambitions in the city to care for her in ways other than material. The girl ends up on a rundown farm, whose caretaker, ex-teacher Jasiek (Zbigniew Zamachowski), has also opted out of busy city life and is searching for alternatives. Stefek is similarly unhappy with the family he has and spends most of his time in the streets on his own. Interestingly, Jakimowski points to the post-Soviet economic transitions as somehow related to the family crisis. In his first film, it is the parents, doing extremely well within the nascent capitalist economy, that become responsible for their child's escape into a semi-imaginary world where squinting one's eyes is a metaphor for the imaginative refurbishment of reality. In Stefek's case, his mother struggles to make ends

Figure 40   In *Squint Your Eyes* (2002), Jakimowski celebrates life in the periphery. Jasiek and Mała enjoy each other's company, while playing a game of cards.

meet in the impoverished provincial town, while his father leaves the family to become a businessman in the city. Both parents are essentially absent in the boy's life. While the mother has not abandoned her children, her long shifts at the shop make her unavailable for Stefek. In Jakimowski's films, the father is temporarily substituted with a decidedly non-patriarchal figure. In *Squint Your Eyes* it is a burnt-out teacher, who spends his days playing cards, drinking and philosophising. In *Tricks*, a teenage girl takes on the demanding parental role. In contrast with the absentee fathers, both substitute figures become true friends and mentors to Mała and Stefek. Instead of material stability, they provide the children with spiritual and psychological skills that enable them to feel confident in what is presented as a terribly hostile world. Disappointingly, both of Jakimowski's films work strenuously to eventually reinstate the classic patriarchal family featuring the breadwinner father at its helm as the ultimate cure for the child's discontent with the world. In *Tricks*, the father–son reunion comes at the expense of Elka's advancement in life. It is suggested that the father stays in town and decides to meet his son thanks to Elka, who performs one of her amazing 'tricks'. She decides to miss her job interview at the Italian corporation, which she has been working for a long time to secure, in order to help Stefek guide the father towards the mother. This female sacrifice of a professional career for the good of the collective is well aligned with the Romantic ethos of *Matka Polka* as the self-sacrificing female, as well as the Catholic ideal of altruistic Virgin Mary.[57]

To conclude this chapter, I would like briefly to discuss Emir Kusturica's film *Time of the Gypsies* as a text where carnivalesque sensibility blends in with magic realism and intertextuality, in a narrative focalised by a child, which celebrates the matriarch over the atrophied patriarch. The film presents a contemporary rite-of-passage story centred on the life of Perhan (Davor Dujmović), a young, somewhat awkward boy who lives with his younger sister, gambling uncle and shaman grandmother in a Roma village on the out-skirts of Sarajevo. The setting is emphatically peripheral; the establishing shot introduces the viewer to a squalid settlement drowning in mud, barely affected by modern technology. In the next couple of deep focus shots, the camera juxtaposes the foregrounded Gypsy village, ensconced in its own 'slow' Gypsy time, with modern-day Sarajevo, visible in the distance, where high-rise blocks of flats and motorway traffic speak of a very different time register. Perhan helps his grandmother Hatidža (Ljubica Adžović) to run the lime kiln, making and selling quicklime. When he is not busy at the kiln, Perhan cares for his sick sister Danira (Elvira Sali), whose deformed leg is a source of chronic pain and much worry for the family. The children are orphans. Their father was a Slovenian soldier passing through town and their mother died in labour. Uncle Merdžan (Husnija Hasimović), who shares the house with his mother and his deceased sister's children, spends his days drinking and gambling.

The main plot of the film concerns Perhan's transition into adulthood. He falls in love with beautiful Azra (Sinolička Trpkova) and, in order to win her hand in marriage, has to make a small fortune. Azra's mother, who repeatedly throws the young suitor out of her house, considers Perhan to be a good-for-nothing bastard with no future. It just so happens that Perhan's godfa-ther, Ahmed (Bora Todorović), known in the village as the Sheik and whose money-making skills are admired by all, manipulates Perhan into joining him in a crime racket that he runs in Milan, Italy. Once Perhan finds out that Ahmed traffics children and forces them into begging and prostitution, he wants to extricate himself from the deal. Ahmed has different plans for the boy. After agreeing to provide Perhan's sister with the best medical treatment in Ljubljana, as a favour to repay Hatidža for healing his infant son, Ahmed backs down on his promise and tells Perhan that he must work for him if he wants the sister to continue receiving her treatment. Perhan is quickly initiated into a life of crime. With time, he masters his trade and takes over the business. When he finally returns to the village to marry Azra, she is found to be preg-nant, as well as rumoured to have cheated on Perhan with his uncle Merdžan. After Azra repeatedly states her undying love, Perhan decides to marry her but refuses to acknowledge her child as his own. The baby, who eventually turns out to be Perhan's son, is sold into white slavery. Like Perhan's own mother, Azra dies in labour. In the film's final scenes, Perhan discovers that his sister never received the medical help promised by Ahmed. Instead she was forced to beg on the streets, along with other kids that Ahmed trafficked. In an act of revenge, Perhan kills Ahmed with a fork, using telekinesis to lodge the utensil in the Sheik's neck. Ahmed's new bride, in turn, shoots Perhan to avenge her husband. The film ends with the scene of Perhan's funeral. The story of the young man's rite of passage is cut short. The grandmother is there to bury the dead and console the surviving. As Andrew Horton comments in his appraisal of gender dynamics within the film, Kusturica's 'women survive and grieve while men pass out, leave, disappear, die,' thus pointing to the alternative vision of gender relations in a non-patriarchal culture.[58]

As in any of Kusturica's cinematic communities, life in the village is imbued with carnival excess: people fight, dance, love, drink and eat with abandon. Weddings and funerals, both celebrated with equal measures of joy and sadness, punctuate the otherwise dreary life of poverty. In a text that evokes and simultaneously suppresses the exoticising / idealising gaze, Kusturica carefully negotiates the existing stereotypes surrounding the most marginalised people of Europe. The result is a film that occupies the precarious space between horror and farce. Kusturica's Gypsies are both victims and victimisers, paupers and rich crime bosses. Their children are vulnerable innocents and precocious 'old souls'. Among them, there are sly tricksters, who cheat at cards and lift a house off its foundations in an angry fit, and venerable shamans, who use black magic to save lives. In their spare time, Kusturica's Gypsies enjoy a Charlie Chaplin impersonation or an ancient pagan tale about the origins of Mother Earth. The village is the space where the utter squalor of miserable material conditions stands in dramatic contrast with the extravagant demeanour of every character. As Goran Gocić persuasively argues, 'even the definitely "primitive" aspects of Balkan lifestyle and its apparent "backwardness" in Kusturica's work are used to their advantage and acquire an inexplicable, charismatic charm'.[59]

Time of the Gypsies is saturated with a magic realist view of the world, where magical occurrences are well embedded in the daily routines of the characters and are accepted as commonplace by those who experience them. As mentioned before, Hatidža is the local witch doctor. At some point, she is summoned by the mafia boss to help save his choking son. Using her hands and the blood extracted from the boy's hand, she performs a healing ritual that brings back the young life. Having inherited his grandmother's supernatural powers, Perhan has the gift of telekinesis. We see him move a tin can across a bench, to the amusement of his girlfriend and the horror of a drunk, who runs away, believing that the can is possessed. Perhan can also communicate with animals, especially the pet turkey that he receives from his grandmother as a token of appreciation.[60] Perhan and his sister see their mother's apparition, who is guiding them on their way out of the village. During childbirth, Azra levitates with Perhan's help, defying pain and the earthly burden of labour. Typical of many magic realist narratives, Kusturica's film refuses to fetishise the supernatural. Magic can be a life-giving force or a medium to charm a turkey into an absurd dance.

Apart from these supernatural occurrences, happening well within the bounds of everyday reality, the film offers poetic dream sequences, which actually convey some key plot events, thus suggesting a fluid relationship between dream and reality. This hybrid storytelling strategy further complicates the sense of the real in the already excessive 'rogue' narrative. One of the most spectacular of the dream sequences depicts the riverside festivities on the eve of St George's Day (celebrated by Orthodox Christians and Muslims of different ethnicities across the Balkans in place of pagan Spring rites). Combining images rich in fire and water symbolism with Goran Bregović's sorrowful version of the famous Gypsy folk song entitled 'Ederlezi' (the Roma word for Spring festival), Kusturica created a scene that functions independently within the text as a cinematic ritual, on a par with the sacramental spectacle of Greek tragedy. Filmed at dusk, using crane and deep-focus shots, the series of atmospheric scenes depict a multigenerational crowd of people, eating, drinking, singing and performing ritual ablutions in the river. In the midst of the festivities, Perhan flies over the river, then slowly descends to find Azra and make love to her in a boat that meanders in close proximity to all the revellers. Perhan's bird's-eye view becomes the viewer's perspective. With his descent, Kusturica's camera merges the view from above with one from within, pulling the viewer into the very centre of the crowd and affording the cathartic experience of plunging from the heights of the sacred into the midst of the profane.

This sudden shift from the heavenly to the earthly is exemplary of the carnivalesque sensibility theorised by Bakhtin as an ideologically informed strategy to promote duality and ambiguity in the manner of viewing and representing the world. Kusturica's volatile camera in this scene (and many other scenes throughout the film) is used to contest the stasis of represented reality. The scene begins with a portrait of a majestic re-enactment of the ritual of baptism, an act of admission into the Christian Church, yet it very quickly morphs into a pagan fertility rite. Through a clever use of cross-cutting, Kusturica erodes the highly choreographed vision of an ecclesiastical feast with vignettes of adolescent sex and young children frolicking on the river bank. If there were a note of sanctimonious gravity evoked by the presence of a floating cross (upon closer inspection, one sees the burning straw effigy of Winter in place of the Christian symbol), it disappears in the course of the scene, which pairs the setting of the cleansing and eternally renewing river with the intimate encounter of the young, desiring bodies. In one especially stunning frame, the camera looks down on to the nude Perhan and Azra lying closely side by side in a semi-embrace, with the outline of the boat creating a new visual boundary for their conjoined body. This new hybrid body forms what Bakhtin called the 'double body', which for him represented the split, anti-dogmatic figure, always exceeding any singular authority or single truth. Furthermore, for Bakhtin, the double body symbolises the 'unfinished metamorphosis of death and renewal'.[61] The double body elicits both sadness and happiness as it simultaneously represents death and conception, past and future. Perhan and Azra's entwined bodies form an entity, which in Bakhtin's words, 'retains the parts in which one link joins the other, in which the life of one body is born from the death of the preceding, older one'.[62] Kusturica signals ambivalence about life's coming and passing by bringing into the scene Perhan's grandmother. A jolly woman by nature, Hatidža is shown here standing on the river bank and crying copiously, witnessing her grandson's rite of passage.

Dynamic transfers between the sacred and the profane, central and peripheral, are also detectable in the manner in which Kusturica's film engages with other films in a rich intertextual dialogue, taking us back to the Bakhtinian notion of textual hybridity or polyphony. As critics have noted, with *Time of the Gypsies* Kusturica intensified his use of intertextuality. In this film, he references over forty different works belonging to a variety of cinematic traditions, both Western and Eastern. Out of those forty references, the most recognisable ones take the viewer (depending of his / her level of cinematic literacy) back to Coppola's *Godfather* films, Charlie Chaplin, John Ford, Bruce Lee, Orson Welles, Jacques Tati, Federico Fellini, Luis Buñuel, Andrei Tarkovsky, Andrzej Wajda, Jiři Menzel, Aleksandar Petrović, Rajko Grlić and Živojin Pavlović. While most viewers will decode the references from the top of the list, simply because they point to filmmakers from the West's cinematic canon, only those with a truly transnational cinematic knowledge will pick up on Kusturica's local and regional references. After discussing the international provenance of Kusturica's intertextual practice and providing the most comprehensive list of the filmmaker's influences to date, Dina Iordanova observes,

> One thing is certain – Kusturica only makes-over the work of recognized cinematic masters. Thus, he demonstrates an excellent background in cinema, in fact better than that of many film scholars who remain compartmentalized and rarely look beyond their narrow research field.[63]

Similarly, Andrew Horton focuses on Kusturica's penchant for referencing the prominent names in filmmaking. He argues,

> Kusturica wishes to celebrate particular masters of the cinema and their works – Yugoslav, Hollywood, and European – but he is also necessarily making it clear that he wishes to be authenticated and included in their company, in the family of national (Yugoslav) and world cinema.[64]

Judging from the many controversial, often self-aggrandising, interview statements by Kusturica, the ambition to be included in the cinematic canon might well be behind the filmmaker's kaleidoscopic use of cinematic references.

However, there might also be a possibility of an altogether different motivation for Kusturica's energetic and polymorphous referentiality, which Goran Gocić describes as 'plundering' and Andrew Horton as 'stealing'.[65] Since Kusturica has always fashioned himself as a deeply political director, more than an aesthete or an intellectual, I would like to consider his use of intertextuality as a political strategy, used to renegotiate the relationship of peripheral cinema to the mainstream Hollywood / Western European centre. I see this political strategy operating in two major ways. Firstly, Kusturica constructs peripheral, or to use Bakhtin's category, profane versions of the scenes, characters and locales borrowed from the sacred vaults of the history of Western cinema, appropriating the canonical texts, often to disclose their profane origins that have been 'bleached' out of cultural history. For example, when uncle Merdžan impersonates Charlie Chaplin for the amusement of his niece and nephew, his performance points to Chaplin's silenced Gypsy ancestry.[66] When Kusturica makes Ahmed, the Gypsy Sheik, into the Balkan version of Coppola's Godfather, who is running his shady operations in the civilised city of Milan, he is commenting on the overlooked history of anti-Italian prejudice in the United States that has been repressed in the course of mythologising the figure of the mobster as part of American self-made identity. Secondly, Kusturica's numerous references to Eastern (mostly Russian and East Central European) cinema empower the local viewer to engage with his films fully, allowing for that level of engagement to become the exclusive right and privilege of the viewer fluent in both global and vernacular cultures. Horton uses David Bordwell's concept of narrative 'communicativeness' to praise Kusturica's films for using Hollywood references to 'translate' his Yugoslav story for the average Western viewer. He also recognises that Kusturica, in using references to local and regional cinemas, 'has purposely built in a "home culture" element that speaks to those who know, without detracting from the pleasure and involvement the film has set up for the non-Yugoslav audiences'.[67] While I agree with Horton that *Time of the Gypsies* offers a rich and satisfying cinematic experience to diverse audiences, there is perhaps a need to question why and how certain cinematic references become global and others remain vernacular in a world where transnational transfers of culture and capital follow the old and the new imperial interests.

NOTES

1. Jean Epstein, 'On Certain Characteristics of *Photogénie*', in Philip Simpson, Andrew Utterson and K. J. Shepherson (eds), *Film Theory Vol. I* (London and New York: Routledge, 2004), pp. 54–5.
2. Jean Epstein, '*Photogénie* and the Imponderable', in Timothy Corrigan, Patricia White and Meta Mazaj (eds), *Critical Visions in Film Theory* (Boston and New York: Bedford / St Martin's, 2011), pp. 254–5.

3. André Bazin, 'The Ontology of the Photographic Image', *Film Quarterly*, 13:4, Summer 1960, pp. 4–9.
4. Walter Benjamin, 'The Work of Art in the Age of Mechanical Reproduction', in Hannah Arendt (ed.), *Illuminations*, trans. Harry Zohn (New York: Schocken, 1969), p. 233.
5. Siegfried Kracauer, *Theory of Film: The Redemption of Physical Reality* (Princeton: Princeton University Press, 1997), pp. 71–2.
6. Maurice Merleau-Ponty, *Sense and Non-Sense*, trans. Hubert Dreyfus and Patricia Allen Dreyfus (Evanston, IL: Northwestern University Press, 1964), p. 58.
7. Roland Barthes, 'The Reality Effect,' *The Rustle of Language*, trans. Richard Howard (Oxford: Blackwell, 1986), pp. 141–8. In this essay, Barthes discusses the referential illusion of realism.
8. Béla Balázs, *Theory of the Film: Character and Growth of a New Art*, trans. Edith Bone (New York: Arno, 1972), p. 55.
9. Theodor Adorno and Max Horkheimer, 'The Culture Industry: Enlightenment as Mass Deception', *Dialectic of Enlightenment: Philosophical Fragments* (Stanford: Stanford University Press, 2002), p. 99.
10. Ibid. p. 100.
11. *Ghost Dance*, film, directed by Ken McMullen, 1983.
12. See Louis-Georges Schwartz, 'Cinema and the Meaning of "Life"', *Discourse*, 28:2 and 3, Spring and Fall 2006, pp. 7–27, and Alan Cholodenko, 'The Crypt: The Haunted House of Cinema', *Cultural Studies Review*, 10:2, September 2004, pp. 99–113.
13. Anne C. Hegerfeldt, *Lies that Tell the Truth: Magic Realism Seen through Contemporary Fiction from Britain* (Amsterdam and New York: Rodopi, 2005), p. 54.
14. For a comprehensive survey of his work on sign classification, see Charles Sanders Peirce, in James Hoopes (ed.), *Peirce on Signs: Writings on Semiotic* (Chapel Hill: University of North Carolina Press, 1991).
15. Barbara Klonowska, 'Far Away From the Present: Magical Realism in Polish Film', *Studies in Eastern European Cinema*, 1:2, pp. 193–4 (pp. 183–96 inclusive).
16. Maggie Ann Bowers, *Magic(al) Realism* (London and New York: Routledge, 2004), p. 21.
17. Robert Stam, *Literature Through Film: Realism, Magic, and the Art of Adaptation* (Malden, MA, and Oxford: Blackwell, 2005), p. 340.
18. Ibid. p. 341.
19. See Dan North, 'Magic and Illusion in Early Cinema', *Studies in French Cinema*, 1:2, 2001.
20. Tom Gunning explores the non-narrative tendency in early cinema that privileged the act of showing itself. He conceptualises the 'cinema of attractions' as a cinema of exhibition, where an image, through its new, cinematic guise, constitutes an attraction in itself. Tom Gunning, 'The Cinema of Attraction: Early Film, its Spectator, and the Avant-Garde', in Robert Stam and Toby Miller (eds), *Film and Theory: An Anthology* (Oxford: Blackwell, 2000), pp. 229–35.
21. Anne C. Hegerfeldt, *Lies that Tell the Truth*, p. 132.
22. David K. Danow, *The Spirit of Carnival: Magical Realism and the Grotesque* (Lexington: University Press of Kentucky, 1995), p. 5.
23. For his theory of the carnivalesque, see Mikhail Bakhtin, *Rabelais and his World* (Bloomington: Indiana University Press, 1984).
24. Marta Dynel, *The Pragmatics of Humour Across Discourse Domains* (Amsterdam and Philadelphia: John Benjamins, 2011).

25. Padraic Kenney, *A Carnival of Revolution: Central Europe 1989* (Princeton: Princeton University Press, 2003).
26. Denise Roman, *Fragmented Identities: Popular Culture, Sex, and Everyday Life in Postcommunist Romania* (Lanham, MD: Lexington, 2003), p. 55.
27. Anikó Imre, *Identity Games: Globalization and the Transformation of Media Cultures in the New Europe* (Cambridge, MA: MIT Press, 2009), p. 205.
28. Mikhail Bakhtin, 'Discourse in the Novel', in Michael Holquist (ed.), *The Dialogic Imagination*, trans. Caryl Emerson and Michael Holquist (Austin: University of Texas Press, 1981).
29. Wendy Faris, *Ordinary Enchantments: Magical Realism and the Remystification of Narrative* (Nashville: Vanderbilt University Press, 2004), pp. 172–3.
30. Anikó Imre, 'Twin Pleasures of Feminism: Orlando Meets *My Twentieth Century*', *Camera Obscura* 54, 18:3, 2003, p. 199.
31. Lucy Fischer, 'The Lady Vanishes: Women, Magic, and the Movies', in John L. Fell (ed.), *Film Before Griffith* (Berkeley and Los Angeles: University of California Press, 1983), p. 341 (pp. 339–54 inclusive).
32. Katarzyna Marciniak, *Alienhood: Citizenship, Exile, and the Logic of Difference* (Minneapolis: University of Minnesota Press, 2006), p. xiv.
33. This reflects the curious gender divide in the post-Communist assessments of the gains and losses of the communist experiment. In casual conversations with members of the postwar generation across East Central Europe, I find women to be more forgiving of the system's ills and more appreciative of the institutions of social support that allowed many of them easy access to education, workplace, childcare and free healthcare services, while the system was still functioning.
34. Catherine Portuges, 'Central European Twins: Psychoanalysis and Cinema in Ildikó Enyedi's *My Twentieth Century*', *Psychoanalytic Inquiry*, 27:4, 2007, p. 530.
35. Anikó Imre, 'Twin Pleasures of Feminism', p. 201.
36. Wendy Faris, *Ordinary Enchantments*, p. 128.
37. Anikó Imre, 'Twin Pleasures of Feminism', p. 191.
38. Katherine Gyékényesi Gatto, 'Her *Twentieth Century*: The Postmodern Cinema of Ildikó Enyedi', *Hungarian Studies Review*, vol. 26, Spring / Fall 1999, at http://epa.oszk.hu/00000/00010/00002/gyekenyesi.htm (accessed 12 September 2011).
39. Wendy Faris, *Ordinary Enchantments*, p. 132.
40. Steven Shaviro, 'My Twentieth Century', *The Pinocchio Theory*, at http://www.shaviro.com/Blog/?p=566 (accessed 21 August 2011).
41. Larry Wolff, *Inventing Eastern Europe: The Map of Civilization on the Mind of the Enlightenment* (Stanford: Stanford University Press, 1994), p. 4.
42. Homi Bhabha, 'Cultural Diversity and Cultural Differences', in Bill Ashcroft, Gareth Griffiths and Helen Tiffins (eds), *The Postcolonial Studies Reader* (London and New York: Routledge, 1995), p. 209.
43. Ibid.
44. Rachel O. Moore, *Savage Theory: Cinema as Modern Magic* (Durham, NC, and London: Duke University Press, 2000), p. 2.
45. Ibid. p. 9.
46. Ewa Mazierska, *Polish Postcommunist Cinema: From Pavement Level* (Oxford: Peter Lang, 2007), p. 226.
47. Ewa Mazierska, 'Between the Sacred and the Profane, the Sublime and the Trivial: The Magic Realism of Jan Jakub Kolski', *Scope*, Issue 20, June 2011, at http://www.scope.nottingham.ac.uk/article.php?issue=jan2000&id=281&section=article (accessed 13 September 2011).

48. Anne C. Hegerfeldt, *Lies that Tell the Truth*, pp. 146–7.
49. David K. Danow, *The Spirit of Carnival*, p. 70.
50. Maggie Ann Bowers, *Magic(al) Realism*, p. 104.
51. Tzvetan Todorov, *The Fantastic: A Structural Approach to a Literary Genre* (Ithaca, NY: Cornell University Press, 1975), p. 120.
52. Wendy Faris, *Ordinary Enchantments*, p. 99.
53. Edgar Morin, *The Cinema, or The Imaginary Man* (Minneapolis: University of Minnesota Press, 2005), p. 72.
54. Ibid. p. 30.
55. Vincent Canby, 'The Tin Drum, Movie Review', *The New York Times*, 11 April 1980.
56. Jean Piaget, *The Child's Conception of the World*, trans. Joan and Andrew Tomlinson (Savage, MD: Littlefield Adams Quality Paperbacks, 1989), p. 133.
57. For an in-depth analysis of the long history of female martyrdom and victimisation in Polish cinema, see Ewa Mazierska and Elżbieta Ostrowska, *Women in Polish Cinema* (Oxford: Berghahn, 2006).
58. Andrew Horton, 'Cinematic Makeovers and Cultural Border Crossings: Kusturica's *Time of the Gypsies* and Coppola's *Godfather* and *Godfather II*', in Andrew Horton and Stuart V. McDougal (eds), *Play it Again, Sam: Retakes on Remakes* (Berkeley: University of California Press, 1998), p. 184.
59. Goran Gocić, *The Cinema of Emir Kusturica: Notes from the Underground* (London: Wallflower, 2001), p. 84.
60. On the significance of the turkey, Dina Iordanova writes

> Perhan's closest friend in *Gypsies* is his turkey, which according to Kusturica is a bird that enjoys special standing in Romani mythology. The moment at which the uncle slaughters the turkey to make soup, Kusturica indicated, was the turning point of the film, the end of Perhan's childhood and the beginning of his maturity. The turkey, symbolising his soul, keeps returning to Perhan's dreams and its white ghost appears to him at the moment of his death. (Dina Iordanova, *Emir Kusturica* (London: British Film Institute, 2002), p. 126)

61. Mikhail Bakhtin, *Rabelais and his World* (Bloomington: Indiana University Press, 1984), p. 256.
62. Ibid. p. 318.
63. Dina Iordanova, *Emir Kusturica*, p. 149.
64. Andrew Horton, 'Cinematic Makeovers and Cultural Border Crossings', p. 179.
65. Goran Gocić, *The Cinema of Emir Kusturica: Notes from the Underground*, p. 144; and Andrew Horton, 'Cinematic Makeovers and Cultural Border Crossings', p. 188.
66. For the full account of Chaplin's Roma heritage, see Joyce Milton, *Tramp: The Life of Charlie Chaplin* (New York: Da Capo, 1998).
67. Andrew Horton, 'Cinematic Makeovers and Cultural Border Crossings', p. 182.

EPILOGUE: THREE ENCOUNTERS

Several texts and experiences have inspired this project, but I would like to isolate three personal encounters that led me to think about the cinema of East Central Europe within the category of magic realism. All three encounters happened during my childhood in the Communist Poland of the early 1980s. Admittedly, a certain amount of nostalgia is therefore involved in this account.

The first encounter was with the effigy of Marzanna, which, as an eight-year-old, I was instructed to carry to the stream behind my primary school building, accompanied by my third-year teacher and all my classmates. This happened on the first day of Spring, in a landscape barren and grey after many months of near-arctic Winter weather. Once we all got to the edge of the water, the teacher proceeded to set Marzanna on fire, while I was holding on to the stick that supported the collection of straw, rags and papier-mâché, all fashioned into a female representation of Winter. With Marzanna set aflame, we burst into a song about her journey back to the sea and the joy of blooming flowers and green meadows that were arriving with Spring. Made with highly flammable materials, Marzanna was burning fast, making me dizzy with excitement and sweaty from the heat that radiated down the stick, on to which I was still holding tight. Then it was time to drown the Winter Witch in the stream. Only the stream was securely iced over. Not wanting to disappoint the teacher, who had entrusted Marzanna into my, obviously, very responsible hands, I hesitated between throwing Marzanna on to the ice, knowing that this would sabotage the drowning, and running into the stream along with my flaming cargo to break the ice cover, so that the drowning would be fully accomplished. Thankfully, a few brave and equally excited classmates read my mind and ran into the stream for me, breaking the ice surface and finally allowing me to deposit Marzanna properly into the water. Thus the ritual was successfully carried out and surprisingly not one of us sustained any injuries. We were supposed to leave the drowning Marzanna in the creek and cautiously not look at her ever again (not even with a single peek), as we made our way back to the school. After nearly turning into a human torch, I was certain that I performed black magic that day. The dubious gender politics inscribed in the ancient custom evaded me then. My parents, one a loyal Communist and the other a Solidarity activist, did not think much of my story when I reported it at the dinner table. The Solidarity activist shrugged his shoulders and mumbled something about the Commies being a bunch of illiterate heathens.

As I accessed this memory later in my life, I wondered how it was possible, in the twentieth century, in a relatively large European city, for a group of Catholic, Jewish and Russian Orthodox children to engage in this blatantly pagan Spring rite within the confines of the institution of public education. I knew that this was not a whimsical activity thought up by our teacher. Most children across Poland participated (and continue to do so) in similar festivities at least once during their childhood. My research on pagan traditions surviving across East Central Europe informs me that the children of Slovakia and the Czech Republic drown their equivalent of Marzanna – the lady Morena. In Ukraine and Russia, people celebrate Maslenitsa. In Romania, it is the holiday of Mărţişor, and in Bulgaria a related observance of the Baba Marta Day. This pagan element persists and inflects contemporary cultural expressions in the region, including film. Within this cultural landscape, modernism and postmodernism have developed unique local formations, quite different from Western models, due to the lasting influence of the premodern element. Contributing to the peripheral identity of the region, the element continues to be repressed in official discourses, including film scholarship.

Taking place a few years after my drowning of Marzanna, the second encounter that inspired my study of liminal cinema in a liminal cultural territory was an encounter with Wojciech Jerzy Has's 1973 film *The Hour-Glass Sanatorium*. When it premièred, the film was awarded the prestigious Jury Prize at the Cannes Film Festival, and ironically it also occasioned Has's forced exile from filmmaking, effected by the Communist authorities (who financed the rather extravagantly expensive production), for the following ten years. I must have been eleven or twelve when I watched this mesmerising surrealist vision on national television. Set at the turn of the twentieth century, the film tells the story of young Joseph (Jan Nowicki), who is travelling in time and space to visit his deceased father Jacob (Tadeusz Kondrat) in a mysterious sanatorium, where the patriarch continues to exist in a post-mortem slumber, along with other patients, who teeter eternally between life and death. The director of the sanatorium, Doctor Godard (Gustaw Holoubek), explains that the time of the sanatorium is separated from outside time by a very special time interval, which situates the patients right in between what was and what is to be. As Joseph begins to tour the sanatorium, he embarks on a phantasmagoric journey of dreams, memories and historical events, all enmeshed in a spatio-temporal labyrinth filled with oneiric figures and talismanic objects. A much darker and catastrophic version of *Alice's Adventures in Wonderland*, Joseph's peregrinations take him through the bloody battlefields, the dilapidated *shtetls* and the exotic provincial marketplaces of Austro-Hungarian Galicia. Has presents this half-real and half-ethereal place as an unfinished, or an already unravelled, dream province of the dead Emperor Franz Joseph I, whose actual imperial domain spread over much of East Central Europe, and is well represented in the bewildering collection of the Emperor's official titles. Those included Emperor of Austria, Apostolic King of Hungary, King of Bohemia, King of Croatia, King of Dalmatia, King of Slavonia, King of Galicia, King of Illyria and Lodomeria, King of Jerusalem, Archduke of Austria, Grand Duke of Tuscany, Grand Duke of Cracow, Duke of Lorraine, Salzburg, Styria, Carinthia, Carniola, the Bukovina, Grand Prince of Transylvania, Margrave of Moravia, Duke of Upper and Lower Silesia, and so on. Interestingly, some of the Emperor's titles were fictional; they did not correspond with the existing administrative units. For example, the Kingdom of Illyria was not in existence during most of the Emperor's rule.

The film impressed me with its paradoxical pairing of the meandering, dream-like narrative with the intensely material, often tactile, *mise-en-scène*, crowded with German Expressionist sets, theatrical interior designs and an excessive agglomeration of idiosyncratic props, from a Prussian helmet, through an array of taxidermied birds, glass eyeballs, clocks, umbrellas, enemas, stamps, scrapbooks, collections of bird eggs, human skulls, wax figures, bolts of fabric, candlesticks, mechanical dolls, and mannequins, to a kettle and a lantern. For the immature viewer that I was at the time, this combination allowed for a wild excursion into the complete unknown (including adult eroticism, religious symbolism and historical controversy), while being securely anchored in the palpable and known reality of the object world. Most importantly, Has's film led me to my third seminal encounter. As the credits rolled, I discovered that Has's film was based on the short stories of Bruno Schulz (1892–1942) – the little-known master of East Central European magic realism, whose prose has influenced generations of artists interested in locating the metaphysical in the fabric of the physical. In my later education, I went on to read, admire, study and write a part of my doctoral dissertation about Schulz's incomparable fiction.

The latest preoccupation with Bruno Schulz's legacy in the context of the cultural memory of East Central Europe deals with his visual art (not his writing), and it was spurred by the aftermath of a historical event that took place in his hometown, Drohobycz, Ukraine, on 9 February 2001. On that day, Benjamin Geissler (a German documentary filmmaker and the son of a Schulz scholar) went to Drohobycz and discovered a group of wall paintings by Schulz. The artist painted these polychromes in the Summer of 1942 for the son of Felix Landau, the Gestapo officer, who had taken a liking to Bruno Schulz and protected him from the Nazi genocidal policies that were directed against the Jewish population of Drohobycz at the time. In exchange for this protection, Landau commissioned art projects and other odd jobs from Schulz. The murals in question represented a fairy-tale scene that spread all over the walls of the nursery in Landau's villa. After the war and the reassignment of borders, Drohobycz, formerly Polish, became a Ukrainian territory, and the villa was subsequently apprehended by Communists and parcelled into cramped flats for the Ukrainian working class. The murals were painted over and forgotten. Even upon their discovery by Geissler (documented in his 2002 film *Finding Pictures / Bilder finden*), these artifacts did not elicit much attention from art critics or the authorities.

What changed this relative indifference was the murals' controversial disappearance soon after. In May 2001, representatives from Yad Vashem Holocaust Museum in Israel arrived in Drohobycz and removed some sections of the murals (those that had already been revealed by the Polish art conservationists). Although Yad Vashem claims to have obtained prior permission from the mayor of Drohobycz, the Ukrainian government (upon external pressure) issued a public statement, which interprets the removal as a criminal activity that broke the international law guiding the proper transfer of priceless art. The debate that followed Yad Vashem's unilateral decision to appropriate Schulz's last creative output (he painted the murals shortly before being shot dead in a street by another Gestapo officer) as a part of the cultural history of the Holocaust can be described as a venomous exchange of more or less nationalistic identity claims among the three parties involved in the conflict: Jews, Poles and Ukrainians. In the course of this dispute, the following questions were insistently asked: 'Whose is Schulz?' 'Was Galicia Polish, Jewish or Ukrainian?' and 'Why and how should we remember Schulz?' Most answers offered to these questions tend to be limited to the collective mythologies of the three nation-states. Schulz's own prerogative of always interrogating myth against history and vice versa somehow got lost in the cries of martyrdom voiced by three peoples whose suffering could never be measured. The complex nature of the place where Schulz lived and worked – the multicultural Galician province of the former Austro-Hungarian Empire – was best defined by the writer himself.

Much like the filmmakers discussed in this volume, whose post-Soviet magic realist art addresses a monumental transformative moment, Schulz used his writing to approach an equally enormous shift in his world. Like the post-1989 magic realist films, Schulz's prose deals with the crumbling of a regime. What began in 1892 as a life of relative conformity, even stagnation, under the Austro-Hungarian Empire assumed a very different tone with the dissolution of that empire at the time when Schulz was writing his stories – the period following the end of World War I. During Schulz's childhood, the Galician world had been efficiently guarded by Emperor Franz Joseph I. Structured by labyrinthine bureaucracy and imperial hierarchy, this economically challenged province functioned as a forgotten backwater for the glamorous centre of the empire: *fin-de-siècle* Vienna. The Austrian administration insisted on Galicia's agricultural economic profile in order to secure a steady food supply for the empire and a market for the industrial products made in the wealthier and more advanced regions of the empire. Franz Joseph I appears in Schulz's fiction as a dichotomous figure. On the one hand, he is the agent of boredom and uniformity; on the other hand, he is also the guarantor of permanence and peace.

The empire enforced conformity, but at the same time it shielded the forgotten province from industrial and political revolutions, allowing small towns like Drohobycz to continue their sleepy existence. At the beginning of the twentieth century, Drohobycz was an anachronism, mostly owing to its outdated economy that relied on the enterprise of a few patrician merchants. Schulz's father was one of those; he owned a draper's. Whenever Schulz's narrator does assume a nostalgic note it is to talk about this anachronistic world that was held in its place by Franz Joseph I and, on a smaller scale, by the Father (the central character in Schulz's stories). During Schulz's youth, Drohobycz earned a livelihood from an assortment of small businesses and agriculture. The local shopkeepers and artisans worked according to early nineteenth-century codes of trade and proudly defended their businesses from modern commercialisation, often at the cost of serious impoverishment.

Schulz's narrator, however, does not remain in the nostalgic past. Much of his storytelling concerns the present, the time when Schulz came of age and began writing: the first decades of the twentieth century. During that period, the world of his childhood all but disappeared. A series of changes altered Galicia and the way of life that its inhabitants were used to. The old world began to vanish around 1904, when Drohobycz and a number of the surrounding towns found themselves in the middle of a newly discovered oil field. Soon followed the development of the international oil industry in Galicia, as well as the formation of its new and numerous working class. The foreign-sponsored industrialisation brought on with this development very quickly disrupted the leisurely rhythm of life in Drohobycz and forcefully transformed it into a grey and uniform industrial base that would service the oil business at the lowest cost possible and with total disregard for the benefits of the local community. The Industrial Revolution reached Poland and other East Central European nations much later than it did the rest of Europe. At the beginning of the twentieth century, those areas of Europe already industrialised were entering the postcapitalist commodity model, while East Central Europe was still making the transition from a precapitalist agrarian economy into the industrial stage.

Without naming the proper names (the words 'Poland', 'Galicia', 'Austro-Hungary' and 'Drohobycz' are never used), or trying to explain the political impetus behind these transformations, Schulz's narrator arrests the transformative moment and, by doing so, tries to subvert the usual inconspicuousness of history. Although the aforementioned changes were world-altering, the news reports and chronicles published at the time were quick to catalogue them into orderly sequences of cause and effect. Instead, Schulz, by employing the motif of metamorphosis, undercuts the classifying impulse and proceeds to reflect the strangeness of the world spinning in the motion of events. As a representative of the East Central European province, and consequently a member of the collectivity that was detached from the centres of power that instigated the changes, Schulz offers a peripheral vision of what transpired. This vision is full of rather irrational (often supernatural) events that, I believe, stand in for actual historical events, or rather for the impressions that these events imprinted on the population of East Central Europe – the people who found themselves in the grip of forces that were incomprehensible and extraneous to their daily lives.

Schulz's very cinematic prose uses metamorphosis to abolish the nineteenth-century trust in certitude, predictability and unity of the Habsburg world. By employing highly metaphoric language and fantastic events in narratives that are otherwise faithful to detail and precise in depicting everyday reality, the writer points out the irrational leaps of knowledge and the arbitrariness of human discourses that led to the formation and subsequent dissolution of the imperial order. The stories, through use of a 'surreal' quality, put in question the boundaries between the real and the imaginary. As the parting words of this narrative, I will let Schulz speak of change, its hopes and its disappointments:

> Then the world stood motionless for a while, holding its breath, blinded, wanting to enter whole into that illusory picture, into that provisional eternity that opened up before it. But the enticing offer passed, the wind broke its mirror, and Time took us into his possession once again . . . Undefined ourselves, we expected something from Time, which was unable to provide a definition and wasted itself in a thousand subterfuges.[1]

NOTE

1. Bruno Schulz, *The Collected Works of Bruno Schulz*, ed. Jerzy Ficowski, trans. Celina Wieniawska (London: Picador, 1998), p. 127.

SELECT FILMOGRAPHY

Barta, Jiří, 1986: *The Pied Piper (Krysař)*.
Buñuel, Luis, 1929: *An Andalusian Dog (Un Chien andalou)*.
Burton, Tim, 2003: *Big Fish*.
Charles, Larry, 2006: *Borat: Cultural Learnings of America for Make Benefit Glorious Nation of Kazakhstan*.
De Sica, Vittorio, 1951: *Miracle in Milan (Miracolo a Milano)*.
Dovzhenko, Alexander, 1930: *Earth (Zemlya)*.
Enyedi, Ildikó, 1989: *My Twentieth Century (Az én XX. századom)*.
Gárdos, Péter, 2005: *The Porcelain Doll (A porcelánbaba)*.
Geissler, Benjamin, 2002: *Finding Pictures (Bilder finden)*.
Gothár, Péter, 1996: *Letgohang Vaska (Haggyállógva Vászka)*.
Grune, Karl, 1923: *The Street (Die Straße)*.
Hanák, Dušan, 1972: *Pictures from the Old World (Obrazy starého sveta)*.
— 1976: *Rose-Tinted Dreams (Ružové sny)*.
Has, Wojciech, 1965: *The Saragossa Manuscript (Rękopis znaleziony w Saragossie)*.
— 1973: *The Hour-Glass Sanatorium (Sanatorium pod klepsydrą)*.
Holland, Agnieszka, 1981: *Fever (Gorączka)*.
— 1993: *The Secret Garden*.
Huszárik, Zoltán, 1971: *Sinbad (Szinbád)*.
Jabłoński, Dariusz, 2008: *Strawberry Wine (Wino truskawkowe)*.
Jakimowski, Andrzej, 2002: *Squint Your Eyes (Zmruż oczy)*.
— 2007: *Tricks (Sztuczki)*.
Jakubisko, Juraj, 1969: *Birds, Orphans and Fools (Vtáčkovia, siroty a blázni)*.
— 1983: *A Thousand-Year-Old Bee (Tisícročná včela)*.
— 1997: *An Ambiguous Report About the End of the World (Nejasná správa o konci světa)*.
Jasný, Vojtěch, 1963: *The Cassandra Cat (Až přijde kocour)*.
Jeles, András, 1984: *Annunciation (Angyali üdvözlet)*.

Jireš, Jaromil, 1970: *Valerie and her Week of Wonders (Valeria a týden divů).*
Kawalerowicz, Jerzy, 1961: *Mother Joan of the Angels (Matka Joanna od aniołów).*
Kędzierzawska, Dorota, 1991: *Devils, Devils (Diabły, diabły).*
— 1994: *Crows (Wrony).*
— 1998: *Nothing (Nic).*
— 2005: *I am (Jestem).*
— 2010: *Tomorrow Will Be Better (Jutro będzie lepiej).*
Kieślowski, Krzysztof, 1985: *No End (Bez końca).*
— 1988: *The Decalogue (Dekalog).*
— 1991: *The Double Life of Veronique (La Double Vie de Véronique).*
— 1993: *Three Colors: Blue (Trois couleurs: Bleu).*
— 1994: *Three Colors: Red (Trois couleurs: Rouge).*
— 1994: *Three Colors: White (Trois couleurs: Blanc).*
Kolski, Jan Jakub, 1991: *Burial of a Potato (Pogrzeb kartofla).*
— 1992: *The Knacker (Pograbek).*
— 1993: *Johnnie the Aquarius (Jańcio Wodnik).*
— 1993: *Magneto.*
— 1994: *Miraculous Place (Cudowne miejsce).*
— 1995: *Playing from the Plate (Grający z talerza).*
— 1995: *The Saber from the Commander (Szabla od komendanta).*
— 1998: *History of Cinema in Popielawy (Historia kina w Popielawach).*
— 2000: *Keep Away From the Window (Daleko od okna).*
— 2006: *Jasminum (Jaśminum).*
— 2009: *Afonia and the Bees (Afonia i pszczoly).*
— 2010: *Venice (Wenecja).*
Kusturica, Emir, 1989: *Time of the Gypsies (Dom za vešanje).*
— 1993: *Arizona Dream.*
— 1995: *Underground (Bila jednom jedna zemlja).*
— 1998: *Black Cat, White Cat (Crna mačka, beli mačor).*
Kutz, Kazimierz, 1970: *Salt of the Black Earth (Sól ziemi czarnej).*
— 1972: *Pearl in the Crown (Perła w koronie).*
— 1994: *Death as a Slice of Bread (Śmierć jak kromka chleba).*
Leszczyński, Witold, 1968: *Matthew's Days (Żywot Mateusza).*
Llosa, Claudia, 2009: *The Milk of Sorrow (La teta asustada).*
McMullen, Ken, 1983: *Ghost Dance.*
Méliès, Georges, 1896: *The Vanishing Lady (Escamotage d'une dame chez Robert-Houdin).*
— 1902: *A Trip to the Moon (Le Voyage dans la Lune).*
Menzel, Jiří, 1968: *Capricious Summer (Rozmarné léto).*
— 1985: *My Sweet Little Village (Vesničko má středisková).*
Němec, Jan, 1966: *Martyrs of Love (Mučedníci lásky).*
Parajanov, Sergei, 1964: *Shadows of Forgotten Ancestors (Tini zabutykh predkiv).*
— 1968: *The Color of Pomegranates (Sayat Nova).*
Passendorfer, Jerzy, 1974: *Yanoshik (Janosik).*
Perrin, Jacques, 2001: *Winged Migration (Le Peuple migrateur).*
Schlöndorff, Volker, 1979: *The Tin Drum (Die Blechtrommel).*
Sophia, Zornitsa, 2004: *Mila from Mars (Mila ot Mars).*
Stuhr, Jerzy, 2000: *The Big Animal (Duże zwierzę).*
Šulík, Martin, 1995: *The Garden (Záhrada).*
— 1997: *Orbis Pictus.*
— 2000: *Landscape (Krajinka).*
Švankmajer, Jan, 1988: *Alice (Něco z Alenky).*

— 2000: *Little Otik (Otesánek)*.
Svěrák, Jan, 1996: *Kolya (Kolja)*.
Tarr, Béla, 1988: *Damnation (Kárhozat)*.
— 1994: *Satan's Tango (Sátántangó)*.
— 2000: *Werckmeister Harmonies (Werckmeister harmóniák)*.
Trajkov, Ivo, 2004: *The Great Water (Golemata Voda)*.
Triffonova, Iglika, 2001: *Letter to America (Pismo do Amerika)*.
Trzaskalski, Piotr, 2002: *Eddie (Edi)*.
Vláčil, František, 1967: *Marketa Lazarová*.
Vulchanov, Rangel, 1970: *Aesop (Ezop)*.
Wajda, Andrzej, 1970: *The Birch Wood (Brzezina)*.
Waszynski, Michal, 1937: *The Dybbuk (Dybuk)*.
Wenders, Wim, 1987: *Wings of Desire (Der Himmel über Berlin)*.
Wiecek, Andrzej, 2002: *Angel in Cracow (Anioł w Krakowie)*.
— 2005: *Angel in Love (Zakochany anioł)*.
Zelenka, Petr, 2002: *Year of the Devil (Rok Ďábla)*.

BIBLIOGRAPHY

Adams, Carol J. (1990) *The Sexual Politics of Meat*. New York: Continuum.

Adorno, Theodor and Max Horkheimer (2002) 'The Culture Industry: Enlightenment as Mass Deception', *Dialectic of Enlightenment: Philosophical Fragments*. Stanford: Stanford University Press, 99.

Andruchowycz, Jurij and Andrzej Stasiuk (2007) *Moja Europa*. Wolowiec: Wydawnictwo Czarne.

Backhaus, Gary (2000) 'The Phenomenology of the Experience of Enchantment', in Analecta Husserliana and Anna-Teresa Tymieniecka (eds), *The Aesthetics of Enchantment in the Fine Arts*. Dordrecht: Kluwer Academic, 31.

Bakhtin, Mikhail (1981), 'Discourse in the Novel', in Michael Holquist (ed.), *The Dialogic Imagination*, trans. Caryl Emerson and Michael Holquist. Austin: University of Texas Press.

— (1984) *Rabelais and his World*. Bloomington: Indiana University Press.

Balázs, Béla (1972) *Theory of the Film: Character and Growth of a New Art*, trans. Edith Bone. New York: Arno, 55.

Ballard, Phil (2004) 'In Search of Truth: Béla Tarr Interviewed', *Kinoeye*, 4, 2, March.

Barthes, Roland (1986) 'The Reality Effect', *The Rustle of Language*, trans. Richard Howard. Oxford: Blackwell, 141–8.

Bauman, Zygmunt (1998) *Globalization: The Human Consequences*. New York: Columbia University Press.

Bazin, André (1960) 'The Ontology of the Photographic Image', *Film Quarterly*, 13, 4, Summer 4–9.

— (2005) *What is Cinema? Volume I*. Berkeley: University of California Press.

Benjamin, Walter (1969) 'The Work of Art in the Age of Mechanical Reproduction', in Hannah Arendt (ed.), *Illuminations*, trans. Harry Zohn. New York: Schocken, 233.

Bertman, Stephen (1999) 'Warp Speed: How Fast Times Are Changing Our Personal Values', *Humanities Research Group Working Papers*, 8, 9.

Bhabha, Homi (1995) 'Cultural Diversity and Cultural Differences', in Bill Ashcroft,

Gareth Griffiths and Helen Tiffins (eds), *The Postcolonial Studies Reader*. London and New York: Routledge, 209.

— (1990) 'The Third Space: Interview with Homi Bhabha', in J. Rutherford (ed.), *Identity, Community, Culture, Difference*. London: Lawrence & Wishart, 207–21.

Bloch, Ernst (1977) 'Nonsynchronism and the Obligation to its Dialectics', *New German Critique*, 11, Spring, 24, 26, 24.

Bowers, Maggie Ann (2004) *Magic(al) Realism*. London and New York: Routledge.

Breton, André (1972) *Surrealism and Painting*, trans. Simon Watson Taylor. New York: Harper & Row.

Buslowska, Elzbieta (2009) 'Cinema as Art and Philosophy in Béla Tarr's Creative Exploration of Reality', in *Acta Univ. Sapientia, Film and Media Studies*, 107–16.

Canby, Vincent (1980) 'The Tin Drum, Movie Review', *The New York Times*, 11 April.

Canudo, Ricciotto (2004) 'The Birth of the Sixth Art', in Philip Simpson, Andrew Utterson and K. J. Shepherdon (eds), *Film Theory*. London: Routledge, 25–33.

Carpentier, Alejo (1995) 'Baroque and the Marvelous Real', in Lois Zamora and Wendy Faris (eds), *Magical Realism: Theory, History, Community*. Durham, NC: Duke University Press, 89–108.

Casanova, Giacomo (1971) *History of my Life*, vol. 10. London: Longman.

Casey, Edward (1996) 'How to Get from Space to Place in a Fairly Short Stretch of Time', in Keith Basso and Steven Feld (eds), *Senses of Place*. Santa Fe: School of American Research, 18.

Cavell, Stanley (1979) *The World Viewed: Reflections on the Ontology of Film*. Cambridge, MA: Harvard University Press.

Chakrabarty, Dipesh (2007) *Provincializing Europe: Postcolonial Thought and Historical Difference*. Princeton: Princeton University Press.

Chanady, Amaryll (1995) 'The Territorialization of the Imaginary in Latin America: Self Affirmation and Resistance to Metropolitan Paradigms', in Lois Zamora and Wendy Faris (eds), *Magical Realism: Theory, History, Community*. Durham, NC: Duke University Press, 168.

Cholodenko, Alan (2004) 'The Crypt: The Haunted House of Cinema', *Cultural Studies Review*, 10, 2, September, 99–113.

Connell, Liam (1998) 'Discarding Magic Realism: Modernism, Anthropology, and Critical Practice', *Ariel*, 29, 2, 102–41.

Danow, David (1995) *The Spirit of Carnival*. Lexington: University Press of Kentucky.

Davis, Norman (1997) 'West Best, East Beast', *Oxford Today*, 9, 2, 28–31.

Deleuze, Gilles and Félix Guattari (1983) 'What is Minor Literature?', *Mississippi Review*, 11, 3, Winter / Spring, 13–33.

Derrida, Jacques (2005) *Paper Machine*. Stanford: Stanford University Press.

Durix, Jean-Pierre (1998) *Mimesis, Genres and Post-Colonial Discourse: Deconstructing Magic Realism*. Houndmills: Palgrave Macmillan.

Dynel, Marta (2011) *The Pragmatics of Humour Across Discourse Domains*. Amsterdam and Philadelphia: John Benjamins.

Engels, Friedrich and Karl Marx (1998) *The German Ideology, including Theses on Feuerback*. New York: Prometheus.

Epstein, Jean (2004) 'On Certain Characteristics of *Photogénie*', in Philip Simpson, Andrew Utterson and K. J. Shepherson (eds), *Film Theory Vol. I*. London and New York: Routledge, 54–5.

— (2011)'*Photogénie* and the Imponderable', in Timothy Corrigan, Patricia White and Meta Mazaj (eds), *Critical Visions in Film Theory*. Boston and New York: Bedford / St Martin's, 254–5.

Faris, Wendy (2004) *Ordinary Enchantments: Magical Realism and the Remystification of Narrative*. Nashville: Vanderbilt University Press.

— (1995) 'Scheherezade's Children: Magical Realism and Postmodern Fiction', in Lois Zamora and Wendy Faris (eds), *Magical Realism: Theory, History, Community*. Durham, NC: Duke University Press, 168.

Fischer, Lucy (1983) 'The Lady Vanishes: Women, Magic, and the Movies', in John L. Fell (ed.), *Film Before Griffith*. Berkeley and Los Angeles: University of California Press, 339–54.

Flanagan, Matthew (2008) 'Towards an Aesthetic of Slow in Contemporary Cinema', *16:9*, 6, 29, November.

Foster Jr, John Burt (1995) 'Magical Realism, Compensatory Vision and Felt History: Classical Realism Transformed in *The White Hotel*', in Lois Zamora and Wendy Faris (eds), *Magical Realism: Theory, History, Community*. Durham, NC: Duke University Press, 270–1.

Foucault, Michel (1994) *The Order of Things: An Archeology of the Human Sciences*. New York: Vintage.

Galt, Rosalind (2006) *The New European Cinema: Redrawing the Map*. New York: Columbia University Press.

Gocić, Goran (2001) *The Cinema of Emir Kusturica: Notes from the Underground*. London: Wallflower.

Guenther, Irene (1995) 'Magic Realism in the Weimar Republic', in Lois Zamora and Wendy Faris (eds), *Magical Realism: Theory, History, Community*. Durham, NC: Duke University Press, 37.

Gunning, Tom (2000) 'The Cinema of Attraction: Early Film, its Spectator, and the Avant-Garde', in Robert Stam and Toby Miller (eds), *Film and Theory: An Anthology*. Oxford: Blackwell, 229–35.

Gyékényesi Gatto, Katherine (1999)'Her *Twentieth Century*: The Postmodern Cinema of Ildikó Enyedi', *Hungarian Studies Review*, 26, Spring / Fall.

Hames, Peter (2001) 'Bringing up Baby: An Interview with Jan Švankmajer', *Sight and Sound*, 11, 10, October, 26–8.

— (2001)'The Melancholy of Resistance: The Films of Béla Tarr', *Kinoeye*, 1, 1.

Hans, Frank (2008) 'Nuremberg Trial Proceedings', *The Avalon Project at Yale Law School*, 3, February.

Hansen, Miriam (1991) 'Decentric Perspectives: Kracauer's Early Writings on Film and Mass Culture', *New German Critique*, 54, Autumn, 49.

Hegerfeldt, Anne C. (2005) *Lies that Tell the Truth: Magic Realism Seen through Contemporary Fiction from Britain*. Amsterdam and New York: Rodopi.

Heidegger, Martin (1971) 'Building, Dwelling, Thinking', in *Poetry, Language, Thought*, trans. Albert Hofstadter. New York: Harper Colophon, 143–61.

Horton, Andrew (1998) 'Cinematic Makeovers and Cultural Border Crossings: Kusturica's *Time of the Gypsies* and Coppola's *Godfather* and *Godfather II*', in Andrew Horton and Stuart V. McDougal (eds), *Play it Again, Sam: Retakes on Remakes*. Berkeley: University of California Press.

Hutcheon, Linda (2000) 'Irony, Nostalgia, and the Postmodern', in Raymond Vervliet and Annemarie Estos (eds), *Methods for the Study of Literature as Cultural Memory*. Amsterdam: Rodopi, 189–207.

Imre, Anikó (2009) *Identity Games: Globalization and the Transformation of Media Cultures in the New Europe*. Cambridge, MA: MIT Press.

— (2003) 'Twin Pleasures of Feminism: Orlando Meets *My Twentieth Century*', *Camera Obscura* 54, 18, 3, 199.

Iordanova, Dina (2003) *Cinema of the Other Europe*. London and New York: Wallflower, 150.

— (2002) *Emir Kusturica*. London: British Film Institute.

— (2008) 'Intercultural Cinema and Balkan Hushed Histories', *Review of Film and Television Studies*, 6, 1, April, 5–18.

— (1999) 'Underground: Historical Allegory or Propaganda', *Historical Journal of Film, Radio, and Television*, 19, 1, March, 69–87.

Irigaray, Luce (1985) *Speculum of the Other Woman*. Ithaca: Cornell University Press.

Jameson, Fredric (1986) 'On Magic Realism in Film', *Critical Inquiry*, 12, 2, Winter, 311.

Kenney, Padraic (2003) *A Carnival of Revolution: Central Europe 1989*. Princeton: Princeton University Press.

Klonowska, Barbara (2010) 'Far Away From the Present: Magical Realism in Polish Film', *Studies in Eastern European Cinema*, 1, 2, 183–96.

Konrád, George (1996) *The Melancholy of Rebirth: Essays from Post-Communist Central Europe, 1989–1994*. San Diego: Harcourt Brace.

Kracauer, Siegfried (1997) *Theory of Film: The Redemption of Physical Reality*. Princeton: Princeton University Press.

Kristeva, Julia (1986) *The Kristeva Reader*, ed. Toril Moi. New York: Columbia University Press.

— (1982) *Powers of Horror*. New York: Columbia University Press.

Kundera, Milan (2005) *The Curtain: An Essay in Seven Parts*. New York: HarperCollins.

— (1984) 'The Tragedy of Central Europe', *The New York Review of Books*, 31, 7, 33–8.

Latour, Bruno (1993) *We Have Never Been Modern*. Cambridge, MA: Harvard University Press.

Lefebvre, Henri (1991) *The Production of Space*, trans. Donald Nicholson-Smith. Oxford: Blackwell.

Lungu, Dan (2010) '"Miserabilism" or Post-Traumatic Realism (in Romania)', *Writer's Notebook*, February.

McKibbin, Tony (2004) 'Cinema of Damnation', *Senses of Cinema*, December.

Malinowski, Bronislaw (1954) *Magic, Science, and Religion, and Other Essays*. Garden City, NY: Doubleday Anchor, 70.

Marchant, Steven (2009) 'Nothing Counts: Shots and Event in *Werckmeister Harmonies*', *New Cinemas: Journal of Contemporary Film*, 7, 2, 137–54.

Marciniak, Katarzyna (2006) *Alienhood: Citizenship, Exile, and the Logic of Difference*. Minneapolis: University of Minnesota Press.

— (2005) 'Second World-ness and Transnational Feminist Practices: Agnieszka Holland's *Kobieta Samotna (A Woman Alone)*', in Anikó Imre (ed.), *East European Cinemas*. New York: Routledge, 6.

Marciniak, Katarzyna and Kamil Turowski (2011) *Streets of Crocodiles: Photography, Media, and Postsocialist Landscapes in Poland*. Chicago: University of Chicago Press.

Mazierska, Ewa (2011) 'Between the Sacred and the Profane, the Sublime and the Trivial: The Magic Realism of Jan Jakub Kolski', *Scope*, 20, June.

— (2001) 'In the Land of Noble Knights and Mute Princesses: Polish Heritage Cinema', *Historical Journal of Film, Radio, and Television*, 21, 2, June, 172.

— (2007) *Polish Postcommunist Cinema: From Pavement Level*. Oxford: Peter Lang.

— (2010) 'Post-Communist Estonian Cinema as Transnational Cinema', *KinoCultura*, Special Issue 10.

Mazierska, Ewa and Elżbieta Ostrowska (2006) *Women in Polish Cinema*. Oxford: Berghahn.

Menton, Seymour (1983) *Magical Realism Rediscovered, 1918–1981*. Philadelphia: Art Alliance.

Merleau-Ponty, Maurice (1964) *Sense and Non-Sense*, trans. Hubert Dreyfus and Patricia Allen Dreyfus. Evanston, IL: Northwestern University Press.

Metz, Christian and Jean-Louis Baudry (1992) in Robert Burgoyne, Sandy Flitterman-Lewis and Robert Stam (eds), *New Vocabularies in Film Semiotics: Structuralism, Post-structuralism, and Beyond*. London: Routledge, 143.

Michalski, Sergiusz (1994) *New Objectivity: Painting, Graphic Art and Photography in Weimar Germany*. Cologne: Benedikt Taschen.

Milton, Joyce (1998) *Tramp: The Life of Charlie Chaplin*. New York: Da Capo.

Moore, Rachel O. (2000) *Savage Theory: Cinema as Modern Magic*. Durham, NC, and London: Duke University Press.

Morin, Edgar (2005) *The Cinema, or The Imaginary Man*. Minneapolis: University of Minnesota Press.

Noriega Sánchez, María Ruth (2002) *Challenging Realities: Magic Realism in Contemporary American Women's Fiction*. Valencia, Spain: Universitat de València.

North, Dan (2001) 'Magic and Illusion in Early Cinema', *Studies in French Cinema*, 1, 2.

O'Pray, Michael (2008) 'Jan Švankmajer: A Mannerist Surrealist', in Peter Hames (ed.), *The Cinema of Jan Švankmajer: Dark Alchemy*. London: Wallflower, 58.

Orr, John (2001) *The Art and Politics of Film*. Edinburgh: Edinburgh University Press.

— (2001) 'Béla Tarr Circling the Whale', *Sight and Sound*, 11, 4, 22–4.

Ouyang, Wen-chin (2005) 'Magical Realism and Beyond: Ideology of Fantasy', in Stephen M. Hart and Wen-chin Ouyang (eds), *A Companion to Magical Realism*. Woodbridge: Tamesis, 13–20.

Peirce, Charles Sanders (1991) in James Hoopes (ed.), *Peirce on Signs: Writings on Semiotic*. Chapel Hill: University of North Carolina Press.

Piaget, Jean (1989) *The Child's Conception of the World*, trans. Joan and Andrew Tomlinson. Savage, MD: Littlefield Adams Quality Paperbacks.

Portuges, Catherine (2007) 'Central European Twins: Psychoanalysis and Cinema in Ildikó Enyedi's *My Twentieth Century*', *Psychoanalytic Inquiry*, 27, 4, 530.

Reddaway, William Fiddian (ed.) (1971) *The Correspondence with Voltaire and the Instruction of 1767*. New York: Russell & Russell.

Richardson, William (1968) *Anecdotes of the Russian Empire in a Series of Letters Written a Few Years Ago, from St. Petersburg*. New York: Da Capo.

Rivi, Luisa (1999) *European Cinema After 1989*. New York: Palgrave MacMillan.

Roh, Franz (1995) 'Magical Realism: Post-Expressionism', in Lois Zamora and Wendy Faris (eds), *Magical Realism: Theory, History, Community*. Durham, NC: Duke University Press, 20.

Roman, Denise (2003) *Fragmented Identities: Popular Culture, Sex, and Everyday Life in Postcommunist Romania*. Lanham, MD: Lexington.

Rousseau, Jean-Jacques (1986) *Considerations on the Government of Poland*, in Frederick Watkins (ed.) *Political Writings*. Madison, WI: University of Wisconsin Press, 159–276.

Rushdie, Salman (1992) *Imaginary Homelands: Essays and Criticism 1981–1991*. Harmondsworth: Granta.

Sandru, Christina (2004) 'A Poetics of the Liminal: Magical Realism and its Horizons of Escape', *American, British and Canadian Studies*, 5, December.

Schifirnet, Constantin (2009) 'The Mass Media and Tendentious Modernity in the Transition Process from the National Society to the European Community', *Civitas*, 9, 1, January, 57.

Schroeder, Shannin (2004) *Rediscovering Magical Realism in the Americas*. Westport: Praeger, Greenwood.

Schulz, Bruno (1998) *The Collected Works of Bruno Schulz*, ed. Jerzy Ficowski, trans. Celina Wieniawska. London: Picador.

Schwartz, Louis-Georges (2006) 'Cinema and the Meaning of "Life"', *Discourse*, 28, 2 and 3, Spring and Fall, 7–27.

Shaviro, Steven (2007) 'My Twentieth Century', *The Pinocchio Theory*, at http://www.shaviro.com/Blog/?p=566.

Shohat, Ella and Robert Stam (1996) 'From the Imperial Family to the Transnational Imaginary: Media Spectatorship in the Age of Globalization', in Rob Wilson and Wimal Dissanayake (eds), *Global / Local: Cultural Production and the Transnational Imaginary*. Durham, NC: Duke University Press, 145–70.

Sobchack, Vivian (2004) *Carnal Thoughts: Embodiment and Moving Image Culture*. Berkeley: University of California Press.

Stam, Robert (2005) *Literature Through Film: Realism, Magic and the Art of Adaptation*. Malden, MA, and Oxford: Blackwell.

Stasiuk, Andrzej (2005) *Jadąc do Babadag*. Wołowiec: Wydawnictwo Czarne.

Stiegler, Bernard (1998) *Technics and Time: The Fault of Epimetheus*. Stanford: Stanford University Press.

Stojanova, Christina (2005) 'Fragmented Discourses: Young Cinema from Central and Eastern Europe', in Anikó Imre (ed.), *East European Cinemas*. New York: Routledge, 213–27.

Todorov, Tzvetan (1975) *The Fantastic: A Structural Approach to a Literary Genre*. Ithaca, NY: Cornell University Press.

Tötösy de Zepetnek, Steven (2001) 'Comparative Cultural Studies and the Study of Central European Culture', in Steven Tötösy de Zepetnek (ed.), *Comparative Central European Culture*. West Lafayette: Purdue University Press, 1–32.

Trifonova, Temenuga (2007) 'Stoned on Mars: Home and National Identity in Bulgarian Post-Communist Cinema', *Cineaste*, 32, 3.

Tsuo, Kurt (2009) 'Unity Under Siege: The European Single Market after the Financial Crisis', *Harvard International Review*, 31, 1, Spring, 32–5.

Tuan, Yi-Fu (1974) *Topophilia: A Study of Environmental Perception, Attitudes, and Values*. Englewood Cliffs: Prentice-Hall.

Vertov, Dziga (2004) 'Kinoks: A Revolution', in Philip Simpson, Andrew Utterson and K. J. Shepherdson (eds), *Film Theory: Critical Concepts in Media and Cultural Studies: Volume I*. London and New York: Routledge, 233.

Wandycz, Piotr (2001) *The Price of Freedom: A History of East Central Europe from the Middle Ages to the Present*. London and New York: Routledge.

Warnes, Christopher (2006) 'Magical Realism and the Legacy of German Idealism', *The Modern Language Review*, 101, 2, April, 488–98.

Weber, Max (2009) *From Max Weber: Essays in Sociology*. London: Routledge.

Williams, Raymond (1973) *The Country and the City*. New York: Oxford University Press.

Wolff, Larry (1994) *Inventing Eastern Europe: The Map of Civilization on the Mind of the Enlightenment*. Stanford: Stanford University Press.

'Wrongly Labelled' (2010) *The Economist*, 394, 8664, 9 January.

Zamora, Lois (1995) 'Magical Romance / Magical Realism', in Lois Zamora and Wendy Faris (eds), *Magical Realism: Theory, History, Community*. Durham, NC: Duke University Press, 544.

Žižek, Slavoj (1997) 'Multiculturalism, or, the Cultural Logic of Multinational Capitalism', *New Left Review*, 225, September, 28–52.

INDEX

Page numbers in *italics* refer to figures.